ADVANCE PRAISE

"Over the past five years, Dr. Reeves has helped our legal department integrate diversity and inclusion into our leadership principles. We are excited about THE NEXT IQ, which is both an analysis of what we need to do to effectively step into today's leadership challenges as well as a guide on how we can actually take individual and organizational action to become better and more inclusive leaders."

Jeff Gearhart
Executive Vice President, General Counsel and Corporate Secretary
Wal-Mart Stores, Inc.

"This book is a must read for any CEO or CLO of a multi-national corporation that is facing the immediate task of creating a leadership pipeline that will forever transform and best position its Company for the challenges of an ever increasing dynamic, diverse, and competitive global marketplace. Dr. Reeves artfully balances intuition, empirical data and pragmatism to make a compelling case for the need of today's leaders to embrace a radically different mindset and approach to leading through inclusion and by seeking many different perspectives in search of all of the right answers and solutions to a problem and not simply selecting one "right answer" to solve the problem. This is exactly the type of mindset needed within DuPont to maximize the growth opportunities that exist in the "developing markets" throughout the world. Simply stated, the leaders of tomorrow can no longer rely upon their innate intelligence. "Inclusive intelligence" will be the hallmark of successful leaders of the future. That is the case made in this treatise and one that could not have been more timely delivered. Thank you, Dr. Reeves"

Thomas L. Sager
Senior Vice President and General Counsel
DuPont Legal

"Dr. Reeves offers us an insightful tool in The *Next* IQ. The book provides any audience, whether they be corporate businesses, law firms, or other organizations seeking tools to grow, with great resources that can transform thinking from many of the traditional notions and biases that we carry in many historical ways of thinking, or Retro IQ, to a journey of introspection and discovery that will help us all in gaining a value-add through this expanded inclusion and diversity lens. Individuals or teams can use the book to expand their collective thinking, open up pre-existing blind spots, and truly become recipients of hidden value that already exists in many organizations. I highly recommend it."

N. Cornell Boggs, III
Chief Responsibility and Ethics Officer
MillerCoors LLC

The myriad books about leadership, and about diversity and inclusion, can leave one with the sense that all insights on those subjects are exhausted. "The *Next* IQ" dispels that impression, from the first page to the last. Dr. Reeves draws upon a wealth of experience and extraordinary insight to demonstrate the interrelation between leadership and inclusion in a most unique way. The thesis of the book—that inclusion is not just a social goal, but the most important tool in achieving and sustaining successful leadership—is compellingly demonstrated through practical advice that easily and effectively can be incorporated into the daily activity of any person seeking to lead, in any field. This is a fabulous work."

William A. Von Hoene Jr.
Executive Vice President, Finance & Legal
Exelon Corporation

"Arin Reeves's new book is not just interesting reading, it's essential reading for any leader coping with the information revolution and the rapid pace of 21st century change. Reeves's observations about our interactions—not just in the workplace, but in society—are perceptive, enlightening, entertaining, and undeniable. "The *Next* IQ" is that rare book that combines revelation with practical advice. After reading this book, you will not approach your colleagues or your decisions in the same way."

Susan Lichtenstein
Senior Vice President, Corporate Affairs and Chief Legal Officer
Hill-Rom Holdings, Inc.

"Dr. Arin Reeves is someone whom I have long considered the leading mind addressing issues of diversity and inclusion in the legal profession. But with this book, Dr. Reeves has transcended the legal profession to squarely establish herself among today's foremost executive management and international business thought leaders. In the 20th Century, Covey taught us the Seven Habits and Thomas Peters and Robert Waterman put us In Search of Excellence. But in the 21st Century, people like Malcolm Gladwell, James Surowiecki, and Jim Collins defined The Tipping Point, The Wisdom of Crowds, and Good To Great, and Dr. Reeves lights a pathway with THE *NEXT* IQ The Next Level of Intelligence for 21st Century Leaders. And she does so with great stories and practical exercises to put the ideas into action. Great work, Arin!"

Veta T. Richardson
President & CEO
Association of Corporate Counsel

"THE *NEXT* IQ is a critical, must-read for anyone interested in maximizing intelligence on a personal or organizational level. Forevermore, our understanding of intelligence will be defined by this book; it is that ground-breaking. Dr. Reeves is so far ahead of the curve in this area, she is defining the path we will all be following for many years into the future. You cannot be an effective leader in any organization without this new understanding of how intelligence, leadership and inclusion work together. It is a revelation that will change everything we know and do in organizations in regards to leadership and much more."

Kathleen Nalty
Executive Director
Center for Legal Inclusiveness

"THE *NEXT* IQ explains why today's leaders must change the way they think about intelligence, leadership and inclusion in order to succeed in the 21st century. More importantly, THE *NEXT* IQ illustrates how today's leaders can change, by providing practical examples and direction on inclusive intelligence that a leader can implement today. THE *NEXT* IQ provides something most valuable and rare: actionable knowledge."

Michael C. Connelly
Senior Vice President, Strategy and Planning
Xcel Energy

"I applaud this provocative, insightful, and perceptive addition to the literature on leadership. It provides an impressive range of thoughtful perspectives and specific strategies from which all concerned leaders, instructors, and students of leadership will benefit."

Diane C. Yu
Chief of Staff and Deputy to the President
NYU

"Arin Reeves has crafted the quintessential treatise on the power of integrated communities to be a force of change and innovation. A must read for any business leader—THE *NEXT* IQ creates and codifies an approach to intelligence that transcends any one individual's contribution, into a broader capacity to problem solve, entrepreneurially leverage opportunities in the marketplace and truly learn from each other."

Scott Filer
Chief Executive Officer
National Children's Center

Through a series of thought-provoking lessons, Arin brilliantly challenges us to view intelligence and its potential for a competitive edge in a new way. Her fresh perspective, THE *NEXT* IQ, is simple and compelling, and essential for learning and leading in a global environment."

Ruth Ann Gillis
Executive Vice President & Chief
Administrative Officer, Exelon Corporation
President, Exelon Business Services Company,
Exelon Corporation

The *Next* IQ:

The Next Level of Intelligence for 21st Century Leaders

The *Next* IQ:
The Next Level of Intelligence for 21st Century Leaders

Arin N. Reeves
Foreword by John W. Rowe
Chairman & Chief Executive Officer, Exelon Corporation

Cover design by Andrew O. Alcala.

Printed in the United States of America.

16 15 14 13 12 5 4 3 2

Cataloging-in-Publication Data is on file with the Library of Congress.

Reeves, Arin N.
  The next IQ / by Arin Reeves. — 1st ed.
     p. cm.
  ISBN 978-1-61438-153-2 (print : alk. paper)
1. Leadership. 2. Organizational learning. 3. Intelligence levels.
I. Title.
  HD57.7.R4364 2012
  658.4'092—dc23

                                    2011052206

Discounts are available for books ordered in bulk. Special consideration is given to state bars, CLE programs, and other bar-related organizations. Inquire at Book Publishing, ABA Publishing, American Bar Association, 321 North Clark Street, Chicago, Illinois 60654-7598.

www.ShopABA.org

for
eric

to
caelan and miles

CONTENTS

FOREWORD
THE *NEXT* IQ:
THE NEXT LEVEL
OF INTELLIGENCE
FOR 21ST CENTURY
LEADERS

by John W. Rowe

Exelon Corporation is one of the nation's largest electric utilities. We have the largest fleet of nuclear power plants in the country, and we serve millions of customers who represent the myriad of experiences, backgrounds, perspectives, and new ideas that comprise the global marketplace of the 21st century. As Chairman and CEO of Exelon, I've been an advocate for inclusive leadership because there is no other way to lead in today's uncertain and challenging environment or to compete effectively in that marketplace.

Many companies deal with inclusion as a "nice to have," but it has always been a "must have" for Exelon because we are stronger, smarter and better when we have diverse voices shaping our strategy, culture and actions. Leadership at the highest levels of any organization, at its core, requires one to be a thought leader and a civic/community leader, and the only way to do that in the complex global environment of the 21st century is to be informed of and attuned to the multitude of needs and interests that are present in our organizations, among our customers, and within our communities. Leadership at the highest levels of any organization is also personal. People pay attention to what you do and how you do it, not just what you say, so if you preach the power of inclusion, you must demonstrate inclusive leadership.

As I have lived these realities of leadership, I have developed my own six critical attributes of leadership. Each of these attributes is founded on the ability to actively seek out and integrate different perspectives into the way we think about and learn from the world around us.

First, you must have an unflagging commitment to learn all there is to learn while recognizing that there is always more to learn. In today's world, it's truly difficult to learn rapidly and comprehensively unless you have different perspectives continuously informing your opinion and intuition from different sources. Have a hunger for finding these perspectives.

Second, you must have a passionate commitment to action, recognizing that you almost always will lack sufficient information on which to act. In order to be able to act with confidence without full information, you have to trust the people around you. Inclusive leadership allows people around you to be confident in their own intelligence and their ability to challenge you. If you have not created a space for people to challenge you, you have not created a space for people to express their full intelligence and potential.

Third, you must cultivate a personal appreciation and regard for all individuals. Diversity is a commitment in the way you lead and the way you respect others. If you respect people for who they are, they will maximize who they are and the talents they bring to the table. That will make your organization and its work stronger.

Fourth, you have to have a total commitment to your vision and values. The way leaders lead provides the pathway through which others can also be their best, and your vision and values have to demonstrate inclusion as a daily practice. Lip service means nothing without courageous action.

Fifth, you must have confidence in the future and certainty of success, despite the harsh realities of the present. The realities of the present are only mediated by thinking of leadership through a future lens.

Sixth, lead somewhere that is worth going. Use the values and goals you have developed to establish a mission, a destination worthy of the effort.

These principles are how I have led, continue to lead and expect those around me to lead as well. That said, inclusive leadership is not always easy to do. The uncertainties, challenges, unanswerable questions and day to day difficulties of leadership pull us back into the comforts of where we feel safe even when the situation calls for something new. That's where Arin and THE *NEXT* IQ come in.

THE *NEXT* IQ is about leadership in the 21st century and how it exists at the intersection of leadership, intelligence and inclusion. Arin's work provides clear research and illustrative examples of how leadership today demands inclusion in order to be effective. Leaders who lead in that way do so more intelligently than those who don't. This book focuses on why it is critical for us to not only embrace different perspectives but to actively seek them out in order to enhance our own ability to learn and lead, and on how we can do this in ways that make sense in our individual lives.

Even when we know what it takes to be a successful leader, we often slide back into what is comfortable, easy and predictable because we are human and we all work in fast-paced stressful uncertain environments. It's easy for people to talk about leadership and inclusion, but the transition from talk to action is difficult. Arin's work with Exelon has enabled our organization to translate our values into action in the workplace. This book offers concrete ideas on how to move from talk to action in a realistic way.

My wife and I are active sponsors of many civic and community endeavors that work to lift voices into conversations where they have previously been absent. We have committed much of our time specifically to activities that advance education and inclusion because these are two pillars on which our society will grow and thrive. We have founded charter schools and supported innovative research and teaching in institutions of higher education. We have done this because we know that without these critical foundations, we cannot grow the next generation of leaders we need. This book gives us the framework to assess leadership in that forward-thinking way and it gives us the tools to be able to do that simply and effectively.

ACKNOWLEDGMENTS

Many authors begin their acknowledgments with "no one writes a book alone," and now I know why! Writing this book has been one of the most amazing, growth-inducing, exhausting, inspiring, and energizing adventures in my life. Neither I nor the book would have made it through if not for the legacy, effort, energy, kindness, encouragement and patience of the people whose faith in me and high expectations for me continue to be daily drivers for being and doing better in all areas of my own life.

I am who I am because of some incredibly talented thinkers, writers and storytellers who are no longer here but live through me and so many others whom they influenced. I thank each of them for a legacy that inspires me every day. I remember you always, and I promise to not let you down.

Eric, thank you. For everything. You are the most amazing best friend, life partner, mentor, first draft reader, editor, and a million other things to me. You are beyond amazing . . . you are be.amazing! I am better as a person because of who you are and who you believe/push me to be. This book would not be here if not for who I am because we are us. Since we talked about those rare perfect moments more than thirteen years ago, the perfect moments keep getting more and more perfect. I love you and am so very grateful for everything about you, *ilya, a.*

Caelan and Miles, thank you so much for your patience when I had to write, your curiosity about the book, your insistence on knowing my page count on a daily basis, your excitement when I finished every draft, your help with the proofreading, your beautiful cards of congratulations, and for everything else that you did to make it possible for mommy to finish this book. The two of you inspire me every day with your humor, imagination, energy, independence and enthusiasm for everything! I love you both so very much. (Oh yeah, and by the way, per your request . . . butt.)

For my amazing family and friends, I know that I require more patience than any of you should be required to exercise in one lifetime, and I am so grateful for each and every one of you. Mom, thank you for your encouragement and for telling me at a very young age that I would never be successful working for anyone other than myself. Adi, thank you for the ideas and edits and for having the courage to think differently on so many fronts. To Krista, Tonya and Abosede, thank you for your encouragement throughout this process and for celebrating the small wins with me. You have supported and nurtured me more than words can express! For all of my other family and friends, I am so grateful for each of you. Thank you. Thank you. Thank you for who you are and for who you inspire me to be.

I am truly fortunate to have the lines between professional colleagues and personal friends blur so frequently because of the incredible people with whom I have had the privilege of working and from whom I've learned so much about so much. I want to thank John Rowe for trusting me enough to write the Foreword for this book and for his personal and professional leadership on inclusion through the years. Bill, Nicole, Veta, Kathleen, Scott, Jeff, Tom, Cornell, Susan, Mike, Diane and Ruth Ann—each of you has taught me, inspired me and slowly but surely become (not always with your consent!) a mentor/friend. With your extremely busy schedules and tremendous demands on your time, I am so very grateful that you invested your time in reading the manuscript and giving me your thoughts (both the private advice as well as the public quotes)! Veta and Kathleen, a special thanks to you for all the ways in which you have helped me to grow and then grow some more over the past few years.

To Cie, thank you for getting this whole process started! I am so grateful that the ABA decided to invest in me and this book. Tim, thank you for your patience with my many many questions! Thank you also to Neal and everyone else who has worked on the design, editing, and the other aspects of getting this book to print. Thank you for making this such an amazing journey for me.

Rolisa and Debbie, you know—without a doubt—that without your contributions, I would be way off schedule and still struggling to get my endnotes formatted correctly! Rolisa, thank you for all of your hard work on the citations and for keeping my life together so that I did not completely lose my mind. Debbie, thank you for keeping me on track, and thank you for jumping in and becoming an integral part of the team so quickly!

Thank you to all of the researchers, scholars, writers, practitioners and visionaries whose brilliance created the foundation for my own ideas. I have always felt that I am one of the luckiest people ever to have had teachers of all walks of life who have challenged me to live my life the way I was meant to and allowed me to learn from their courage and wisdom as I developed my own. Some of you I've met and you've invested in me personally. To the ones I have not met but have been moved by greatly, I've learned from you through your life stories and your work. All of you have taught me to always see and think differently, to see and think in my own way. Thank you.

Finally, to all of you who will read this book—thank you for your interest in these ideas. I hope that you are inspired to see the world and yourself in different ways as you read, and I am grateful for the opportunity to have this conversation with you.

All my best,
Arin

INTRODUCTION

A result of the research and work that I have done with individuals, teams, and organizations for over a decade, THE NEXT IQ is that next level of intelligence that you need in order to think, learn, and lead in the increasingly seamless global marketplace of the 21st century. Whether intelligence refers to individual capacity (intelligence quotient), strategic information (intelligence à la Central Intelligence Agency), best practices (business intelligence), or effectiveness in human relationships (emotional intelligence), THE NEXT IQ is about *making intelligence more intelligent for the way the world works today.*

> It is what we think we already know that often prevents us from learning.
>
> Claude Bernard (French physiologist, 1813–1878)

The events in 2011—from the use of Twitter and Facebook in the protests in Egypt to the immediate volatility in the global financial markets caused by economics in Greece one day, a natural disaster in Japan another day, and political wrangling in the United States on a different day—have illustrated how the world has indeed become inextricably interconnected in the ways in which we access information, impact each other's lives, and depend on each other for stability and prosperity. This interconnectedness has changed the ways in which we respond and react, but it must also change the ways in which we think and learn so that we can lead proactively and not reactively. THE NEXT

IQ introduces you to these new ways of thinking through an integrated exploration of research studies, stories, learning experiences, and tested solutions. In the pages that follow, you will learn that The Next IQ is a shift from intelligence as information to intelligence as actionable insight, and this shift will transform leadership that is rooted in individual expertise to direction and guidance formed from multiple and diverse perspectives.

The Next IQ is the start of a conversation on how to make our individual and collective intelligence more intelligent by changing the way we think. This conversation begins with a personal story.

A few years ago, I switched from Starbucks to one of its competitors for my morning dose of hot caffeine. I switched even though everything I cared about was better at Starbucks—the coffee, the ambience, and the service. So, why did I transfer my loyalty? The coffee cup lids.

The lids at Starbucks have an open hole made for easy sipping; however, the hole made it just as easy for spilling . . . on me, my clothes, my car, my children in their stroller, and my fellow commuters when I got jostled on the train. The frustration mounted quickly enough for me to call the Starbucks customer service line to complain about the lids; the woman who answered my call gently told me that the lids were one of the most frequent sources of complaints that she heard. I asked the baristas at my local Starbucks why the coffee cup lid situation was not being fixed given the number of complaints that seemed to be mounting. The baristas encouraged me to order my drink in a larger cup to create "splash room." But, my dosage of choice—Venti—was already the largest dose possible. Starbucks didn't have any larger cups that could decrease my spill probability.

One day, the barista offered to give me less coffee in my cup to prevent spillage! That was the day I switched to the competitor because the competitor's coffee cup lids had little flaps that I could close when I was not moving. Even though I preferred the coffee at Starbucks, I knew that the competitor's coffee would not spill when I was walking or driving or being jostled on the train.

When I first walked into the competitor's coffeehouse, I was surprised to find many of my former linemates from Starbucks. I asked a few of them why they had switched, and I was amazed to find that avoiding the morning spill had also motivated them to walk across the street. So, I drank coffee that I did not really like for a couple of months until a friend of mine told me about the splash stick. The what? She told me there were now splash sticks available at Starbucks to plug the holes in the lids so that coffee didn't splash everywhere.

Of course! A splash stick! This brilliant idea came from a customer who had figured out how to stop the splashing and shared the idea on MyStarbucksIdea.com, the new interactive site that Starbucks set up to solicit ideas from its customers to improve its products, services, and anything else that customers wanted to improve.

MyStarbucksIdea.com was launched on March 19, 2008, at a time when Starbucks appeared to be on the decline. Embroiled in stiff competition with Dunkin' Donuts and McDonald's, Starbucks had hit massive lows in its stock prices ($17.38) and was planning store closures. When Howard Schultz, founder and former CEO of Starbucks, returned to the helm in 2008, he told *CNNMoney* that Starbucks needed "to put ourselves in the shoes of our customers. That is my new battle cry. Live and breathe Starbucks the way our customers do."[1] The company had amassed organizational expertise, but it had lost connection with the perspectives of the people it served. So, under Schultz's second reign, Starbucks began listening.

What was the very first idea implemented as a result of MyStarbucksIdea.com? Splash sticks—because of the input of more than 10,000 submissions! On April 9, 2008, the Starbucks product development team posted "Be Splash Free" on MyStarbucksIdea.com. It read: "Thanks for your many ideas and comments about providing something for our lids to minimize coffee splashes . . . Based on an overwhelmingly positive customer and partner response, we are rolling out splash sticks nationwide this week . . . We hope this helps keep your car and clothes a little cleaner on your rush to work; enjoy and let us know what you think."

From March 2008 to March 2010, the stock price had risen significantly (from $17.38 to $24.97, a 43.67 percent increase at a time when the S&P 500 averaged a 10.67 percent decline)[2] and the Starbucks siren was again welcoming the return of the masses with her mysterious smile. In July 2009, *BusinessWeek* reported that Starbucks was ranked as the brand most engaged with its customers, with its innovative MyStarbucksIdea.com as the major spark that moved the engagement needle.[3]

Of course, there were many factors that contributed to the turnaround at Starbucks, but the power of the splash sticks in bringing people back to Starbucks cannot be overestimated!

MyStarbucksIdea.com is not just a site where Starbucks customers can post ideas. It is a community space where customers can submit, discuss, and vote for improvements in products and experience direct involvement and extensive collaboration with the product development teams at Starbucks. When you enter the site, you can see all the ideas that have been submitted as well as any given idea's current "position" within product development. Icons indicate if the idea is "under review," "reviewed," "in the works," or "launched." You can see how many votes each idea has garnered, and you can see the comments from the community as well as candid profiles and comments from the "idea partners," the members of the Starbucks product development team who are specifically tasked to be liaisons with the online community.

MyStarbucksIdea.com is a powerful example of *Next* IQ intelligence gathering where the transition from individual expertise to inclusive intelligence is fully visible, and the competencies for the development team include the ability to actively seek and include the customers' ideas into future development opportunities. The site is also a powerful example of innovating in a period of uncertainty, which ironically can bring about stability, instead of waiting for certainty before daring to think innovatively.

Starbucks, with its consistent appearances on lists of "best to work for" companies, does not lack in its ability to hire the best and brightest into its product development team. Starbucks can and does hire the best available individual intelligence in the labor market, but that intelligence is based only on individual knowledge and expertise. The individual intelligence level (expertise) of the people who came up with the next generation of products, experiences, and involvement was certainly high in early 2008, but their intelligence was raised to the next level when they included perspectives different from their own, perspectives not necessarily derived from a product development expertise. On the heels of MyStarbucksIdea.com's success, Starbucks sponsored a contest through BetaCup (www.thebetacup.com) for a coffee cup redesign that would make the disposable cups more environmentally sustainable and user friendly. Take note: more perspectives, more intelligence, and the more diverse the perspectives, the more intelligent the intelligence.

This next generation of intelligence, THE *NEXT* IQ with its *global mindset and deliberate intelligence*, is what we will explore together in this book. That said, in order to discuss THE *NEXT* IQ fully, we have to also understand what I call the RETRO IQ, the reliance on individual expertise of a selective few instead of on the collective wisdom of the global many. Let's take a look at an example of the RETRO IQ in action.

During the same period that Starbucks was expanding the number of perspectives to form its business intelligence, Circuit City was narrowing the number of perspectives influencing its business decisions. In January 2007, Circuit City's stock price averaged about $20.00 a share, and it was known for its experienced and knowledgeable salespeople who listened to customers. In March 2007, Circuit City decided—in spite of extensive feedback from inside and outside the company—to fire 3,400 of its most successful people.[4] Customers rebelled, employee morale plummeted, and Circuit City was thoroughly criticized by market analysts, shareholder advocates, and other stakeholders. So, what did Circuit City do? It fired more people, insisting that it was on the right track because it had an expert leadership team that knew what it is doing.[5]

By March 2008, one year after the mass firing of talented salespeople, Circuit City shares were trading at about $4.00 per share, a 75 percent decrease in value from just one year prior. In November 2008, the company filed for bankruptcy and by March 2009, shares were averaging less than 1 cent per share. Meanwhile, Circuit City's closest competitor, Best Buy, was implementing internal company-wide prediction markets (idea generation and speculation models designed to predict future outcomes) to collect perspectives from across all business units, hierarchies, and functions so that it could increase its collective intelligence. We will discuss more about Best Buy's program in a later chapter, but it is important to note that Best Buy weathered the economic storm between 2007 and 2009 instead of closing its doors.

In the same period, during economic uncertainty that affected all industries and sectors, Starbucks chose to listen to more people, and it thrived. Best Buy chose to listen to more people, and it found ways to survive. Circuit City chose to listen to fewer people, and it went out of business. Integrating multiple perspectives in an inclusive way increases intelligence, both individual and organizational, and impacts success.

This next generation of intelligence is about actively soliciting and then harnessing the power of diverse perspectives that may or may not be rooted in specific individual education, experience, and/or expertise. Product development teams may be the best experts at design, but their ability to design a better cup or a better lid doesn't necessarily mean that it will occur to them to plug the hole so the coffee stays in the cup. Business analysts may be the best experts at showing how cost cutting improves the bottom line, but cost cutting done with a narrow perspective also cuts down on the perspectives that allow you to know and deliver what the customer wants. The intelligence you need to solve any problem is already available, if you know how to look for it and use it. Your *Next* IQ is your ability to seek out that intelligence and include it into how you think, learn, and lead.

This book, The *Next* IQ:

- Explores how our understandings of intelligence, leadership, and inclusion have evolved and intersected to create a new level of intelligence that is critical for leaders in this new millennium.
- Presents the global mindset, CORE (intellectual **C**ourage, intellectual **O**penness, intellectual **R**eflection, and intellectual **E**mpathy), and how to cultivate the deliberate intelligence (seeking and including diverse and contrasting points of view) necessary to think, learn, and lead in the 21st century.
- Delves into why we tend to *not* expand the circle of perspectives that can inform our intelligence even when it seems like common sense to do so.
- Examines why we resist seeking and including diverse and contrasting perspectives even when it is in the best interest of our own intelligence and why leaders in the global marketplace of the 21st century cannot be intelligent if they are not *inclusively* intelligent.
- Illustrates how inclusive intelligence in action has a dramatic, positive impact with examples of how leaders from all walks of life have used collective and inclusive intelligence to transform themselves, their teams, their organizations, and even their countries.
- Underscores how the stickiness of the Retro IQ fights the active engagement of your *Next* IQ.

- Presents tested solutions for inclusive intelligence that can be implemented by individual leaders and/or organizations to think, learn, and lead for maximum impact.

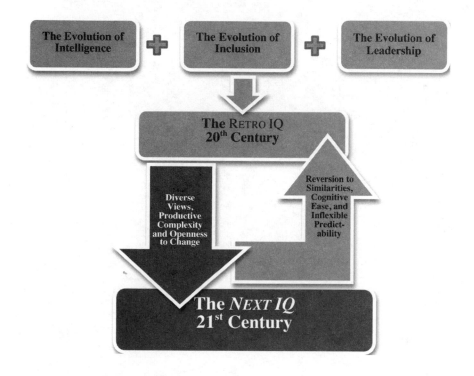

CHAPTER 1

THE *NEXT* IQ—A PREVIEW

The IQ. We know what it is even if we don't know (or agree with) all the technical details about how to define it, measure it, or fully understand it. We know it has to do with intelligence, and we know that a higher score means more intelligence. We know that, in general, we would hire or promote someone with a high IQ over someone with a low IQ. We know that if we took an IQ test, we would hope to get a high score. This is the nature of our familiar but often unexamined relationship with the IQ: IQ equals intelligence; higher IQ is better than lower IQ.

> Globalization has changed us into a company that searches the world, not just to sell or to source, but to find intellectual capital—the world's best talents and greatest ideas.
>
> Jack Welch (former chairman & CEO, General Electric)

This is what I call the RETRO IQ. It is the framework of intelligence that dominates our thinking right now. Although there is much about the virtues and value of the RETRO IQ that can be debated, this book is not about the merits of measuring and analyzing intelligence in the RETRO IQ way. THE *NEXT* IQ is about letting go of this old framework of understanding intelligence altogether and forging a new mindset that brings our relationship with intelligence into the 21st century.

1

The RETRO IQ was effective in the preindustrial agrarian societies (18th and early 19th centuries) when you were born into your social status and your options for work were determined by that status. These societies had limited mobility and communication between different communities. The ability to transfer goods, services, or even ideas across regions or nations was constricted to all but the highest of social classes. The upper classes were the only ones with the means to transcend these various limits. In these early economic structures where production was governed by individual craftsmanship (as opposed to mass production), and education was not accessible to the overwhelming majority of people, your IQ was the sum of what you had access to learn and what you did with what you learned. The environment then did not require more than that from its leaders or their followers.

The RETRO IQ continued to be effective even during the Industrial Revolution when quantum changes in manufacturing, technology, transportation, and societal structures shifted activity and populations away from rural agrarian areas into newly forming urban centers where goods were being mass produced, knowledge and culture were being transferred with relative ease across different communities, and trading across regional and national boundaries was becoming increasingly frequent. Individual expertise had tremendous value even in the industrialist societies (19th and 20th centuries) because people were communicating more, but the levels of education among the masses had not yet shifted dramatically. So, your IQ continued to be the sum of what you had access to learn and what you did with what you learned. The environment for the masses still did not require more than that, but the shift for leaders to think beyond their zones of familiarity was starting to occur.

It is in the transition from the industrial culture to the information culture (20th and 21st centuries) that the RETRO IQ started to lose its relevance. In an information society, the primary resource fueling the economic engines is information, which becomes knowledge when filtered through intelligence. Alvin Toffler, writer and futurist, states that "[i]n a Third Wave economy, the central resource—a single word broadly encompassing data, information, images, symbols, culture, ideology, and values—is actionable knowledge."[1]

This concept of actionable knowledge—the ability to take information and make it into knowledge and transform that knowledge into action—is the key to success as we move away from industry as the economic engine. Actionable knowledge becomes even more critical when we consider the interconnectedness of global economies and the rapid transmission of information across national, cultural, language, and other boundaries.

In the latter part of the 20th century, we saw the information economy begin to break down social, cultural, economic, language, and even interpersonal barriers. In its place, we are witnessing the formation of a truly global society where, as Thomas L. Friedman has articulated in *The World Is Flat: A Brief History of the Twenty-First Century*, competition is unfettered by geographical boundaries and where individuals and organizations need to think and behave differently if they want to thrive in a flat marketplace that affords admission easily to all competitors.[2] It is in this increasingly flattening world where individual expertise and unilateral intelligence—the RETRO IQ—becomes a competitive irrelevance because more people than ever before have access to the information anyone needs to build an individual perspective.

So, what does it take to compete and lead in this flat, open, boundaryless (a term coined by Jack Welch of GE) global marketplace of the 21st century? It takes a global mindset, and the CORE of this global mindset is intellectual **C**ourage, **O**penness, **R**eflection, and **E**mpathy. Leaders must use this CORE to actively seek and then include different and contrasting perspectives. Sounds easy, right? It can be if your workplace, your team, your own professional network, and your personal network already have diverse perspectives that you can begin to include and integrate into your own thinking. Most of us, however, find that when we take a close look at the environments and networks in which we find ourselves, we see similarity more so than diversity. Humans naturally gravitate toward similarity. This is where THE *NEXT* IQ enters. An individual's *NEXT* IQ is *the cultivation of intellectual courage, openness, reflection, and empathy and the ability to actively seek and include different and contrasting points of view from diverse perspectives to create innovative high-impact solutions.* THE *NEXT* IQ begins with the fundamental understanding that no matter how much you know, how brilliant you are, how skilled you are, or how much experience you have amassed, you are not as intelligent as you can be unless you have cultivated an intellectually global mindset and have actively sought out and included different perspectives into your outlook and analysis.

The *Next* IQ is a new way of thinking about intelligence, and nowhere is this new way of thinking more necessary than in leaders who want to lead for impact in this new millennium. As Steve Ballmer, CEO of Microsoft Corporation, once commented about leadership: "Our people, our shareholders, me, Bill Gates, we expect to change the world in every way, to succeed wildly at everything we touch, to have the broadest impact of any company in the world."[3] Ballmer was not talking about just hiring the programmers with the greatest expertise; he was asserting Microsoft's vision for creating impact. The former operates on the Retro IQ; the latter requires The *Next* IQ.

The ability to have impact starts with the ability to cultivate a global mindset. In 2010, James Turley, chairman and CEO of Ernst & Young, stressed that the "[economic] crisis has mandated that we rethink how we have always done business. We need to develop a new global mindset. Topping the list of what we need to examine are talent management and development, and the connection between diversity of thought and innovation."[4] Turley also warned that "the knee-jerk reaction is to relegate diversity to the realm of human resources, associated with fair hiring practices and good corporate citizenship. But any company that clings to that old-fashioned notion of diversity risks limiting its creative potential and ultimately losing its competitive edge. In a globalized world, diversity is more than just a question of race or gender. It is a spectrum of attributes . . . And research shows that capitalizing on these differences is a powerful factor in encouraging innovation."[5]

THE GLOBAL MINDSET: *A CLOSER LOOK*

The global mindset is generally agreed to be a mindset "that combines an openness to and awareness of diversity across cultures and markets with a propensity and ability to synthesize across this diversity."[6] Or, as Kewal Handa, chief for Pfizer and Wyeth, has been quoted as saying, a global mindset is "learning how to compete for everything, everywhere, with everyone."[7] There are many scholarly and industry articles on what a global mindset entails; however, there are very few guides on how exactly to develop a global mindset.

To cultivate a global mindset, you have to start with four key intellectual attitudes that allow you to effectively seek and include diverse perspectives: intellectual **C**ourage, intellectual **O**penness, intellectual

Reflection, and intellectual **Empathy**. Together, these four attitudes comprise the intellectual CORE needed to develop a global mindset and to make your intelligence more intelligent.

- Intellectual **Courage** is the stepping outside of your intellectual comfort zone to challenge your beliefs, thoughts, perspectives, and experiences. It is the willingness to proactively explore these differences knowing that the exploration could create confusion, fear, anger, or other negative emotions. The opposite of this attitude—intellectual cowardice—is the refusal to explore beyond your comfort zone in order to avoid potentially negative emotions.
- Intellectual **Openness** is the exercise of patience and suspension of judgment to be fully open to all beliefs, thoughts, perspectives, and experiences and to analyze them on their own terms and merits instead of as comparatively right or wrong to your own mindset.
- Intellectual **Reflection** is the filter through which you view what you think are facts and analyze how much your past experiences, opinions, and prejudgments about the world have made your perspectives appear like facts to you.
- Intellectual **Empathy** is the process by which you look at your conclusions reflectively and ask yourself if someone else with the exact same set of inputs could have perhaps arrived at a completely different conclusion. This empathy allows you to know that you may be right while others are right, too.

These four intellectual attitudes set the foundation you need in order to seek and include diverse perspectives in a way that allows for a more intelligent intelligence as a leader. Your intellectual CORE will enable you to cultivate the global mindset required to compete and thrive in a world that is increasingly "boundaryless."

THE NEXT IQ has emerged as a critical skill in the 21st century, rooted in the evolution of how we understand and think about intelligence, leadership, and inclusion. Where the RETRO IQ grew out of historical definitions of intelligence and adhered itself to leadership while skimming the edges of inclusion, THE NEXT IQ organically grows out of and connects intelligence, leadership, and inclusion.

Let's take a look at one analysis comparing the RETRO IQ and THE *NEXT* IQ through a sample (RETRO) IQ test question: "In certain IQ tests, [you are] given **two** points for 'categorical' answers, **one** point for 'descriptive' answers, but **no** points for 'relational' answers. So, in response to *'How are a cat and a mouse alike?'* you get two points for 'they are both animals,' one point for 'they both have tails,' and nothing at all if you say 'they both live in houses.'"[8] Further, any creative answers like "they both have starring roles in *Tom and Jerry*" or "they both can be pets" will net you no credit at all.

Translated as a *Next* IQ question, the sample above becomes **"Describe all the ways in which a cat and a mouse are alike,"** and we expect multiple right answers. Whereas the Retro IQ asks you to pick one right answer, The *Next* IQ asks you to generate many answers from as many different perspectives as possible. How would a 5-year-old respond? How would a resident of Shanghai respond? How would a 50-year-old farmer in Peoria, Illinois, respond? How would a veterinarian respond? How would an animal rights activist respond? How would a cartoonist respond?

What if you were leading a team that had to decide new animal safety policies for household pets? Would you want your team to think in terms of one answer or would you want them to generate as many answers as possible before creating a workable solution? *Leading in the 21st century requires a global mindset and the active seeking and including of different and contrasting points of view from diverse perspectives in order to create innovative high-impact solutions.*

In some ways, The *Next* IQ is not so new, and its intertwined integration of intelligence, leadership, and inclusion is visible in many of the 21st-century models of communicating and connecting such as Web 2.0 (with Britannica Online being Web 1.0/limited knowledge and Wikipedia being Web 2.0/collective and growing knowledge)[9] and crowdsourcing (using collective intelligence to solve problems). If you have explored any of these areas individually, you will see some familiar concepts as you continue reading, but the value of this book does not lie in the isolated understanding of intelligence, leadership, and inclusion; it lies in recognizing the impact that is possible when your actions spring from the powerful intersection of intelligence, leadership, and inclusion.

> Wit consists in seeing the *resemblance* between things which differ, and the *difference* between things which are alike.
>
> Madame de Staël, French author and political propagandist, 1766–1817

The *Next* IQ is written from the perspective of how people really learn, so there are stories where you may expect statistics and anecdotes where you may expect analysis. That doesn't mean that you won't get the statistics and analysis, but it may not be where you expect to get it and it may not look the way it has looked in other books. I've deliberately adopted a style of writing where the concepts are presented through stories, metaphors, and other learning constructs that make sense with our lives today and illustrate how The *Next* IQ works.

In The *Next* IQ, it's not what you know that counts. It's not who you know that counts. It's who you know and what they know and how you put it all together that counts! Would you like to try it out before you read further? Here is a simple exercise that will preview The *Next* IQ for you.

---
1 + 1 = 11

Next IQ thinking is not about changing *what* you think about; it's about changing *how* you think about whatever you think about. You can do this exercise with a significant other, child, coworker, friend, teacher, student—any person who is willing to sit down with you for ten minutes. Eight concepts are presented below. You can work with just one concept at a time or with all of them together. You can add more concepts or you can add contexts that narrow the focus of a concept.

The guidelines are simple: Select a concept or concepts and a partner. You and the "second opinion" will take three minutes to individually write down your perspectives about each concept. It is important to write down your perspectives instead of just thinking about them, and both of you should do it at the same time. After three minutes, set aside your individual perspectives and discuss the concept for six minutes collectively to arrive at a perspective that is agreeable to both of you.

Once you have finalized the joint perspective, compare it with your individual perspectives and note how each differs from or is similar to the joint perspective. In thinking about the differences between your individual and the joint perspectives, ask yourself if your perspective changed or whether a particular dimension of your perspective was revealed because of the conversation.

Do this exercise with different people and notice what happens to your perspective with different people.

Concept	My Perspective	Another Perspective	Our Perspective
Success			
Family			
Security			
Ambition			
Peace			
Power			
Control			
Happiness			

The joint perspective that you create is THE NEXT IQ in action. That joint perspective is not a perspective you could have arrived at on your own even though it is what you believe. More importantly, each time you do the exercise with the same concept, the joint perspective from the previous time now becomes part of your individual perspective, which gets further enriched by the new joint experience. If you take even one concept and do this exercise with five people, your personal intelligence about that concept will deepen many times over. Yet, you are not learning anything new per se about the concept; you are just seeing more facets to what you already know and believe. You are, however, learning new things about the person who is doing the exercise with you, and that knowledge will enhance the relationship between the two of you, simply because you had the conversation.

This exercise is useful not just because it generates multiple answers to the same question, but because it creates new answers that are not possible without going through the efforts of identifying the many diverse perspectives.

When you actively seek and use your NEXT IQ, you are deliberately using your intelligence differently than when you simply remember what you know, like adding 1 + 1 and getting 2. With the 1 + 1 = 11 exercise, the more that the joint perspective surprised you, the more that second opinion was different from your own. The more you actively seek those surprises, the more prepared you are to compete and lead and win in the seamless global environment of the 21st century.

This next level of intelligence allows leaders to quickly think differently by leveraging the multiple channels of information they have available to them. By starting the process of thinking with multiple perspectives, you will find your thinking actually shifts from processing information to creating actionable insights.

THE *NEXT* IQ INSIGHTS

THE *NEXT* IQ	The RETRO IQ
THE *NEXT* IQ is bold vision, global perspectives, diverse inputs, and collective wisdom.	The RETRO IQ is narrow focus, individual knowledge, and singular expertise.
THE *NEXT* IQ is an inclusive intelligence that lives at the intersection of intelligence, leadership, and inclusion.	THE RETRO IQ was an asset in agrarian and industrial economies but is a liability in a rapidly changing and increasingly global knowledge-based economy.
THE *NEXT* IQ requires a global mindset (intellectual CORE: **C**ourage, **O**penness, **R**eflection, and **E**mpathy) and *deliberate intelligence* (seeking and including diverse and contradictory perspectives).	

THE *NEXT* IQ ACTIONS

- Do the 1 + 1 = 11 exercise with at least two people.
- Ask your team to generate a list of 10 words that are important to your organization (i.e., innovation, excellence, quality, growth, etc.). Encourage individuals to do the 1 + 1 = 11 exercise with those words.

CHAPTER 2

THE *NEXT* IQ
IN ACTION

Let's explore some examples of THE *NEXT* IQ in action on the global stage. Each of the examples in this chapter highlights leaders and organizations that approached their decision-making processes with a global mindset and inclusive actions. These different approaches underscore both the flexibility of THE *NEXT* IQ as well as the creativity with which it can be applied.

IBM JAMS

JAM SESSIONS

"Since 2001, IBM has used 'jams' [massive electronic brainstorming and problem-solving events] to involve its more than 300,000 employees around the world in far-reaching exploration and problem-solving [because] 'In a world where innovation is global, multidisciplinary and open, you need to bring different minds and different perspectives together to discover new solutions to long-standing problems.'

ValuesJam in 2003 gave IBM's workforce the opportunity to redefine the core IBM values for the first time in nearly 100 years. During IBM's 2006 *Innovation Jam*™—the largest IBM online brainstorming session ever held—IBM brought together more than 150,000 people from 104 countries and 67 companies. As a result, 10 new IBM businesses were launched with seed investment totaling $100 million."

IBM Jam Program Office: https://www.collaborationjam.com

For most of the 20th century, innate intelligence—the ability to take information from the world around you and synthesize it into the right answers—was the primary prerequisite for learning and leading.[1] In the first half of the century, psychologists focused on defining intelligence and creating measurement tools through which to determine the *intelligence quotient* (what I'm calling the RETRO IQ) for individuals. The RETRO IQ model was a breakthrough for educators and employers who had been seeking standardized ways in which to group individuals for teaching and training purposes. According to the American Psychological Association, "[i]n the last century, IQ and achievement tests have changed the face of education and employment all over the industrialized world."[2]

Let's take a closer look at what the RETRO IQ actually tells us. The underlying premise of the intelligence in this RETRO IQ model is that the more information (of the kind being tested) you have had the opportunity to explore, gather, and analyze, the better your answers. In other words, as Harvard psychologist E. G. Boring asserted, "[i]ntelligence is what the tests test."

> If the Aborigine drafted an I.Q. test, all of Western civilization would presumably flunk it.
>
> Stanley Marion Garn
> (professor of physical anthropology, 1922–2007)

There has been much written in favor of and against IQ tests, their applicability, their relevancy, and their accuracy in predicting intelligence. Toward the end of the century, theorists moved away from this narrow definition of intelligence and offered multifaceted models of intelligence and its connections to learning and leading, but intelligence continues to be what the theorists define and what the tests test.

The RETRO IQ measured how you gathered, synthesized, and used information in contexts created by academic theorists. However, only a few—by luck, privilege, or opportunity—had access to the information they needed to have the option of being intelligent. Even in the RETRO IQ's heyday, critics like Walter Lippmann, the Pulitzer Prize–winning journalist, were wary of the incompleteness of and the possible biases in this way of thinking about intelligence.[3] Yet, in spite of the critiques and many revisions in response to the critiques, the RETRO IQ dominates our impression of who is intelligent and how intelligence is connected to leadership. (Think about how much the IQ tests of today—the SAT, LSAT, GMAT, GRE, MCAT, etc.—determine who gets the opportunities to be perceived as intelligent.) The RETRO IQ is inadequate, not because it doesn't measure what it seeks to measure, but because what it seeks to measure is incomplete in measuring what it takes to be a leader in today's global marketplace.

With all of its access to the best minds that the RETRO IQ can deliver, IBM uses *NEXT* IQ tools to generate cutting-edge business ideas. Why? Because no matter how powerfully qualified an individual or group is under the RETRO IQ model, the best ideas are generated through the number of diverse perspectives brought together, not the amount of time or energy spent by any one perspective or even a small group of similar perspectives.

In the 21st century, information is no longer a privilege of the few. It's available to almost anyone who can access the Internet, and much of the information has already been synthesized for easier consumption and translated into intelligence for quick digestion. So, as our collective access to information has increased, so has our collective intelligence. According to groundbreaking research by James R. Flynn, the mean IQ of the world has been increasing almost 10 IQ points per decade.[4] Moreover, Flynn found in the analysis of one test that a score that placed in the top 10th percentile a hundred years ago would place in the bottom 5th percentile today.[5]

So, did people get smarter or did the test get dumber? The answer probably lies in the middle; nonetheless, the test matters less now than it did a hundred years ago. The RETRO IQ, even though it continues to be held in high esteem, is not very useful in helping us identify the leaders of today, let alone tomorrow.

If the RETRO IQ focused on gathering and synthesizing—a process hastened now by Google and Wikipedia—THE *NEXT* IQ, the Inclusion Quotient, focuses on the ability to seek and know the multiple perspectives necessary to create a dynamic solution for rapidly changing contexts. THE *NEXT* IQ is the ability to replicate IBM's "jams" on a daily basis at the micro and macro levels. THE *NEXT* IQ for leaders is about the ability to "jam" creatively and consistently in leading teams, inspiring innovation, solving problems, and advancing the core mission of an organization or project.

James Surowiecki writes about this notion of collective intelligence in his book, *The Wisdom of Crowds: Why the Many Are Smarter Than the Few and How Collective Wisdom Shapes Business, Economies, Societies & Nations*.[6] Surowiecki argues that crowds are indeed wiser than individuals; however, he differentiates between unwise crowds (mobs) and wise crowds. Wise crowds, according to Surowiecki need to have individuals who have diversity of opinion, independence of thought, decentralization of knowledge, and an aggregation mechanism to translate individual opinions into a collective judgment/decision. The IBM model works because its process has integrated the characteristics of a wise crowd, and once you have a wise crowd, the wise crowd is wiser than any of its individual members regardless of the brilliance of any individual member.

This ability to create and tap into the wisdom of wise crowds is more critical than the RETRO IQ in predicting who will be effective and excellent leaders in today's world.

MORE INTELLIGENT INTELLIGENCE

INTELLIGENCE FOR THE INTELLIGENCE COMMUNITY

Wikipedia is often cited as the most visible and utilized wisdom derived from diverse and varied perspectives; Intellipedia is its lesser known but equally powerful cousin that serves as the collaborative data-sharing site for the United States intelligence community. Intellipedia officially launched in 2006, and by November of that year, it had over 3,600 independent users in the intelligence community whose collective edits to information totaled around 1,000 edits per day.

As *USA Today* reported on November 2, 2006, "[w]hen New York Yankees pitcher Cory Lidle crashed his plane into a Manhattan apartment building this month, officials from the Transportation Security Administration and eight other agencies updated information on the accident 80 times in two hours. The crash wasn't a terror threat, but authorities didn't know that at first."[7]

Edits are attributed to specific authors, and perspectives and opinions are encouraged in addition to facts. Within a year and a half of its official launch, the *New York Times* reported that "the top-secret version of Intellipedia has 29,255 articles, with an average of 114 new articles and more than 4,800 edits to articles added each workday."[8]

With Intellipedia, when people in the intelligence community are trying to gather information on a topic, they are not limited to asking questions of people that they know or mining sources to which they have access. Like the IBM Jams, Intellipedia opens up the spigot of information for everyone to access as soon as they need the information, and it allows intelligence analysts to share in each other's diverse networks.

As the former Defense Intelligence Agency's Deputy Director for Intelligence, Robert Cardillo, said in 2007, "I can say, without reservation and I tell every new analyst that joins my organization that your value as an analyst to our business and to your customer is directly proportional to the depth and diversity of your network. All right, and no offense, not your IT network; your analytic network: who you work with, who you interact with, where you get expertise from, who you ask questions of."[9] Intellipedia instantly expands the depth and diversity of networks for each and every intelligence professional, and with each level of expansion, Intellipedia makes intelligence professionals . . . more intelligent.

LINUS'S LAW

In the modern day fable *The Cathedral and the Bazaar*, Eric S. Raymond coins and uses the term Linus's Law—"given enough eyeballs, all bugs are shallow"—to create the new rules of developing software in the 21st century.[10] Linus's Law, named for Linus Torvalds, creator of the Linux operating system, playfully makes the point that the number of people (eyeballs) with different perspectives working to solve a problem make bugs (coding/programming errors) shallow—that is, because of the many eyeballs errors rise to the surface thereby becoming easy to locate and fix.

In the computer programming world, "a bug is an error, flaw, mistake, failure or fault in a computer program that prevents it from working correctly or produces an incorrect result."[11] All programming code has some bugs, and some of these bugs are easy to find (shallow) but many are quite difficult to find (deep). If you have enough eyeballs searching for the bugs from lots of different perspectives, even the deep bugs become shallow. Without enough eyeballs, the bugs stay buried and are often deemed unsolvable by experts, not because they truly are unsolvable but because they were unfindable through limited eyeballs.

Multiple and diverse perspectives analyze, diagnose, and solve problems faster than individual perspectives.

The essence of Raymond's essay is that the more widely available the programming code is to the public (the Bazaar model), the faster the bugs are discovered and fixed; the more cloistered the code is to a few select experts (the Cathedral model), the harder and longer it takes to find the bugs and fix them. Raymond explains that the problem in developing software is the "mismatch between the tester's and the developer's mental models of the program; the tester, on the outside looking in, and the developer on the inside looking out. In closed-source development they're both stuck in these roles, and tend to talk past each other and find each other deeply frustrating." The differences in perspectives make communication difficult unless you actively bridge the differences by making everyone a part of the thought process. Although Raymond's rules were developed for developing software, take a look at his rules and see if *The Cathedral and The Bazaar*'s take on intelligence could enhance the way people learn, work, and lead in your organization:[12]

1. Every good work of software starts by scratching a developer's personal itch.
2. Good programmers know what to write. Great ones know what to rewrite (and reuse).
3. "Plan to throw one away; you will, anyhow."
4. If you have the right attitude, interesting problems will find you.
5. When you lose interest in a program, your last duty to it is to hand it off to a competent successor.
6. Treating your users as co-developers is your least-hassle route to rapid code improvement and effective debugging.
7. Release early. Release often. And listen to your customers.
8. Given a large enough beta-tester and co-developer base, almost every problem will be characterized quickly and the fix obvious to someone.
9. Smart data structures and dumb code works a lot better than the other way around.
10. If you treat your beta-testers as if they're your most valuable resource, they will respond by becoming your most valuable resource.

11. The next best thing to having good ideas is recognizing good ideas from your users. Sometimes the latter is better.
12. Often, the most striking and innovative solutions come from realizing that your concept of the problem was wrong.
13. "Perfection (in design) is achieved not when there is nothing more to add, but rather when there is nothing more to take away."
14. Any tool should be useful in the expected way, but a truly great tool lends itself to uses you never expected.
15. When writing gateway software of any kind, take pains to disturb the data stream as little as possible—and *never* throw away information unless the recipient forces you to!
16. When your language is nowhere near Turing-complete [rough translation: tested and validated], syntactic sugar [rough translation: language that is easy to understand] can be your friend.
17. A security system is only as secure as its secret. Beware of pseudo-secrets.
18. To solve an interesting problem, start by finding a problem that is interesting to you.
19. Provided the development coordinator has a communications medium at least as good as the Internet, and knows how to lead without coercion, many heads are inevitably better than one.

LINUS'S LAW IN ACTION

In 1991, Linus Torvalds, a computer science student at University of Helsinki in Finland, posted a message to a newsgroup for computer programmers that began with: "I'm doing a (free) operating system (just a hobby . . .)." This was the birth of the Linux operating system and the beginning of Linus's leadership in open-source software.

Open-source software is software that is licensed to give all users the freedom and rights to use, study, change, and redistribute the original and/or altered program without owing royalties to the original and/or previous developers; any modified and redistributed software is required to retain full and royalty-free openness. This unrestricted access to the source code allows programmers to collaboratively develop, correct, update, and enhance the software openly and transparently, while proprietary/closed software can only be fixed, modified, and improved by a limited number of individuals who have access to the code.

Open-source software is often wrongly presumed to be noncommercial, and many open-source programs these days are "commercial programs, supported by one of many for-profit companies."[13] In other words, open-source is collaborative and profitable—in fact, open-source software business models can be even more profitable than proprietary software business models because the cost of developing the software is far cheaper.

As a leading example of open-source software, the Linux operating system has benefited from the thousands of developers from all over the world who have contributed their talents and problem-solving skills to the continued improvement of Linux.

Though the open-source process has been criticized by many of the proprietary software companies as messy, unstable, and risky, studies actually have shown that open-source code is often better than proprietary software code,[14] that Linux is more reliable than its closed-source counterparts,[15] and that the overwhelming majority of the large companies using Linux are extremely satisfied.[16] In 2006, ZDNet, a major news source for all things computers, declared that "the war is over and Linux won" in coverage of a major IBM study that showed that the majority of server technology in large companies was Linux-based with the trend lines poised to show greater growth for Linux than any of its closed-source competitors.

Linus's Law: More eyeballs, shallow bugs, more success.

Open source is not only giving consumers better products, it is changing the software development industry and the business models in it. Inclusion leads to success, innovative success.

The RETRO IQ is the socially acceptable measure of a person's intelligence as indicated by one of several intelligence tests. Interestingly, none test for the ability to seek out and integrate different (and often conflicting) perspectives into one's way of seeing and analyzing the world. In our schools, our workplaces, and our communities, we have allowed the world of intelligence and the world of inclusion to exist separately and independently.

What if the two worlds need to fuse together in order for each to make sense? What if the ability to be inclusive is a form of intelligence, and what if intelligence is not—well, intelligent—if it is not inclusive?

Radical? Maybe, but it is not a completely new concept.

The IBM Jams and Linus's Law push us to think beyond what we can know by ourselves, but they can often be misunderstood to mean that the intellectual capital of any one person is not important. On the contrary, in both the Jams and Linus's Law, the intellectual capital brought to the collective process is critical but it is not enough by itself. Individual expertise may suffice to find one right answer to a problem in the now, but individual expertise alone does not allow you to generate all the possible answers you need to solve for the now and the next.

TUMOR BOARDS

A Japanese proverb that predates all our modern work on intelligence research simply and elegantly states that "none of us is as smart as all of us." So, those of us who rely on seeking out the perspectives of others, especially others who have had the benefit of different experiences and perspectives, are tapping into a collective intelligence that is more expansive and extensive than any one individual IQ.

THE PATHOLOGIST, THE ONCOLOGIST, AND THE POWER OF MULTIPLE PERSPECTIVES

A diagnosis of cancer is difficult for a doctor to deliver and devastating for a patient to hear. We have made dramatic advancements in how cancer is medically treated, but one of the most profound advancements in cancer treatment is not a medical one. It is one of inclusion: tumor boards.

Although they have been around for a few decades, tumor boards—multidisciplinary teams of physicians representing various specialties, social service professionals, alternative care professionals, and patients themselves—have become a critical component of care in meeting the complex health needs of patients with cancer. Tumor boards meet at various points during a patient's journey from diagnosis to treatment to remission to retreatment to end-of-life decisions to discuss and analyze the full range of options available to a patient. There is often disagreement—that is, the pathologist disagrees with the oncologist, the oncologist disagrees with the holistic medicine expert—and there are rarely clear answers. The dialog flows from one of information sharing to one of understanding the differences in the interpretation of the information. Even when there is some agreement on what the data is, the advice given to the patient is often very subjective: "If it was me, this is what I would do." Tumor board discussions are not conducted to build consensus; they are engaged to give a patient the ability to make the best decision possible when there are no right answers to be found.

The individual intelligence of any one person who serves on a tumor board is less intelligent than the collective power of the diverse and often divergent perspectives that are raised. As one physician who serves on a tumor board said to me, "Once the door is opened to a new world, I am better for knowing what is in that world even if I choose to not go through that door. And, in these matters of life and death, having these doors opened to you is a gift that means more than being right."

THE *NEXT* IQ does not impugn the importance of intelligence as we have always understood it. (The importance of the oncologist's expertise in oncology does not fade.) THE *NEXT* IQ does, however, challenge the traditional understanding of intelligence as incomplete and outmoded for the 21st century, and it offers a new way to lead that stretches from intelligence to inclusive intelligence. (The oncologist's expertise is not complete without the pathologist's, the psychologist's, and the patient's perspectives.) THE *NEXT* IQ is not about tweaking the way you think about intelligence. It is about radically shifting the way you *approach* thinking about intelligence, especially as intelligence relates to leadership.

In his book, *The Difference: How the Power of Diversity Creates Better Groups, Firms, Schools, and Societies*, Scott E. Page differentiates identity diversity (who you are) from cognitive diversity (how you think) even though he unequivocally connects how identity diversity can influence and impact cognitive diversity.[17] According to Page, diversity in cognitive perspectives can be broken down into four categories: diverse perspectives (how we see things), diverse interpretations (how we analyze and categorize things), diverse heuristics (how we think about and generate solutions to problems), and diverse predictive models (how people logically make their way through a set of criteria to figure out what can or will happen next). According to Page, "when we meet people who think differently than we do ... we should see opportunity and possibility. We should recognize that a talented 'I' and a talented 'they' can become even more talented 'we.' That happy vision rests not on blind optimism, or catchy mantras. It rests on logic. A logic of diversity."[18]

Jim Turley, chairman and CEO of Ernst & Young, has found that "[l]eading companies have shown that visible benefits to the bottom line result from leveraging inclusive ways of thinking. But care is needed because diverse teams are rarely mediocre—they are either highly successful or highly unsuccessful. Developing an inclusive culture where all team members can successfully bring their perspectives to the table becomes essential. The research is clear: Well-managed, diverse teams will outperform homogenous teams."[19]

> It is not the strongest of the species that survives, nor the most intelligent that survives. It is the one that is the most adaptable to change.
>
> Charles Darwin

As ideal as THE NEXT IQ sounds, there is a reason why not all hospitals have tumor boards and why even the ones that do limit the people who can serve on them. For example, many tumor boards do not allow patients or patient representatives to attend the meetings. The RETRO IQ is familiar, easy, and predictable. It takes less energy to understand because it is deeply embedded in how we have learned to think, work, and lead. For its survival, the RETRO IQ relies on our collective attachment to our comfort zones and our collective resistance to change. So, it is important to note that THE NEXT IQ doesn't ask you to do away with the comforts of the RETRO IQ; it just asks you to allow the RETRO IQ to not dominate the way you think, learn, and lead. In many ways, the core principle of "multiple rights" in THE NEXT IQ allows THE NEXT IQ to exist alongside the RETRO IQ in a supportive and collaborative way instead of competing with it to arrive at one right answer.

THE NEXT IQ feels unfamiliar and difficult at first. It seems to take more energy, more time, and a greater willingness to leave our zones of comfort. Pathologists and oncologists have existed for many decades in their individual spheres of expertise and influence. Bringing them together in one room and encouraging them to disagree and contradict each other requires leadership competencies that are not yet universally embraced. Each doctor can be effective on his or her own, but the patient is served with excellence when an answer informed by diverse perspectives is forged from the productive discord. THE NEXT

IQ challenges us to change the ways in which we learn, think, and lead because the change leads to better results. It pushes us to strive for excellence even if effectiveness is within reach. But, it delivers innovative solutions, and it does so quickly.

So, what does it take to lead with impact in the 21st century?

It takes a shift from the RETRO IQ to THE *NEXT* IQ. In the 21st century, our world is a seamlessly global environment of multiple coexisting right answers, competing contexts, and rapidly changing landscapes where you always have more information than necessary and less time than you need in order to learn and lead. In the 21st century, intelligent leadership needs inclusion in order to be truly intelligent—and to lead well.

THE CHACÓN JOLT

As of this book's publication, a Google search of "leadership" nets you roughly 500 million hits. There are many academic theories, numerous assessments, and a mountain of practical advice for individuals and for organizations. At first glance, it seems there are as many different perspectives on leadership as there are hits on the search term, but a closer look reveals an interesting observation: leadership can take many forms, but all forms seem to require one primary characteristic—intelligence. Research on this connection between leadership and intelligence shows that of 59 characteristics including honesty, charisma, and kindness, intelligence shines as the key characteristic that people perceived as critical for all leaders.[20]

It takes intelligence to be a leader. Intuitive, right?

Well, not quite. It turns out that we (the collective "we" of individuals, organizations, and societies) don't really have any way of definitively, accurately, and consistently discerning who is or is not intelligent, so we generally default to whom we *perceive* to be intelligent in order to determine who actually *is* intelligent. Moreover, once we perceive them to be intelligent, we then presume that they are better leaders, so we are more likely to see and accept them in leadership roles.[21] Simply put, if you are perceived to be intelligent, you are more likely to be perceived as a good leader, and you are more likely to end up in a leadership role.[22]

This creates an interesting cycle. Our historical perceptions of intelligence and leadership are based on the people we have seen in leadership positions throughout history. These leaders from the past play(ed) a critical role in selecting the leaders of today, and our perceptions of leadership going forward are based on the leaders of today. As was, so is and so will be. This is the essence of the RETRO IQ—looking back to look ahead.

This cycle not only validates and perpetuates our perceptions, but it fuses our perceptions with the identities of the people who have historically occupied the positions in question. The perceptions, therefore, don't just become prerequisites for leadership; they become connected with certain identities and characteristics that are more likely to be seen as part of the makeup of viable future leaders because those identities have been visible in past leaders. Invariably, the leaders themselves are not incentivized to break this cycle because challenging the cycle can mean questioning the validity and/or credibility of their own leadership.

THE NEXT GENERATION OF LEADERSHIP

Imagine a minister of defense.

Who did you picture? A man or a woman?
In our research study, about 2 percent pictured a woman.

Now, imagine a visibly pregnant woman leading the troops in Afghanistan. In our studies, about 95 percent responded with various versions of "I can't." The other 5 percent just did not respond.

As *Time* reported in 2008: "When Spanish Prime Minister José Luis Rodríguez Zapatero's new cabinet members took their oath of office before King Juan Carlos on Monday, one of them, the recently-appointed Defense Minister, stood out from the rest. Literally. Carme Chacón, 37, is not only the first woman to head Spain's armed forces. She is also seven months pregnant . . . the sight of Chacón inspecting troops on her first day in office, with her rounded belly covered in a stylish maternity blouse, came as a jolt."[23] (See photo in endnote of Minister Chacón in Afghanistan visiting Spanish troops.)

A pregnant woman as a minister of defense for a major European country is a "jolt" not because of Minister Chacón's intelligence or qualifications but because we cannot perceive what we have never seen. She looks strange and out of place, not because she is either of these things, but because a minister of defense looks like a man, and we cannot begin to even envision her as the leader of the Spanish military until we realize that our perceptions are based on historic vision, and it is difficult to see what we have never seen before.

I'm not suggesting that people who rise to leadership in the RETRO IQ model are not effective leaders. (We have had some excellent ministers/secretaries of defense who have been men!) Many who are perceived to be intelligent and land in leadership roles may be quite effective in those roles, but what if our perceptions lull us into selecting leaders who look like they could be good leaders instead of leaders who could be truly amazing leaders? What if we are settling for sporadic effectiveness by relying on perceptions of leadership informed by history (the RETRO IQ) when we could be striving for consistent excellence by allowing our imagination to guide our perspectives on leadership (THE NEXT IQ)?

Many people in Spain were taken aback when Chacón was appointed as minister of defense, but in 2010, two years after she was sworn in, Chacón polled as the second highest politician in Zapatero's cabinet in a study conducted by Spain's Center for Sociological Research (CIS). Moreover, Spaniards reported trusting the armed forces, under Chacón's leadership, more than any other institution in Spain even though Spain continues to be embroiled in Afghanistan, a policy that is not supported by most Spaniards.[24]

Leaders who strive for excellence and impact must and can shift from the RETRO IQ to THE NEXT IQ (even if they don't fully let go of the RETRO IQ). Upon her appointment, Chacón's abilities and even her politics were questioned far less than her "pregnant status." In order to lead in the 21st century's global arenas, leaders have to solicit different perspectives and integrate those perspectives into the way they lead, and this starts with the ability to envision leaders themselves as looking different than they have in the past. Zapatero's choice for minister of defense showed his ability to see beyond what was to what could be, and in that vision is where THE NEXT IQ comes alive and thrives.

Each of the previous examples of the THE NEXT IQ in action demonstrate how intellectual courage, openness, reflection, and empathy can lead to new levels of intelligence and innovation that could not have been achieved through traditional intelligence mechanisms.

THE *NEXT* IQ INSIGHTS: CHAPTER 2

THE *NEXT* IQ	The RETRO IQ
The ability to "get" all of the possible right answers and create multiple solutions. (IBM Jams, Intelligent Intelligence)	The ability to select one right answer to solve a problem.
Focusing on the solution as the source of power for many individuals. (Linus's Law)	Focusing on an individual's knowledge as a source of power.
The ability to visualize the possibilities of all potential outcomes and solutions in order to make best decision. (Tumor Boards)	An individual's ability to predict the probability of success or failure of one particular event.
Perspectives on leadership informed by imagination of what the present and future truly need. (The Chacón Jolt)	Perceptions of leadership informed by leaders in history.

- The inclusive intelligence possible through THE *NEXT* IQ does not do away with individual intelligence; it transcends it. Inclusive intelligence works better when all the intelligences included are operating at full potential.

THE *NEXT* IQ ACTIONS: CHAPTER 2

- Identify which of the examples in this chapter really resonate with you and why. Is there any aspect of your life to which you can apply the lesson extracted from this example?
- Create your own list of THE *NEXT* IQ in action. Think about the stories and legends of courage, innovation, entrepreneurship, and so on, in your life, family, or organization, and you will find THE *NEXT* IQ in action. Use the list to remind yourself that the next level of intelligence is not something you wait for; it is something you cultivate deliberately.

CHAPTER 3

THE EVOLUTION OF INTELLIGENCE

The Enigmatic Elephant (Part I)

One day an elephant walked into a village where none of the villagers had ever seen an elephant before. The villagers were frightened by the beast and asked the most intelligent men in the village—six blind men renowned for their intellectual skills as well as their courage—to examine the elephant so that the villagers could figure out what the beast was and what they should do with it.

The six blind men were led to the elephant and they formed a circle around it to examine it. Each man reached out and touched the part of the elephant that was in front of him; one touched the side, one touched an ear, one touched a tusk, one touched a leg, one touched the trunk, and one touched the tail. Each man spent ample time getting to know the various nuances of what he was touching, and each was satisfied that he now knew the full and true nature of the beast.

"I know for sure that this beast is like a wall," said the man who had touched the side, and he went on to discuss what that meant.

"Not at all like a wall," interrupted the man who had touched an ear. "I know for sure that this beast is like a large fan."

"Both of you are clearly wrong," said the man who had touched a leg. "This animal is much more like a solid tree."

"I think you all are quite confused. It may not even be an animal," said the man who had touched a tusk. "This creature is hard as stone and sharp as a spear."

"I think perhaps you are the one that is confused," replied the man who had touched the trunk. "This beast is very much alive, and it is like a large snake."

"Not a snake, but maybe a rope," said the man who had touched the tail.

Then, the six men began to argue about the true nature of the beast.

(continued in Chapter 4)

Philosophers and pragmatists alike have pondered the concept of intelligence long before social scientists sought to understand and quantify it. From Socrates (469–399 BC), who asserted that "I know I am intelligent because I know that I know nothing," to the Indian proverb that warns "when there is a glut of words, there is a lack of intelligence," the journey to comprehend intelligence has been an ancient and global endeavor. That said, the transition from trying to understand intelligence to measuring it has been a relatively recent phenomenon that began in Europe and blossomed in America. The question of "what is intelligence?" evolved into "how do we know if someone is intelligent?" which transitioned into "what is one's intelligence quotient?"

History of the IQ and Intelligence Theories

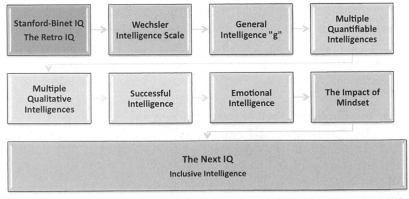

Copyright © 2011 Nextions LLC.

In 1882, France passed a series of laws mandating that all children between the ages of 6 and 14 attend school, but the schools were not adequately equipped to deal with the varying degrees of literacy and learning capacities of the students who flooded their buildings. In a strategic attempt to understand the different learning needs of the country's children, Alfred Binet, a leading French psychologist, was asked to create a test instrument through which a student's learning ability could be measured for the purposes of enhancing the teaching methods in French schools. Binet joined with his colleague, Theodore Simon, to create the Binet-Simon scale, a testing instrument that measured a student's "mental age," the student's "intelligence" in comparison to the average abilities of the student's chronological age group. The student's mental age allowed schools to place the student with his or her learning peers if the child did not test according to his or her chronological average. Binet was excited to contribute to this new way of thinking about learning capacity and teaching, but he expressed doubts about the instrument's ability to pinpoint a *permanent* level of intelligence for any child given Binet's belief that intelligence was a dynamic concept that changed as the child and his or her circumstances changed.[1]

In spite of Binet's concerns, the Binet-Simon scale became the foundation upon which the concept of "quantifiable intelligence"—or IQ as we know it today—was born and future intelligence tests were built. In the early 1900s, the Binet-Simon scale was standardized for the American population by Lewis Terman, a psychologist at Stanford University, and the Stanford-Binet Intelligence Scale was introduced to the world as the first intelligence test to give people of any age a discrete intelligence quotient, an IQ.

In 1955, American psychologist David Wechsler published the next generation of intelligence measurement, the Wechsler Adult Intelligence Scale (WAIS), which provided a composite IQ score, a verbal IQ score, and a performance IQ score. Wechsler was deeply dissatisfied with the narrowness of the Stanford-Binet test because he, like Binet, believed that intelligence involved "the global capacity of a person to act purposefully, to think rationally, and to deal effectively with his environment,"[2] and he believed that having multiple scores that revealed multiple capacities gave a fuller picture of a person's true intelligence. Further, given his specific criticism of the Stanford-Binet test that children learned differently than adults, Wechsler also developed two tests specifically for children, the Wechsler Intelligence Scale for Children (WISC) and the Wechsler Preschool and Primary Scale of Intelligence (WPPSI). The latest revision of the WAIS, the WAIS-III, has greatly influenced the revisions of the Stanford-Binet test and is the standard test used for both educational and professional purposes.

Theories of Intelligence

As our collective understanding of intelligence continues to build on and evolve from Binet, Terman, and Wechsler, differing theories of the definition and/or composition of intelligence itself have developed. Four of the most influential theorists and their theories on this topic are outlined below.

- Charles Spearman (1863–1945), a British psychologist, formulated the concept of a "general intelligence," a *g factor* that demonstrated a general cognitive ability regardless of context.[3]
- Louis L. Thurstone (1887–1955) believed that intelligence could never be a single ability. Instead, he identified seven different primary mental abilities that he thought collectively contributed to one's overall intelligence: verbal comprehension, reasoning, perceptual speed, numerical ability, word fluency, associative memory, and spatial visualization.[4]
- Howard Gardner (b. 1943), similar to Thurstone, put forth a theory of multiple intelligences, but unlike Thurstone, Gardner moved away from using purely numerical scores for intelligence altogether and integrated articulations of intelligence from other cultures to create his eight distinct intelligences: visual-spatial, verbal-linguistic, bodily-kinesthetic, logical-mathematical, inter-personal, musical, intra-personal, and naturalistic.[5]
- Robert Sternberg (b. 1949) agreed with Gardner that intelligence had multiple facets, but he felt that many of Gardner's intelligences were better classified as talents. Sternberg viewed intelligence as an active dynamic force in a person's life, and he identified three factors that he believed led to "successful intelligence": analytical intelligence (problem-solving abilities), creative intelligence (capacity to deal with new situations), and practical intelligence (ability to adapt to change).[6] As Sternberg summarizes his own research, "we did lots of studies where we show practical intelligence doesn't correlate with G [General IQ]. We have prob-

ably two dozen studies that practical intelligence better predicts job success than IQ."[7]

As these theories illustrate, the issue of intelligence continues to perplex psychologists and researchers who want to capture the concept and study it in a contained way. Adding complexity to this intellectual stew has been the recent introduction of "emotional intelligence" as both a part of and separate from IQ. Emotional intelligence, often referred to as EI, consists of the ability to understand and regulate emotions and empathy. Keith Beasley, a contributor to Mensa International, even coined the term Emotional Quotient (EQ) to challenge the dominance of IQ as an intelligence measure. The pioneers of EI, Peter Salovey and John D. Mayer, have defined emotional intelligence as "the subset of social intelligence that involves the ability to monitor one's own and others' feelings and emotions, to discriminate among them and to use this information to guide one's thinking and actions."[8] According to Salovey and Mayer, the perception of emotion, the ability to reason using emotions, the ability to understand emotion, and the ability to manage emotions are the four components of emotional intelligence. The emotional intelligence movement has gained considerable momentum in the past few years with the release of Daniel Goleman's book *Emotional Intelligence: Why It Can Matter More Than IQ.*[9]

CONTEMPORARY DEFINITIONS OF INTELLIGENCE

From Binet to Goleman, from IQ to EQ, all the hard work and research on understanding intelligence must have resulted in some universal definitions of intelligence, right? Absolutely not! The definitions of intelligence vary as much today as they have since the 19th century:

- "capacity for learning, reasoning, understanding, and similar forms of mental activity; aptitude in grasping truths, relationships, facts, meanings, etc." (www.dictionary.com)
- "capacity for understanding; ability to perceive and comprehend meaning" (Collins English Dictionary)
- "ability to learn or understand or to deal with new or trying situations; the ability to apply knowledge to manipulate one's

environment or to think abstractly as measured by objective criteria, as tests" (Merriam-Webster)

- "capacity to acquire and apply knowledge, especially toward a purposeful goal; an individual's relative standing on two quantitative indices, namely measured intelligence, as expressed by an intelligence quotient, and effectiveness of adaptive behavior" (American Heritage Dictionary)

These representative definitions cover everything from "grasping truths" to "quantitative indices" to "adaptive behavior," but they all do begin with the *ability* or *capacity* to do these varying things. So, whether we are talking about testing for learning potential or we are considering the coexistence of multiple intelligences (including emotional intelligences), we begin with an individual's ability to take in the world around her and express what she has absorbed in the form of answers to test questions, solutions to business problems, or adaptation to changing environments.

This ability, according to recent research by Carol Dweck, is not a fixed capacity. It is a flexible process based on an individual's mindset.[10] Dweck, a professor at Stanford University, has found that people's understandings of intelligence have a tremendous impact on their ability to learn.[11] People with a "fixed mindset" on intelligence believe that their abilities are connected to a fixed intelligence so they tend to focus on what they think they can or can't do instead of focusing on what they can learn. People with a "growth mindset" see their intelligence as constantly expanding so they tend to focus on what they can learn. In the long run, the "fixed mindset" people—even if they are highly intelligent based on traditional measures—tend to underperform their "growth mindset" peers.

In the business context, Laura Kray and Michael Haselhuhn studied the impact of fixed mindsets and growth mindsets on people's abilities to negotiate, and they found that negotiators with growth mindsets were better negotiators who achieved better results.[12] With respect to how supervisors view the ability of those that they are leading, research by Peter Heslin and Gary Latham found that supervisors with a growth mindset were far more likely to see higher levels of potential as well as improvement in their employees in comparison to supervisors with a fixed mindset.[13] Supervisors only see potential and improvement in others when they believe that intelligence is growing instead of fixed.

If we connect all the intelligence dots, it becomes evident that intelligence requires both a growth mindset and the ability to absorb data of all sorts from the environment and to express the processed data as personal insights. While the 19th- and 20th-century definitions of intelligence helped us identify the various dots, connecting these dots in the 21st century requires THE *NEXT* IQ. Leaders need to cultivate a global mindset (a growth mindset that has no boundaries) and exercise the ability to seek and include multiple and often contradictory streams of data in order to learn and lead successfully in an environment where information is in excess and new insights are in demand.

As the fable at the beginning of the chapter illustrates, the power of THE *NEXT* IQ is the power for each of the "blind men" to know that their knowledge is true even if someone else's knowledge contradicts it. Further, they can come to understand that the contradictory knowledge is true even if it sounds false. THE *NEXT* IQ is the shift from asking "which of us is right?" to "what does it look like if each of us is right?"

RE(DEFINING) INTELLIGENCE: THE *NEXT* IQ

Let's visit another typical intelligence test question to demonstrate the contrast between 19th- and 21st-century thinking.

How would you answer the following question?

Which doesn't belong? clam, pig, oven, rose

The correct answer to this IQ test sample question is "oven" because it is not a living thing whereas the others are. Now, taken from the perspective of a child (or a chef), the answer may be "rose" because all the others have to do with food. Yet another perspective—perhaps an oceanographer's—would claim that the answer should be "clam" because you can find all the other items on land whereas a clam is found in water.[14] Recall from "Tunnel Vision IQ" in Chapter 1, as C. George Boeree has explained, in some IQ tests points are given for categorical answers and descriptive answers, but no points are given for relational answers.

So, which is the most *intelligent* answer? If you were the leader of a team, would you want your team to argue for one "right answer" or would you want them to generate all the possible answers? Which approach would make your team more intelligent? Which approach would make your team more competitive?

The RETRO IQ tests one's ability to process information. THE *NEXT* IQ captures one's ability to take in information from varied and often conflicting sources and arrive at a new insight in which multiple perspectives coexist and new information is generated.

Let's explore Linus's Law through Eric S. Raymond's essay, *The Cathedral and the Bazaar.* Recall from Chapter 2 that Linus's Law states, "given enough eyeballs, all bugs are shallow." The following is the revised version of Raymond's bazaar-style creation and use of intelligence that we utilize with our clients:[15]

1. Every good work starts with the curiosity of a person. Every great work starts with the collective curiosity of many people.

2. Good innovators know how to get good ideas. Great innovators know not to reinvent the wheel when they don't need to.

3. Plan to throw at least one idea away; you will, anyhow. The more ideas you get from more sources, the more you will know which one(s) to throw way.

4. If you have the right attitude, interesting problems will find you.

5. When you lose interest in anything, your last duty to it is to hand it off to a competent successor. Before you lose interest in anything, your first duty is to make sure that you are developing competent successors on your team.

6. Treating your clients/customers/constituents as part of the problem-solving team is your most effective route to solving the problem.

7. Communicate early. Communicate often. Ask and listen.

8. If you include enough people in solving a problem, someone will quickly find the best way to see the problem, and someone will find the best way to solve the problem.

9. Great information and a good problem solver is better than a great problem solver and good information.

10. If people know that what they say is valuable, they will say valuable things.

11. The next best thing to having good ideas is recognizing good ideas from your clients/customers/constituents. Sometimes the latter is better.

12. Often, the most striking and innovative solutions come from realizing that your concept of the problem was wrong.

13. Perfection (in design) is achieved not when there is nothing more to add, but rather when there is nothing more to take away.

14. Any tool should be useful in the expected way, but a truly great tool lends itself to uses you never expected.

15. If you don't understand the filters through which you view information, you don't understand the information.

16. The most profound of ideas are also the simplest. The more eyeballs, the more you see.

17. Secrets are not a source of power or security. Openness and transparency can lead to greater security than secrets.

18. To solve an interesting problem, start by finding a problem that is interesting to you. To solve an interesting problem quickly, start by finding multiple perspectives that also find the problem interesting.

19. Many heads are inevitably better than one.

LINUS'S LAW IN ACTION

Every year, the *American Lawyer*, a leading publication for the legal profession, does a survey of the satisfaction levels of mid-level associates in the country's largest law firms. This mid-level gauge is particularly critical because, for most firms, the majority of voluntary or involuntary attrition of associates occurs in this mid-level range, and law firms care about this survey because it gives them valuable insights into the morale and perspectives of their associates. Law firms also care about this survey because the *American Lawyer* ranks the law firms based on the overall average rates of associates' satisfaction, and the rankings (publicly available data visible to all, including clients of the firms) then impact how the firms retain their top talent and recruit the next generation of top talent.

After this survey was released in 2010, I got a call from a managing partner of a law firm that had not fared well in the rankings. He had assembled a group of partners who had been tasked with developing and implementing programs in the firm that would raise their scores for the next year. He wanted me to advise them in this endeavor.

At the very first meeting of this working group (me and eight partners), I asked each person in the room to briefly write down what he or she thought was the cause of the low satisfaction scores among the associates. Before they shared their individual written responses with the group, I reviewed Linus's Law with them—"given enough eyeballs, all bugs are shallow"—and I asked them, as a group, to select 5 of the 19 suggestions set forth by Eric Raymond as the framework within which we would work. They selected:

- *If you have the right attitude, interesting problems will find you.*
- *Treating your clients/customers/constituents (mid-level associates) as part of the problem-solving team is your most effective route to solving the problem.*
- *If you include enough people in solving a problem, someone will quickly find the best way to see the problem, and someone will find the best way to solve the problem.*
- *If people know that what they say is valuable, they will say valuable things.*
- *Often, the most striking and innovative solutions come from realizing that your concept of the problem was wrong.*

After the lengthy discussion that resulted in the selection of these five principles, I asked them to review their written responses as to the problem statement and see if they wanted to revise them. All the partners wanted to revise their statements, not because they had changed their minds, but because they now realized that they did not have information and/or perspectives (eyeballs) to make up their minds in the first place (identify and solve the bugs).

The discussion revealed to them how little associate perspectives were sought and included in the programs that the firm designed for associate satisfaction and morale! Through the discussion, the partners realized that there were many others among the professional staff who would have great insights into what the associates wanted because they were the ones to whom the associates reported their concerns.

The collective RETRO IQ of this firm prioritized the perspectives of partners and brought in expert consultants from the outside when the partners felt that they were lacking expertise. The partners never looked at all the perspectives within their organization that could have provided the intelligence they were seeking.

A shift to THE *NEXT* IQ included appointing associates and other professional staff to all groups working on associate issues in order to seek and include "many eyeballs" into what the firm planned and did.

It is neither coincidence nor chance that the majority of surveys that measure employee satisfaction illustrate that greater participation in decision-making and greater transparency into how decisions are made have the most direct relationships with high satisfaction. Employees are happier when they feel more involved and integrated, but organizations and the leaders at their helms are also more intelligent when everyone is more engaged.

> I not only use all the brains that I have but all that I can borrow.
>
> Woodrow Wilson (U.S. president, 1913–1921)

THE LEADERSHIP ELEPHANT IN YOUR ORGANIZATION

Identify individuals at multiple levels, in varying functions, and from different backgrounds within your organization and create an anonymous mechanism by which the individuals can answer the following three questions with as much detail as they can. Ask all the senior leaders in the organization to complete this exercise as well, and have them compare their answers with the collective responses from the organization.

1. What does a leader look like in our organization?

   _____

   _____

2. What three characteristics must a person have to be a leader in our organization?

   _____

   _____

3. What does a person have to accomplish in order to be seen as a potential leader in our organization?

   _____

   _____

Similar to the "1 + 1 = 11" exercise, this exercise is powerful not because of any one individual's answer but because the differences between the answers give you a peek into the potential of your organization's NEXT IQ. It is only in understanding the differences in these answers that you can understand the answers at all.

The RETRO IQ is equivalent to the ability to walk into a store and select the best product the store has to offer that meets your needs. THE *NEXT* IQ, on the other hand, is equivalent to the ability of knowing what is in different stores so that you can go to the right store to select the product that is best for you. The best product available in a limited universe is not always the best product available in an unlimited universe. The RETRO IQ limits your universe of choices while THE *NEXT* IQ expands your universe of choices before you have to begin choosing.

THE *NEXT* IQ INSIGHTS: CHAPTER 3

- The definitions and measurement systems of intelligence have evolved over the last two centuries, and contemporary definitions of intelligence have expanded to include both mindset and abilities.
- Given the amount of information that any leader has to process in the 21st century in order to make effective decisions, a growth mindset (intelligence is always growing) and multiple abilities (use all the brains you have and also all that you can borrow) are critical.
- THE *NEXT* IQ illustration of Linus's Law in Action (a law firm's intent to raise associate satisfaction) shows how expanding the number of perspectives expands the number of possible solutions.

THE *NEXT* IQ ACTIONS: CHAPTER 3

- Identify one challenge to which you can apply the Linus's Law problem-solving technique. Which of the 19 suggestions do you think will be particularly helpful for the challenge you have selected?
- Do the Leadership Elephant in Your Organization exercise to discover the various ways that leadership and leaders are perceived by different people in the organization. In what ways can you use this information to help the leaders become more self-aware?

CHAPTER 4

THE EVOLUTION
OF LEADERSHIP

A TIMELESS INDIAN FABLE

The Enigmatic Elephant (Part II)

As the six blind men argued about the true nature of the creature, the other villagers waited anxiously to find out which of the men was right. The longer they argued, the stronger each of the men clung to what he knew to be true based on his experience.

"It is a spear. How could you possibly think a spear is a wall?"

"A spear? It is clearly a tree. Why can't you admit that you were mistaken?"

"A mistake has surely been made, but not by me. This creature is most like a snake."

"All of you are wrong. You should listen to me. I am the oldest among us, and I say it is a tree-like creature."

"You may be the oldest, but I solve puzzles faster than you, so I am right. This creature is like a rope."

And on and on the argument continued . . .

(continued in Chapter 5)

Leaders need intelligence in order to lead, and intelligence needs inclusion in order to be intelligent. This is the core of the transition from the RETRO IQ to THE *NEXT* IQ. This transition is foundational to surviving and thriving in the 21st century, but it is especially critical for leaders who often need to make decisions with incomplete information under increasingly pressurized and narrowing time constraints. There has always been a presumption that our leaders are intelligent, but leaders today can no longer survive on the Retro IQ model of intelligence. Leaders need to be inclusively intelligent in order to be effective and excellent; however, this conclusion can be fully understood only after following the evolution of leadership and the contexts in which leadership has been defined, measured, and developed. As Max De Pree, former CEO of Herman Miller and author of *Leadership Is an Art*, so eloquently framed the foundation on which to study leadership: "One examines leadership beginning not with techniques but rather with premises, not with tools but with beliefs, and not with systems but with understandings."[1]

We begin by exploring the evolution of leadership theory as it has worked to keep up with changes in demographics, greater opportunities for education, and unlimited access to information. The fascination with leaders and leadership has a long history, but as with intelligence, the recorded scientific inquiries into the mechanics of leaders and leadership began roughly in the early 20th century.

Prior to the 19th century, the premise of leadership was primarily rooted in its articulation as the absolute authority over other people. Whether the authority flowed from religion, royalty, or force, authority and leadership were inextricably intertwined in that a person had to be given the authority to lead in order to exercise leadership. Moreover, this authority was derived from ". . . an outside source, the power of the original source of delegation or control—divine, delegated, hereditary, or raw force."[2] Although a few of the great philosophers such as Socrates and Lao-Tzu have pondered the internal intellectual and moral characteristics of leaders, these philosophies were often considered an alternative way of thinking about leadership while authority continued to be the only avenue to legitimate leadership.

GREAT MAN AND TRAIT THEORIES OF LEADERSHIP

In the 19th century, Scottish historian and writer Thomas Carlyle framed leadership from the perspective of the "great men" or "heroes" who he believed had changed the course of history. He pointed to the lives of those he considered heroes such as Oliver Cromwell, William Shakespeare, Dante, Napoleon, Jean-Jacques Rousseau, Martin Luther,

and Muhammad to argue that "great men" led because they were great.[3] Leadership, according to Carlyle's argument, must be understood historically after a leader has led because it is in the hero's mythical and destined ascent into leadership that we can see what leadership actually means.

Even though the great man theory had its critics in the 19th century, it was the dominant perspective on leadership until the trait theory came along in the early 20th century (~1920s to 1930s). The trait theory of leadership begins with the premise that in order for men to become leaders, they had to possess certain physical, personal, and moral traits that made leaders different from their followers. Many of these traits (such as intelligence) were connected to the great man theory in that the heroes that Carlyle described became the blueprint from which leadership trait templates were built. By the middle of the 20th century, research on trait theory was adding up to show that traits were far less illuminating of leadership than the dynamic environment in which leaders operated.[4]

BEHAVIORAL AND CONTINGENCY
THEORIES OF LEADERSHIP

The trait and great man theories of leadership were similar in that they both looked to leaders to understand leadership without fully exploring the organizational contexts, the people who were being led, and the objectives the leaders were trying to achieve. As the reliability of the trait theory began to waver, a new model of leadership, the behavioral theory, emerged (~1940s to 1950s). The behavioral theory was a quantum leap for leadership theory because it focused on what leaders did instead of simply focusing on who they were. From understanding the difference between autocratic and democratic leaders[5] to analyzing the consequences of leaders' actions on the people they are leading,[6] the behavioral theory of leadership studied leadership from both the actions that the leaders took as well the differentials that various actions had on those being led. One of the key thrusts of the behavioral theory was that leaders could be made by teaching people the right behaviors.

In studying the behaviors of leaders, researchers quickly discovered that the same actions by leaders led to dramatically different consequences depending on the organization and the context. The frustration that behavioral theory alone could not lead to a comprehensive understanding of leadership led to the development of the contingency theory and situational theory of leadership (~1950s to 1970s). Joan Woodward, a British sociologist, was one of the pioneers (and one of the first women's voices in leadership theory) of transitioning the leadership dialog from behavioral theory to the contingency theory and situation theory of leadership. Woodward connected the technologies and structures in an organization to the type of traits that leaders needed to have and use in order to effectively lead in different contexts within different organizations.[7] The contingency theory of leadership, further expounded upon by Fred Fiedler (Fiedler Contingency Model), asserted that there was no leadership style that was equally effective in all situations, and individual variables in each situation needed to be analyzed in order to identify the leadership style best suited for that particular set of circumstances and needs.[8]

The contingency theory of leadership spawned additional theories such as the situational theory, substitutes-for-leadership theory, and path-goal theory, all of which basically posited that effective leadership was contingent upon the circumstances and the context regardless of the characteristics of the leader.

RELATIONAL AND LMX THEORIES OF LEADERSHIP

In the wake of the research done on contingency theory, several researchers became interested in the contingencies of personal relationships. Based on studies examining the relationships between subordinates and supervisors as the core to effective leadership,[9] a new theory, the relational theory (~1970s to 1980s) was constructed. This theory evolved into the leader-member exchange theory (LMX theory) (~1980s to 1990s).[10] One of the key tenets of LMX theory is the understanding of in-groups (subordinates who have high-quality trusting and respectful relationships with leaders) and out-groups (subordinates who have low-quality relationships with leaders that feel more contractual than trusting). LMX theory has shown that leadership can be measured as outcomes of behaviors instead of evaluations of leaders themselves. In this context, when leaders have high-quality relationships with their subordinates, there are more positive leadership outcomes than when they have low-quality relationships with their subordinates, regardless of the personal traits of the leaders or the situations in which they have to lead.

Research on in-groups and out-groups has also helped us understand the limitations of LMX theory in that although we know that the outcome of behaviors can tell us a lot about the leaders, we don't fully know what motivates the behaviors that led to the outcomes. When in-group identification is based on visual cues such as racial differences, research shows that in-group members—once they have identified someone of a different race—lose their motivation to read the other person's facial expressions or emotional cues.[11] The effect is subtle and it is so instantaneous that the person becomes designated to out-group status immediately upon recognition that he or she is of a different race, and the out-group status demotivates the in-group member to communicate with the individual through normal social communication channels such as reading facial expressions, picking up on nonverbal cues, and so on. This creates the obvious challenge that without conscious awareness or choice in how leaders are creating and reacting to out-groups, LMX theory can help us understand when leaders are not connecting with certain individuals, but it cannot help us fully comprehend why they are not connecting and how to create connections in the future.

As leadership theory headed into the 1980s and 1990s, theorists began to question many of these theories, wondering whether the study of leadership was a self-fulfilling cycle in that the leaders who are studied become the de facto models for effective leadership. In other words, if you want to study the characteristics of fruit, and you go to a fruit market where they primarily sell citrus fruit, you would create a model of fruit that is based on citrus fruit thereby making it difficult for grapes or kiwi or bananas to be easily evaluated as fruit. Since much of the research on leadership has focused on certain types of organizations, the skeptics theory of leadership (~1970s through 1990s) challenged the existing leadership models as incomplete and perhaps even inaccurate.[12]

SKEPTICS, TRANSFORMATIONALISTS, AND BEYOND

The skeptics theory influenced the study of leadership dramatically by refining the ways in which leadership was researched and how the perspectives of the followers should be accounted for in the measurement of leadership effectiveness. As we entered the last decade of the 20th century, a new wave of leadership research refocused attention away from leadership outcomes and back onto the leaders. Arguing that previous leadership research focused too much on transactional leadership (leadership through transactional obligations), the transformational leadership theory strove to study leadership from the outcomes on followers when leaders led by sense of purpose and unified vision.[13] In many ways, transformational leadership theory brought back traces of trait theory, contingency theory, and relational theory; however, it introduced impact on followers as the key measurement of leadership effectiveness. A transformational leader is measured by his or her ability to understand followers as individuals and personally stimulate, motivate, and incentivize individuals to believe in a common mission and achieve collective objectives.[14] Transformational leadership theory is perhaps the dominant leadership model used today in both organizations and in leadership research, and there are several variations on transformational leadership such as servant leadership[15] (see Southwest Airlines at www.southwest.com as an example of servant leadership in a corporation) and integral leadership (see Ben & Jerry's at www.benjerry .com as an example of integral leadership in a corporation).[16]

As we now work our way out of the 20th century and through the various models of transformational leadership, the 21st century presents us with unprecedented challenges in *whom* the leaders must lead and how they must lead in order to lead with excellence. The emerging issues in leadership as we enter the second decade of the 21st century are the contextual factors in leadership (related to identity, culture, and demographic changes), the ethics of leaders, alternative conceptualizations of intelligence in connection with leadership, and the interdisciplinary work necessary to understanding leadership.[17]

THE *NEXT* IQ INDIVIDUAL LEADERSHIP ASSESSMENT

Complete the following self-assessment using a scale of 1–5 (never, rarely, sometimes, often, always). A total of 27–135 points are possible.

1. I gather different perspectives on an issue before I make a decision.
2. I am open to hearing points of view that contradict my own.
3. I try to imagine the problem from perspectives other than my own before reaching a conclusion.
4. I have access to trusted diverse perspectives in my close professional network.
5. I have access to trusted diverse perspectives in my close personal network.
6. I actively seek out contradictory points of view to better understand my perspective before I finalize a decision.
7. I articulate a clear leadership style and vision for myself.
8. My actions and behaviors are consistent with the leadership vision I have for myself.
9. I seek feedback from my colleagues in the workplace about my leadership.
10. I can clearly articulate my professional strengths.
11. I can clearly articulate my professional challenges.
12. I can clearly articulate my personal strengths.
13. I can clearly articulate my personal challenges.
14. I build self-confidence in those around me.
15. I consider it a personal success when those around me succeed.
16. I give second chances easily when people make mistakes.
17. I am comfortable leading people who are a different gender than me.
18. I am comfortable leading people who are a different race/ethnicity than me.
19. I am comfortable leading people who seem to have different personal values than me.
20. I am comfortable leading people who have different personal characteristics than me.
21. I am comfortable leading people who are a different religion/spiritual faith than me.
22. I am comfortable being led by people who are a different gender than me.
23. I am comfortable being led by people who are a different race/ethnicity than me.

24. I am comfortable being led by people who seem to have different personal values than me.
25. I am comfortable being led by people who have different personal characteristics than me.
26. I am comfortable being led by people who are a different religion/spiritual faith than me.
27. I believe that I am more intelligent when my perspectives are informed by different views.

THE *NEXT* IQ ORGANIZATIONAL LEADERSHIP ASSESSMENT

Complete the following assessment for an organization using a scale of 1–5 (never, rarely, sometimes, often, always). A total of 20–100 points are possible.

1. Leaders in the organization have clearly articulated and communicated the values and mission of the organization.
2. Leaders in the organization are held accountable for the values and mission of the organization.
3. Leaders in the organization are open to receiving feedback about their leadership styles.
4. Leaders in the organization actively seek the perspectives and opinions of diverse groups of people before making a decision.
5. Leaders in the organization are willing to admit mistakes and take responsibility for their mistakes.
6. Leaders in the organization encourage dialog and dissent when decisions are being made.
7. Leaders in the organization want to see those around them succeed.
8. Leaders in the organization work hard to empower those around them to succeed.
9. Leaders in the organization represent a diverse array of backgrounds, experiences, and perspectives.
10. Leaders in the organization have informal networks in the organization that are comprised of people from diverse backgrounds, experiences, and perspectives.
11. Leaders in the organization generally say what they mean and mean what they say.
12. Leaders in the organization are trusted by the people they lead.
13. Leaders in the organization are willing to take risks to try new ideas.

14. Leaders in the organization are willing to accept different ways in which people work.
15. Leaders in the organization are willing to share responsibilities for setting meeting agendas and running the meetings.
16. Leaders in the organization reward people who take risks to be innovative.
17. Leaders in the organization reward people who are willing to disagree with them.
18. Leaders in the organization are open to learning new things through trainings and dialog.
19. Leaders in the organization have implemented a robust 360° evaluation system that is connected with their performance management.
20. Leaders in the organization value people over process.

These assessments provide a quick temperature check of how you lead personally and how leaders in an organization lead. The lower the score on either assessment, the more the room for improvement. The higher the score, the more inclusive you are (individually or as an organization), but even for those with relatively high scores, there is always room for improvement. If you score over 60 on the individual assessment or over 50 on the organizational assessment, I would recommend not taking your scores seriously until you ask someone else to give you feedback on your subjective perceptions! So, get a second opinion before you conclude your opinion is valid.

LEADERSHIP INPUT VERSUS LEADERSHIP IMPACT

A few years ago, I did an organizational assessment for a large private company that had just settled a lawsuit. A woman had accused the organization of discriminating against women who were seeking advancement into the highest levels of leadership. In the quantitative analysis done by her attorney, data spanning a three-year period showed that of the 18 women who had been assessed for leadership positions, only 1 had been advanced. On the other hand, of the 37 men who had been assessed for leadership positions, 21 had been advanced.

The senior leaders were as perplexed by the data as they were disturbed by it. They perceived their evaluation and promotion process as fair and objective, and they sincerely believed that none of them was trying to prevent women from advancing. To the contrary, they believed that they were actively seeking to increase the representation of women in leadership with the caveat that they would not "lower the standards for leadership" to advance more women.

In my assessment, I found, among other things, that ambiguously defined input was evaluated in performance reviews much more than impact. People were being assessed based on what they did, not on what they actually accomplished. This was especially true for people who were being evaluated for leadership potential.

Inputs such as "Takes Initiative," "Goes the Extra Mile for Colleagues," and "Inspires Confidence" were attached to people without any consideration of what taking initiative, going the extra mile, or inspiring confidence actually meant or achieved. There was no direct connection between these things that potential leaders did and the actual impact on the organization.

When I pushed the evaluators to drill down into the specific behaviors, they discovered that "going the extra mile" included behaviors such as staying late to lend a hand to a colleague working toward an imminent deadline or pitching in when a colleague needed to be out of the office. Once a few behaviors were identified for each of the evaluation inputs, we went back to the evaluators and asked them if the women expressed these behaviors. Many of them said yes!

Men and women were doing the same things and having a similar impact on the organization with their achievements, but men looked different to the senior leaders (who were predominantly men) when they expressed the same behaviors as women.

As we assessed the various inputs, we discovered many examples where women were doing the exact same thing as the men, but they were not being perceived as leaders. In some instances, women's actions had a more positive impact on the organization, but the men were still rated as having more leadership potential than the women.

The research on the multiple skills required by leaders today is indisputable, yet we are bombarded with the vestiges of archaic "intelligence = leadership" models in business, politics, and other arenas. Headlines in 2011 such as "Is Rick Perry Dumb?" referring to Republican presidential candidate Rick Perry's educational pedigree,[18] and "Was Barack Obama Smart Enough to Make It as an Air Force Pilot?" referring to President Obama's roots in academic (versus practical skills) settings[19] remind us that although research, scholarship, and dialog on leadership is evolving, we have not yet fully moved away from its foundations of static trait-based leaders.

With The *Next* IQ, the point of departure for present and future leadership is imagination, not history. Instead of articulating needs in terms of what we have always had, we start with a vision of the tomorrow we want to create as the basis of determining who we need our leaders to be. We have studied the evolution of intelligence and the evolution of leadership. Where these intersect in the 21st-century global arena reveals that our dialogs on both have been limited in being able to understand how leadership is necessary to deliberately develop intelligence and how an intelligent intelligence is necessary for effective leaders. As we are learning, leaders must have a global mindset sustained through their CORE, intellectual courage, openness, reflection, and empathy. This mindset will ensure that leaders actively seek and include diverse perspectives, and the addition of inclusion principles to this critical intersection of intelligence and leadership allows us to understand each of these components in a more detailed and comprehensive way.

The *Next* IQ Insights: Chapter 4

- The evolution of leadership has progressed from understanding leadership as an innate trait to evaluating leadership through behaviors and context. The more modern theories of leadership have included focusing on the relationships between leaders and the people they are leading as well as their abilities to impact and transform those relationships.

- Historically, leadership has been defined by studying past leaders. The *Next* IQ approaches leadership from a future-facing perspective by asking what kinds of characteristics and abilities leaders will need to meet the challenges of the future. The *Next* IQ leadership begins in the imagination, not in history.

- The *Next* IQ approach to leadership prioritizes the impact and outcomes achieved by a leader instead of the actions taken by the leader. This allows leaders to sustain a global mindset and a deliberate intelligence because actions are flexible and require the input of multiple perspectives in order to achieve the desired outcome.

The *NEXT* IQ Actions: Chapter 4

- Take The *NEXT* IQ Individual Leadership Assessment. What is your reaction to your score? What three statements on the assessment could you begin to work on in order to increase your score?
- Take The *NEXT* IQ Organizational Leadership Assessment. What is your reaction to the score? Distribute the assessment to several people in the same organization and see how the responses vary.
- Explore how the Leadership Input versus Leadership Impact case study may be playing out in your organization. Examine your evaluation and leadership development tools—is your organization measuring input or impact?

CHAPTER 5

THE EVOLUTION
OF INCLUSION

A TIMELESS INDIAN FABLE

The Enigmatic Elephant (Part III)

As the six men continued to argue about which of them had captured best the true nature of the beast, a young boy walked up to them and listened to their conversation earnestly. He finally interrupted the discussion to say, "From what I can see, it looks like all of you are right. The beast has a body like a wall, two ears like large fans, two tusks like spears, four legs like large trees, a trunk like a snake, and a tail like a rope."

The men were silent as they digested what the young boy had just said. They wondered if they could all truly be right, so they decided to walk around the elephant and see if they felt the different things that they had heard described. After circling the elephant a few times, the men congratulated the young boy for having the vision to overcome their intelligence.

Building on the historical evolution of how we have come to understand intelligence and leadership, THE *NEXT* IQ now asks, In today's world, are intelligence or intelligent leadership possible without inclusion? In other words, if you don't have a global mindset and are not inclusive in the ways you gather and analyze information today, is it possible for you to be truly intelligent? Is it possible for you to lead effectively?

The test of a first-rate intelligence is the ability to hold two opposed ideas in mind at the same time and still retain the ability to function.

F. Scott Fitzgerald
(20th-century
American author)

To answer these questions, we have to trace the evolution of inclusion just as we traced the evolution of intelligence and leadership. The history of inclusion begins with our individual and collective reaction to differences. It is the evolution of our relationship to the differences (real or perceived) that exist among us, differences that allow us to see ourselves as different from many others and be identified as similar to a certain few.

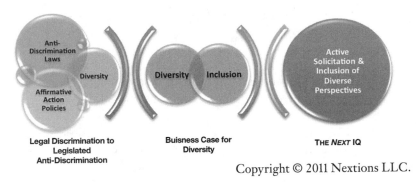

Copyright © 2011 Nextions LLC.

FROM LEGAL DISCRIMINATION TO LEGISLATED ANTI-DISCRIMINATION

Many nations continue to deal with the legacies of legislated discrimination based on differences. From race-based slavery to discrimination along caste, gender, religion, and ethnicity lines, legal discrimination has been an unfortunate reality in most countries and cultures. As some nations moved toward more egalitarian societies, the natural friction between mandated inequality and ideals of individual freedom and equality caused many countries to enact anti-discrimination laws that rolled back codified discrimination. These new laws were necessary, but deeply engrained social norms built upon the foundations of discrimination could not be legislated away easily or rapidly.

FROM ANTI-DISCRIMINATION TO AFFIRMATIVE ACTION

As these anti-discrimination laws began to be enforced in key social arenas such as education, workplaces, housing, and politics, many nations turned to affirmative action programs in order to hasten the shifting of social norms into alignment with their mandates of equality. In the United States, affirmative action is connected with correcting the vestiges of discrimination against racial/ethnic minorities and women.[1] In India, affirmative action is used to ensure that members of the lowest caste are given preferential treatment in education and employment until the social norms shift.[2] In Sweden, affirmative action is employed to accelerate the gender parity in the number of women serving on corporate boards.[3] In France, affirmative action is utilized to prod along the advancement of socioeconomic parity in selective educational institutions.[4]

In 2004, when King Juan Carlos of Spain swore in José Luis Rodriguez Zapatero as prime minister, Zapatero made history by appointing 8 women to his 16-member cabinet. When Zapatero was reelected four years later in 2008, he created an additional cabinet position, the Equality Ministry, and he broke his own gender parity record by appointing 9 women to this now 17-member cabinet, thereby creating a female majority.

This would be radical enough, except that Zapatero appointed a woman to the minister of defense position while Spain was actively involved in military operations in Afghanistan. Carme Chacón became the first woman to serve as Minister of Defense for Spain or any other country. This would be beyond radical enough, except that Carme Chacón was visibly seven months pregnant when she was appointed, and she traveled to Afghanistan to meet with the troops while she was "highly pregnant" as the Spanish media liked to say.

As MSNBC reported after the 2008 election, "Chacón is now one of the most visible members of a government that has enacted sweeping social legislation designed to rid traditionally male-dominated Spain of gender discrimination . . . [it] forced political parties to field more female candidates and passed a law designed to promote women in the workplace and pressure companies to put more of them in their boardrooms."[5]

While women's groups around the world lauded Zapatero's proactive move to create gender parity on his cabinet, the reaction from a conservative commentator who referred to Zapatero's cabinet as a "battalion of inexperienced seamstresses" highlighted the sentiment that the ushering in of gender parity in politics would be accompanied by an equal dose of gender bashing. Although none of the new female ministers were any less educated, experienced, or accomplished than any of their past or current male counterparts, Zapatero's actions branded him as a feminist, in the not so nice use of that term.

Although Prime Minister Zapatero viewed his selections as appointments of merit, the sudden shift in gender demographics created a perception of affirmative action designed to accelerate social change. This type of affirmative action (intended or perceived) also has ushered in a backlash of perceived reverse discrimination.

Query: If you are affirmatively positive toward a group of people, are you naturally "discriminating" against the people who are not the beneficiaries of your "affirmative action"? People who are critical of affirmative action are most often not against the action itself but are likely to perceive that their group will have to lose opportunities in order for another group to gain opportunities.[6]

In spite of the articulated purpose of redressing historical wrongs, affirmative action has been met with cultural resistance because of the perception that merit was being compromised in order to help those who were not helping themselves. In other words, it was charged that those it was meant to help were wrongfully taking opportunities away from those who worked for and deserved them.

In the Netherlands, for example, efforts to assist immigrants—especially Muslim immigrants—incited a backlash against Muslims that anti-immigration politicians rode into power.[7] In America, affirmative action has been a political hot potato that keeps mutating in ways that triggers backlash among opponents, confusion among supporters, and division among politicians.[8] In Sweden, the dialog on advancement of women is peppered with questions of whether men are being disadvantaged with mandated participation of women on corporate boards. In France, the discussion of creating socioeconomic equity has been consistently paired with the undertone of decreasing the excellence of education in the elite schools affected by the laws.[9]

Anti-discrimination. Affirmative action. Reverse discrimination. These words continue to be the subject of ardent debate and the cause of intense division, but the reality of what these terms really mean or the history from which they emanated doesn't matter. Once the perception of unfairness is felt, even by a few, the effort loses its ability to effectively drive its mission. An unfair thing cannot bring about fairness. Regardless of your beliefs on the substance of these issues, it is critical to recognize that, when it comes to human beings, there is no single reality, only different perceptions. This is where we begin to see the evolution of intelligence intersecting with (or crashing into, depending on your perspective) the evolution of inclusion.

FROM AFFIRMATIVE ACTION TO DIVERSITY

While political and legal systems were struggling with strengthening anti-discrimination laws, economic systems were discovering the impact of global demographic changes in consumer markets. Organizations began to understand diversity beyond the boundaries of groups identified and affected by anti-discrimination laws. The workforce of the 21st century is broadly diverse and characterized by a flood of workers from demographics (women, racial/ethnic minorities, national origins, languages, cultures, younger generations, etc.) that were not represented when the structures and cultures of many workplaces were designed and defined. Now, this diverse workforce was beginning to determine who the "employers of choice" were based on how they approached and integrated diversity into their corporate values. Similarly, the diverse needs and increasing purchasing power of consumers in the global marketplace were rivaled only by the diversity of options available to these consumers. The definition of diversity evolved beyond representing the underrepresented into representing the multitude who comprised an organization's current and future workforce and consumer base.

Diversity started becoming less associated with fairness and more connected with "business intelligence."

VALUE PROPOSITION FOR DIVERSITY

Statement on Diversity from CHUBB GROUP (2011)

"Those who perceive diversity as exclusively a moral imperative or societal goal are missing the larger point. Workforce diversity needs to be viewed as a competitive advantage and a business opportunity. That's why Chubb makes diversity a business priority and strives to achieve a fully inclusive diverse workforce.

"As our U.S. and global customer base becomes steadily more diverse, significant portions of Chubb's future growth must come from tapping into these diverse markets. If we are to form lasting business relationships with our customers and become a true global leader in the industry, we must understand our customers' diverse cultures and decisional processes, not merely their languages."[10]

Statement on Diversity at SIEMENS GLOBAL (2011)

"The megatrends of urbanization, demographic change and climate change are transforming the face of our world. Siemens is well-positioned to respond to the challenges posed by these developments—but being able to respond to issues such as these demands that Siemens continually works to strengthen its position as an innovation leader.

"Siemens is in contact with over two million customers daily. These customers, in every corner of the globe, expect Siemens to understand their unique needs and concerns. This requires the best people. And this is precisely what the Diversity Initiative aims to do: help Siemens build superior teams with broad strengths and a wide range of skills.

"In order to successfully compete in our increasingly globalized economy, businesses must understand and incorporate diversity. Those who do this successfully will be able to take advantages of growth opportunities, and will be better able to respond to customers. Siemens does business in 190 countries throughout the world.

"For Siemens to succeed in such an international marketplace, its employee base must reflect the diversity of its customer base. Just in the ten largest Siemens Regional Companies alone, people from 140 different nationalities work together."[11]

The idea that diversity of perspectives was critical to the success of business entities given shifts in demographics, purchasing power, consumer needs/wants, and so on, gained significant momentum in the late 1980s and throughout the 1990s. The "business case" for diversity—as articulated in the statements from Chubb and Siemens—became ubiquitous in discussions on "business intelligence," especially when it came to corporate workforces, consumer marketing, sales, and advertising. As Scott Page asserts: "The bottom line: Diversity can improve the bottom line. It may even matter as much as ability."[12] In experiments Page conducted at California Institute of Technology, he found that "[d]iverse groups of problem solvers—groups of people with different perspectives and heuristics—consistently outperformed groups composed of the best individual performers."[13] A 2009 report by McKinsey & Co. demonstrated that companies with three or more women in senior management positions perform significantly better on nine criteria for organizational excellence when compared with companies that had no women in their senior management.[14]

Although diversity efforts were also spreading in the government sectors, educational institutions, and not-for-profit organizations, the business case argument was most loudly heard in the global marketplace. As companies like Wal-Mart, Shell, Coca-Cola, McDonald's, General Mills, and others began to understand their business cases for diversity (for talent and consumers), they created the business case for the vendors who depend on their business. As diversity efforts evolved in the corporate arena, supplier diversity efforts began to permeate the B2B marketplace; corporations made it known that they would hire vendors (from office supply stores to law firms and consulting firms) based on the diversity in the vendor's employee ranks. As discussions grew more intense, and diversity programs grew more numerous, the realization that the business case for diversity had increased diversity programs but not necessarily diversity of perspectives and thought in these organizations began to emerge from the shadows of robust diversity programs.

FROM DIVERSITY TO DIVERSITY *AND* INCLUSION

Diverse perspectives were being invited into organizations, but were these perspectives given the same access to resources, information,

> Diversity: the art of thinking independently together.
>
> Malcolm S. Forbes
> (publisher, *Forbes* magazine)

and networks they needed to become integrated into and successful within the organizations? Initial research suggests that the focus on attracting diverse people (especially through the business case model) never fully accounted for shifting organizational structures to actually integrate diverse perspectives.[15] In spite of well-intentioned diversity initiatives, individuals who have historically been excluded and who are presently underrepresented don't have the same access to networks of information, professional development opportunities, or sponsorship by leaders in the organization, nor are they afforded the ability to influence important decisions.[16]

On the gender front, a study done by Deloitte in 2010 found that "72% [of global executives surveyed] agree that there is a direct connection between gender diversity and business success, but only 28% document it as a top-10 priority for senior leadership. And while many leading companies have a number of women-focused initiatives in place at any given moment, they do not seem to be achieving the goal of consistently moving women into key decision-making and leadership roles—the roles that have the most impact on business success."[17] For racial and ethnic minorities, the Attrition and Retention Consortium ((ARC); www.retentionconsortium.org) conclusively found that Fortune 500 companies are losing minority professionals and managers at a much higher rate than they are losing whites at the same levels. According to Peter Hom, a professor of management who researched and analyzed the attrition data for ARC, "[g]reater corporate flight among women and minorities during early employment . . . hampers progress toward a more diversified workforce in corporate America."[18] Diversity brought diverse perspectives in the door, but organizations began to realize that they needed something more in order to keep those diverse perspectives in the room.

That something more is where intelligence and leadership intersect—inclusion. In a seminal study on inclusion, L. H. Pelled and her colleagues analyzed existing research and created the following definition of inclusion: "the degree to which an employee is accepted and treated as an insider by others in a work system."[19] A study by Cornell University's Center for Advanced Human Resource Studies found that "diversity focused primarily on heterogeneity and the demographic composition of groups and organizations, while definitions of inclusion focused on employee involvement and the integration of diversity into organizational systems and processes."[20] This research also found that "diversity in organizations may be supported by sets of practices to manage fair treatment issues, increase stakeholder diversity, and demonstrate leadership's commitment to diversity while inclusion may be supported by practices to integrate diversity into organizational systems and processes and encourage the full participation and contribution of employees."[21] In 2002, Frederick Miller and Judith Katz framed inclusion as "about creating an environment in which employees share a sense of belonging, mutual respect, being valued for who they are, and supportive energy and commitment from others so that they can do their best work."[22] Currently, this is the prevalent definition of inclusion utilized by organizations.[23]

As industries are becoming more aware of the differences and interconnectedness between diversity and inclusion, they are building models that help organizations understand how to chart their own progression from anti-discrimination to affirmative action to diversity to diversity *and* inclusion. In the legal profession, the Center for Legal Inclusiveness is leading the way with an innovative model entitled "Advancing Inclusiveness Model (AIM) for Excellence" that charts the path of an inclusive organization and connects inclusion to excellence.[24]

Business intelligence today requires organizations to expand their definitions of diversity to include a wide variety of identities, experiences, and perspectives. Leaders in this new environment need to actively seek and include diverse perspectives into daily operations and interactions in order to realize their full potential.

I use a simple metaphor with my clients to help them understand the differences and the relationship between diversity and inclusion. If you think of your organization as a garden that has the spectrum of flora that you need in order to attract the visitors and fauna you desire, you have to build the garden with two key ingredients in mind. You need the right seeds (workforce), and you need the right soil (workplace) where all the seeds you plant can flourish to their maximum capacity. You can select the best seeds available, but without soil that has the right ingredients for all the seeds to grow, the garden can end up much more homogeneous than intended. The selection of the seeds is diversity, but creation of an optimal environment for all the seeds to grow in is inclusion. Diversity is about the workforce (the people), and inclusion is about the workplace (the structures, the culture, and the individual interactions that make your organization unique). Diversity is about recruiting, and inclusion is about retention, development, and visible leadership by people with diverse perspectives.

In professional service organizations, the gap between diversity (representation) and inclusion (integration) resulted in years of high recruitment rates for racial/ethnic minorities and women and equally high attrition rates. In the legal profession, for example, women have comprised about 50 percent of law school classes for more than twenty years, and they have constituted almost half of all new hires into law firms for the last ten years. Yet, they comprise only about 19 percent of all partners in law firms. Similarly, racial/ethnic minorities have comprised about 20–25 percent of law schools for more than twenty years, and they have constituted about 25 percent of all new hires into law firms for the last ten years. Yet, they comprise only about 6 percent of all partners in law firms.[25] This lopsided ratio of the number of women and racial/ethnic minorities among new hires to the number of women and racial/ethnic minorities among the leaders of organizations is eerily similar in consulting firms, accounting firms, and architectural firms.

Among the companies in Standard & Poor's 100 Index (S&P 500), the percentages of women and racial/ethnic minorities in the boardroom and executive suite have stayed flat for several years even though there has been a marked increase in the deployment of diversity initiatives, policies, and programming.[26] In Fortune 500 companies, a recent boardroom census study reported that "[w]hile research points decisively to the benefits of a diverse boardroom—including enhanced financial performance—white men continue to dominate corporate boards and have, in fact, increased their presence since 2004. Women and minorities are still vastly underrepresented."[27] The study also noted that the "number of board seats remained relatively flat between 2004 and 2010, with only 16 seats added. Significantly, white men gained 32 board seats, while African-American men lost 42 seats. Although women gained 16 board seats, their increase of 1.1 percentage points was not appreciable."[28]

A 2010 study by Calvert Investments found that "[w]hile women make up approximately 18% of director positions within the S&P 500, they represent only 8.4% of the highest paid positions within the same group of companies, positions that provide the opportunities to develop the expertise and networks needed for future board-level appoint-ments."[29] Furthermore, the 18 percent of women in director positions is less than 50 percent of the percentage of women who occupy the posi-tions a couple of levels below that of the directors.

This gap between diversity and inclusion is not just evident in busi-ness and law. In a 2003 report entitled *Unequal Treatment: Confronting Racial and Ethnic Disparities in Health Care*, the Institute of Medicine (IOM) found that a primary contributor to the disturbing disparities in the healthcare received by whites and racial/ethnic minorities was the lack of racial/ethnic minorities in the ranks of healthcare provid-ers.[30] The IOM report led to the formation of the Sullivan Commission on Diversity in the Healthcare Workforce: "Named for former U.S. Secretary of Health and Human Services, Louis W. Sullivan, M.D., the Commission [was] composed of 16 health, business, higher educa-tion and legal experts and other leaders. Former U.S. Senate Majority Leader Robert Dole and former U.S. Congressman and Congressio-nal Health Subcommittee Chairman Paul Rogers serve[d] as Honorary Co-Chairs."[31] The Sullivan Commission found that "[w]hile African Americans, Hispanic Americans, and American Indians, as a group, constitute nearly 25 percent of the U.S. population, these three groups account for less than 9 percent of nurses, 6 percent of physicians, and only 5 percent of dentists."[32] They also discovered that the dismal num-bers persisted even though diversity efforts were underway in recruit-ing students and professionals in nursing, medicine, and dentistry. After holding multiple hearings on the topic, a critical conclusion reached by the Sullivan Commission was that without changing the environments in the educational realm and workplaces to retain the minorities that were being recruited, we would be able to increase neither the diversity in our healthcare workforce nor the quality of healthcare of our country's racial/ethnic minority populations.

Inclusion has evolved from anti-discrimination efforts and is now in a place where, in order to be understood and implemented effectively, it has to be separated from anti-discrimination efforts altogether. If diversity is the presence of multiple perspectives, interpretations, heuristics, and predictive models, inclusion is the ability of a person or environment to solicit and allow those multiple views to be included, engaged, and integrated into a larger dialog. Diversity can be created without inclusion, but it will not last because different voices will stop speaking up if they are not included. Inclusion can also exist without diversity because it is often easy to be inclusive when people share perspectives. We are at a point in our evolution in this area where our work needs to include both diversity (getting different seeds) and inclusion (ensuring that the soil will allow all the seeds to flourish).

In recent years, the field of collective wisdom, advanced in books like *The Wisdom of Crowds* by James Surowiecki and *Crowdsourcing: Why the Power of the Crowd Is Driving the Future of Business* by Jeff Howe, has focused on the same message as inclusion advocates, but it has done so without the baggage of anti-discrimination, affirmative action, and identity diversity. Surowiecki, in fact, stresses the need for diverse perspectives in order for crowds to become wise, but because he is not affiliated with the diversity and inclusion field, his work has been embraced for its content without becoming embroiled in the debates that diversity and inclusion usually bring to a discussion.

THE JURY EFFECT

The 1957 movie *12 Angry Men* is a story about how a jury of 12 men negotiate their personal perspectives, prejudices, and experiences as they deliberate a murder case. Directed by Sidney Lumet, the movie is a classic from a cinematic perspective and was selected by the U.S. Library of Congress in 2007 for the National Film Registry, honored for being a significant contribution to American culture. But more than that, its anthropological take on how people behave in groups and how majorities form and break down and how minority voices rise and fall continues to influence how we think about and study groups today. The movie dramatically portrays how we initially exclude and how we eventually include when we are pushed out of our comfort zones.

Juries are particularly interesting groups for social scientists to study because juries represent groups that have usually been randomly selected and have no historical connection to each other. Juries are also tasked with making decisions using facts presented in an adversarial system that forces them to go beyond just evidence to form beliefs from lawyers they trust. Jury deliberations are intense because the pressure to make a decision is high while the consequences of that decision are serious. It is in this powerful brew of uncertainty, pressure, and consequence that human beings show their best and worst tendencies, their proclivities toward exclusion and their preferences for inclusion.

A 2006 study on diversity in mock juries revealed some interesting insights on the impact of differences in juries. According to Samuel R. Sommers, the author of the study, "placing white jurors in diverse groups raised their performance level, encouraging them to cite more facts, make fewer mistakes, deliberate longer, and conduct broader and more accurate discussions."[33] The interesting finding in this study was that the visibility of race differences triggered more critical thinking in the deliberation for all participants regardless of the individual perspectives of any juror. In other words, we can leverage the power of how differences affect the way we think without generalizing that all people of a particular identity think a particular way.

One of the powerful aspects of *12 Angry Men* is that the deliberation slowly unveils the differences among the men because their visible social identities are homogeneous. Yet, once the differences are unveiled, the critical thinking processes kick in reminding us that as much as similarities comfort us, our differences better us.

From Diversity and Inclusion to The *Next* IQ

Inclusion has coalesced into a rich field of understanding that borrows from many disciplines but transcends them all. In this mosaic, diversity is correctly understood as the differences between people as opposed to specific identities labeled as diverse. Diversity is the quantity and quality of the differences in the network of any particular group of people. Race, ethnicity, gender, sexual orientation, and other identities contribute to diversity because they impact people's experiences and perspectives, but they do not solely comprise diversity. Diversity, by definition, is the collective differences within a particular group, and inclusion is the active leveraging of those differences in order to create the next level of intelligence.

THE *NEXT* IQ is the maturation of inclusion in a way that both integrates the need for representing those who are underrepresented as well as recognizing that all our differences are not visible. THE *NEXT* IQ understanding of inclusion is that not everyone who shares a particular identity shares the same characteristics, perspectives, or experiences, but that we are still dealing with presumed similarities that make some people more comfortable with people they feel are similar to them. Inclusion, then, becomes about the individual—every individual—without consideration of visible differences while still recognizing that we, often unconsciously, superimpose characteristics, perspectives, and experiences onto individuals because of the groups with whom they share their identities.

This evolution of diversity and inclusion to THE *NEXT* IQ begins with a clear understanding of why THE *NEXT* IQ is important in the 21st century. While civic and moral arguments undergirded anti-discrimination and affirmative action efforts, economic arguments boosted the rise of diversity and eventually, inclusion. *The driver for THE NEXT IQ is neither moral/civic nor economic; it is personal. The driver for THE NEXT IQ is about being as smart as you can be, individually or as an organization.* THE *NEXT* IQ is about achieving the next level of intelligence, not just because increasing intelligence is a powerful motivator but also because the moral/civic and economic drivers simply don't work in the arenas of leadership and inclusion.

If your state had a blood shortage and asked for volunteers to donate blood, would you donate? What if your state had a blood shortage and offered to pay people for their blood? Would you sell your blood? If so, what do you think would be a fair price for a pint of your blood? A recent study in a long line of studies on this topic of prosocial (intrinsic motivation such as altruism) versus proeconomic (extrinsic motivation such as monetary compensation) behaviors found that when money is offered for blood, the number of blood donors actually decreases as does the quality of the blood.[34] When blood donation is only voluntary, the number of donors increases as does the quality of the blood. Researchers involved in this study note that the data is so overwhelming that the

World Health Organization has "set a goal for all blood donations to be collected from unpaid volunteer donors by 2020."[35]

So, can the number of blood donors be increased by having both paid and volunteer donors? Interestingly, the answer is no. When people donate blood, they do it for intrinsic motivation (altruism) and image motivation (the desire to be liked, respected, and valued by others). Researchers have found that "with extrinsic incentives, the signal of a prosocial act gets diluted . . . The image value decreases, and the incentive becomes less effective."[36] If money is introduced as an incentive, it dilutes the desire of those who are intrinsically motivated, and it really drives away those who do it for image motivation since it's no longer automatically assumed to be prosocial behavior. This is true for blood donations (unpaid versus paid donors), hybrid cars (tax incentives versus concern for the environment), charitable donations (tax deductions versus altruism), and many other areas where the presence of economic incentives dilutes the drive to act in prosocial ways.

Inclusion, with its roots in the moral argument for equality and its current dance with economic drivers, has languished as window dressing when it should have been integrated into the foundation. By trying to argue for both the moral case and the business case, we have neutralized the power of both. The people who have always felt strongly about the moral case are losing interest because of the business case and people who are paying attention because of the economics keep wondering how much compensation is enough to make the economic case a strong enough driver to change how they learn and lead.

THE NEXT IQ focuses on the personal driver of maximizing intelligence at the individual or organizational level as the motivator for cultivating a global mindset and actively seeking and including diverse perspectives.

> Never hire or promote in your own image. It is foolish to replicate your strength and idiotic to replicate your weakness. It is essential to employ, trust, and reward those whose perspective, ability, and judgment are radically different from yours.
>
> Dee W. Hock (founder and former CEO of Visa)

A global mindset recognizes that information is no longer the prize—the ability to quickly gather, analyze, and transform information into actionable insights is the prize. This ability is not possible as a singular endeavor in the 21st century, and it requires diverse and contradictory perspectives to intelligently analyze and transform information.

THE *NEXT* IQ is as much about intelligence as it is about inclusion, and when inclusive intelligence is developed, the ability to lead expands by quantum leaps.

THE WISDOM OF WHY

A large multinational corporation with whom I worked had a strong diversity and inclusion mandate that required all its vendors to clearly demonstrate a commitment to diversity and inclusion in order to stay on the company's preferred provider list. The CEO and his executive leadership team communicated this mandate frequently and fervently, and they had stern conversations with vendors who were not meeting this commitment, especially in the demographic composition of the teams that served the corporation. The company also had a complex compensation bonus system that rewarded diverse vendor teams for their diversity.

In one particularly heated exchange between the chairperson of a large law firm and the CEO, the CEO shouted with frustration about the "all white team" that had been assembled to tackle a particular legal matter. "Where is the diversity?" he shouted. "I don't understand why you all can't pull together a diverse team when I've asked over and over again for a diverse team." The chairperson of the law firm shrugged helplessly. "We tried. We will keep trying. You just have to understand that there are real challenges out there in recruiting and retaining diverse lawyers." A few profanities and much shouting later, the CEO told the chairperson that unless he saw some diversity in the next team that the law firm assembled, the corporation would begin the process of taking the firm off the company's preferred provider list.

When the CEO and I debriefed after the meeting, he asked me if I thought that he should fire the firm immediately. "If we keep letting them get away with this, they are never going to change!" When I asked him *what* he wanted them to change, he looked at me with increasing frustration and shouted, "I want a diverse team!" Then I asked him *why* he wanted a diverse team.

"Because we are committed to diversity," the CEO responded. I pushed back some more and asked why the law firm should have a diverse team simply because the company was committed to diversity.

"They should do it because it is important to us," he stated with evident frustration.

I pointed out that although the company had done an excellent job communicating *what* it expected from its vendors, it had never articulated *why* it wanted diverse teams. The conversation between me and CEO went something like this:

"So, why do you want them to have diverse teams?"

"Because diversity is important to us."

"So, why do you want them to have diverse teams?"

"Because we have a diverse workforce and we have diverse customers. And, it's a diverse world that is getting more diverse by the minute."

"Why should that make it necessary for them to have diverse teams?"

"Because they would understand us as a business and our needs better if they had a diverse team that looked like our workforce and our customers."

"Why would a diverse team understand you better?"

"Because a diverse team would have the diverse perspectives necessary to understand all the perspectives in our company, with our consumers, and the marketplace overall."

"Why would a team comprised of diverse perspectives be better for you?

"Seriously? They would be able to see the various sides they needed to see so that they could solve our problems better."

"So, diverse perspectives on a team would make that team smarter?"

"Yes."

I asked the CEO if he had ever had that full conversation with any vendor—not just the *what* of wanting a diverse team but the *why* of the underlying reasons for wanting a diverse team. As we talked about how diversity and inclusion were currently being articulated in the marketplace, he realized that the business case that the company had been pushing, "we want diverse teams so you should give us diverse teams," was actually antithetical to the company's overall diversity and inclusion mission.

This corporation had done internal research that showed that diverse teams produced better results within the company, but it had never shared that research with its vendors. It was using an economic motivator (more money if you are diverse) when it needed to be using a competency standard (you are smarter and give us better results if you have diverse perspectives). This shifted the focus from the identities on the team to the perspectives on the team, and it shifted the conversation from "do it because we told you to" to "we need you to be smarter than you are."

This shift in communication illustrates the difference between the RETRO IQ and THE *NEXT* IQ dialogs on inclusion. Not only did this shift make it easy for the CEO and his senior executives to have more productive discussions on this topic with their vendors, but the shift from the *what* to the *why* aligned their internal inclusion strategies with their external ones.

The evolution of inclusion has resulted in an environment where the intrinsic and extrinsic motivators have been rendered ineffective, but leaders who want to lead on this issue can continue to advance the ball by changing the focus from the business case to the "intelligence case." The *why* drives the *what* because people are only motivated to figure out the *how* if they buy into the *why*.

THE *NEXT* IQ INSIGHTS: CHAPTER 5

- The evolution of inclusion began in the legal arena with anti-discrimination legislation and affirmative action. The underlying driver for this journey through the legal system was moral/civic motivations.
- Inclusion evolved out of the legal arena and entered the economic arena through a focus on demographic diversity for the sake of economic success, creating what is now commonly referred to as the business case.
- The failure of diversity programs in actually creating diversity led to diversity being paired with inclusion. Diversity is the "seed" and inclusion is the "soil" in a heterogeneous garden. The diversity and inclusion phase attempts to blend both the moral/civic and economic motivators to drive change.
- THE *NEXT* IQ moves beyond the moral case for equal treatment and the business case for demographic diversity to create a new imperative for inclusive intelligence as more intelligent than narrow intelligence. The *NEXT* IQ is the culmination of the evolu-

tions of intelligence, leadership, and inclusion and focuses on the global mindset and deliberate intelligence that effective leaders need in the 21st century.

THE *NEXT* IQ ACTIONS: CHAPTER 5

- Watch the movie *12 Angry Men* with your team and ask individuals to articulate the leadership lessons they can take away from the movie.
- For every objective that you are trying to accomplish (individually or as a team), ask why—à la The Wisdom of Why example—that objective is critical to achieve. Ask "why" for every answer until the answer is concise, clear, and utterly simple.

CHAPTER 6

WHY THE *NEXT* IQ MATTERS MORE THAN THE RETRO IQ

THE *NEXT* IQ PERSPECTIVE

In February 2009, Ben Bernanke, chairman of the Federal Reserve, gave a talk on the economy, and the following four headlines show the variance in how different news outlets perceived and reported his words:[1]

USA Today:	Bernanke Sees Possible End to Recession in 2009[2]
New York Times:	Fed Chairman Says Recession Will Extend Through the Year[3]
CNNMoney:	Bernanke: Recovery Will Take Years[4]
Reuters:	Bernanke Says Recession to Linger but Banks Will Survive[5]

So, did Bernanke say that the recession would end in 2009, 2010, or even later? The headlines seem to be so very different that they cannot all possibly be correct. What he actually said per the official transcript posted by the Federal Reserve was in part:

> If actions taken by the Administration, the Congress, and the Federal Reserve are successful in restoring some measure of financial stability—and only if that is the case, in my view—there is a

reasonable prospect that the current recession will end in 2009 and that 2010 will be a year of recovery . . . These values are all notably different from the central tendencies of the projections for 2010 and 2011, reflecting the view of policymakers that a full recovery of the economy from the current recession is likely to take more than two or three years.[6]

So, he did say that the recession could end in 2009, and he also said that a full recovery could take a few years. If you viewed these headlines and the transcript through the RETRO IQ, the urge would be to try and find which of the headlines best captured Bernanke's true sentiments. You might even try to assign interpretational bias to the headlines based on your impressions of the news outlets.

> I am not struck so much by the diversity of testimony as by the many-sidedness of truth.
>
> Stanley Baldwin (British politician and prime minister, 1867–1947)

If you viewed the same headlines and transcript through THE *NEXT* IQ, you would have the mindset to accept as natural (not bad or good, just natural) that different outlets would cover Bernanke's speech differently, so you would actively seek out the opportunity to read the (sometimes contradicting) points of view to arrive at a perspective that has benefited from many worldviews. When I have conducted leadership trainings with senior leaders in organizations, I always ask them if they would prefer that their subordinates read one source or several sources to get their daily dose of current events and professional updates. Every leader has always selected the latter option even if the leader does not follow his or her own preference.

In their most recent report on globalization outlining global market trends and priorities for organizations, Ernst & Young summarized the current global market as marked by "greater integration of trade, capital, culture and labor across borders."[7] The report goes on to state: "Cross-border investment flows are broadening and deepening, and opportunities and competition are now spread more evenly between developed and emerging markets. This convergence of market potential between East and West, along with a gradual economic recovery and growing interdependencies between sovereign states and multinationals, will ensure that globalization continues to deepen over the coming years."[8] Ernst & Young's report is entitled "Winning in a Polycentric World," a complex world with many centers and a multifaceted one that requires many perspectives in order to be understood.

So, not only does it make sense to have many sources of information feeding your intelligence, but it is in your best interest to have a polycentric stream of information sources and relationships that inform your perspectives and your experiences. Based on their research, Ernst & Young's report concludes that:

> The business leader of the future must be comfortable with complexity and multiple perspectives across the organization. They will need to ensure that every task force, management program and leadership team is diverse and know how to harness that power. "Business leaders will have to figure out how to manage multiple viewpoints and perspectives across the company," says Radjou. [Navi Radjou, Centre for India & Global Business at Cambridge Judge Business School] "But rather than trying to seek convergence, which is the easy route, companies will need to encourage divergence, because divergence leads to diversity and diversity leads to more innovation. If you want to fight complexity, the answer is not simplicity."[9]

Ernst & Young's report focused on how companies can succeed in an increasingly global marketplace, and the business necessity for creating and maximizing diversity and inclusion is one of their four key pieces of strategic advice to their clients. What Ernst & Young is recommending that companies build, in other words, is the intelligence of THE NEXT IQ.

Intelligence is not what you do; it's not the vehicle you drive or the destination you set as your goal. Intelligence is the fuel that allows you to get better results on your journey. Intelligence is how you do things. Your NEXT IQ, then, is your ability to do the things you want to do in a way that maximizes your success and impact. Whether you are building your individual or an organization's NEXT IQ, the critical intelligence that is necessary for the 21st-century marketplace lives and thrives at the intersection of intelligence, leadership, and inclusion. It borrows the best from all three even as it changes the way we think about each of these evolving categories.

THE *NEXT* IQ INTERSECTION

Copyright © 2011 Nextions LLC.

Intelligence

THE *NEXT* IQ keeps our understanding of intelligence moving forward by defining it as a global mindset combined with the deliberate intelligence necessary to actively seek and include different and contrasting perspectives. While the RETRO IQ celebrates the depth of individual expertise, THE *NEXT* IQ lauds the depth, breadth, and magnitude of collective wisdom. Even the most recent shifts in our understanding of intelligence such as the introduction of multiple intelligences and emotional intelligence focus primarily on individual expertise, albeit a more nuanced individual expertise. THE *NEXT* IQ suggests that no matter how aware you are of your specific intelligences, you should not consider your intelligence fully intelligent until you have formed your own crowd whose wisdom informs your perspectives.

As lawyer and author John Jay Chapman muses: "I want to find someone on the earth so intelligent that he welcomes opinions which he condemns."[10] The ability to actively seek perspectives that challenge and contradict one's own is rooted in the intellectual CORE (Courage, Openness, Reflection, and Empathy) of a global mindset, and together they comprise THE NEXT IQ. It is not enough in today's rapid information world to simply know what you can know and see what you can see. *You have to deliberately plug into ways of knowing what you cannot know and seeing what is not visible to you.*

Since information is now accessible by almost everyone, intelligence has to be about the ability to think about and act on information, not merely access data or gather facts. Information has become passive while intelligence has to be actionable in order to be intelligent. Intelligence also has to be the ability to combine and synthesize different perspectives in order to reach many accurate conclusions, not one right answer.

Intelligence, then, is not an individual characteristic but the ability to not consider your perspective complete until it has benefited from perspectives different and even contradictory to your own.

Leadership

THE NEXT IQ encourages leaders to actively solicit different opinions in order to pursue their vision. It begins with knowing that no matter how intelligent you are, you are still only as intelligent as you can be by yourself, which is not reflective of the comprehensive intelligence you need in order to be a leader. As leadership thought leader Margaret Wheatley has written: "Our willingness to acknowledge that we only see half the picture creates the conditions that make us more attractive to others. The more sincerely we acknowledge our need for their different insights and perspectives, the more they will be magnetized to join us."[11] Leaders need intelligence to lead, and intelligence needs inclusion in order to be intelligent.

Steve Case, cofounder and former chairman of AOL, has observed that "the strength of a team is different people with different perspectives and different personalities."[12] In order to lead in the 21st century, leadership requires more than one's own expert intelligence. It truly requires all the intelligences from diverse sources that can be brought together and synthesized in order to infuse the leadership with inclusive intelligence.

Inclusion

THE *NEXT* IQ, while recognizing inclusion's connections to historical discrimination and ongoing anti-discrimination efforts, requires us to redefine the different but connected components of diversity and inclusion, not just in who we visibly are (race/ethnicity, gender, age, physical ability, etc.) but also our invisible identities (sexual orientation, national origin, native tongue, religion, etc.) as well as our experiences, our learning styles, our communication preferences, our perspectives and our priorities. As archaeologist Howard Winters mused: "Civilization is the process in which one gradually increases the number of people included in the term 'we' or 'us' and at the same time decreases those labeled 'you' or 'them' until that category has no one left in it."[13]

From the perspective of the RETRO IQ, inclusion is what one did for others in order to include them in the folds of privilege. THE *NEXT* IQ posits that the ability to include is a skill critical to excellence, so you seek and include diverse perspectives to maximize your own intelligence, not to advance a social cause or gain an economic benefit.

THE NEXT GENERATION OF INTELLIGENCE

Generational differences are a popular topic of interest and consternation in workplaces today. These differences on how, when, and where to work seep into discussions on recruiting, hiring, professional development, leadership development, and succession planning, and they confound the sensibilities of the older generations who occupy the leadership positions in many organizations. In my line of work, I often hear the following questions from each side of the generation coin:

- "Why do they always ask about working from somewhere else when we have a perfectly fine office for them?" versus "Why do they always want me to come into the office when I can work perfectly well from anywhere I want?"
- "Why do they email me instead of coming by my office when I ask them to get in touch with me?" versus "Why do they never

respond to my emails when I try to show them that I responded to their requests quickly and thoughtfully?"
- "Why do they leave the office before I do?" versus "Why don't they appreciate that I always check in and finish up work at night to make sure that they know I'm always available?"
- "Why do they text when they can pick up the phone and call me?" versus "Why do they call me and leave messages on my voicemail when it would be faster to just text me?"

Sound familiar? My research on generational differences in the workplace shows that generational differences—at their core—are communication differences that are interpreted and internalized as personal slights. For example, when a law firm partner asks an associate to get in touch with him immediately, the associate does so by email, and the partner interprets the email as an act of disrespect because he expected the associate to come see him in person. When an associate asks for guidance by email, she sees it as unnecessary that the partner requires a face-to-face meeting to discuss the issue. Communication differences, on their own, are usually benign, but communication differences rooted in generational differences are perceived as subtle signs of disrespect or disregard based on one's own perspective of interaction protocols.

A senior marketing executive once commented to me that he saw it as blatant disrespect if one of his direct reports went home if he was still in the office working on a project. Even if that direct report met all of her deadlines and turned in exemplary work, the executive viewed the work product from the lens of "how could she go home when I'm still here." The direct report, on the other hand, knowing that she would be logging in later to ensure that all work product was completed impeccably, had no idea that her work was being filtered through such a lens.

As much as research on generational differences has informed us on how to create workplaces that work for different perspectives, the focus on differences based on birthdates reinforces the focus on differences. When working with professionals of any generation that find themselves irritated by the actions of someone in another generation, I begin by asking about why they think the irritating party is doing what they are doing. It is easy to focus on the actions as conflicting with our expectations, but trying to connect with the motive behind the actions usually reveals that the same drivers of excellence, creativity, responsiveness, and so on undergird the expectations and actions of professionals regardless of their generational identities.

When we focus on the "what" of an individual's actions, it is easy to become irritated by the differences between our expectations and their output, but when we focus on the "why" of an individual's actions, our eyes are opened to the reality that the same drivers can result in different actions. Our disappointment is more often a reflection of our limited perspectives. A shift to understanding the "why" expands our intelligence about the many possible expressions of any given driver. A drive to be responsive may result in an email because an email is faster than a face-to-face meeting, and the drive to be excellent may result in finalizing work product in the evening after a period of reflection.

In my experience, generational differences are not so much challenges to be dealt with as they are opportunities to learn how we can do different things while following the same mission. If we are smart enough to view generational differences as the opportunities that they are, we become even smarter for being able to hold different (and seemingly conflicting) perspectives as connected dots that form a more intelligent whole.

Why The *Next* IQ Matters More Than the Retro IQ for Leaders and Organizations in the 21st Century

As the fable about the blind men and the elephant in the last few chapters illustrates, each man's ability to describe what he felt intelligently and immaculately did not create the opportunity for any of them to understand the full beast individually or collectively until each saw his intelligence as incomplete without the perspectives of the others. We will discuss in greater detail in later chapters why we have such difficulty in seeing our perspectives as incomplete, but the fable illustrates what we know to be true in our own experiences and observations: It is difficult to feel that you are right while acknowledging that someone who clearly disagrees with you can be as right as you are.

A VISUAL EXAMPLE DEMONSTRATING
——— DIFFERENT PERSPECTIVES ———

We use the accompanying graphic in many of our trainings to illustrate how different perspectives can completely change what is visible to the person.[14]

Suppose a leader places a paper with the number 3 in the middle of the table and proceeds to talk with the team about the 3 without realizing that each team member sees something completely different. Any understanding that results from the meeting begins with a misunderstanding. If the leader in this instance proceeds with a discussion about 3 without realizing that what she is calling a 3 looks like an E or M or W to others around the table, then that leader is leading with a lower level of intelligence than if she started the meeting asking each team member to articulate what he or she sees. Gaining those perspectives and even walking around to see each perspective personally increases that leader's capacity to lead the team in a way that is more inclusive, more intelligent, and more effective.

If you replace the 3 with a new workplace policy, a new product, a new consumer market, and so on, you can begin to understand the difference between leaders who seek all perspectives and proceed with full intelligence of multiple perspectives and leaders who assume that everyone sees what they see.

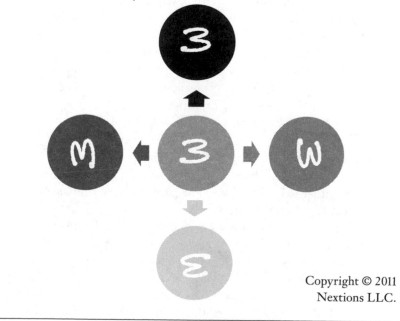

Naturally, the individual intelligence quotient and individual expertise of a leader is important in the way the leader approaches, analyzes, and solves critical problems. A leader's intelligence quotient and expertise, however, decrease in importance as time constraints tighten, information is incomplete, and the world gets flatter. They also decrease in importance when leadership is required to innovate and create new solutions, not merely solve problems. As Wayne Gretzky has said about hockey players, "A good hockey player plays where the puck is; a great hockey player plays where the puck will be."[15] Good leaders solve problems that are occurring right now; great leaders innovate for future opportunities. The RETRO IQ adequately prepares you for the former; THE *NEXT* IQ equips you for the latter.

THE *NEXT* IQ IN ACTION: EXPERTISE VERSUS INTELLIGENCE

While I was working on a leadership development initiative with a large professional services firm, one of the firm's major clients told the firm that it was about to announce the selection of a different firm as the lead on a major upcoming deal. As the six senior partners who worked for this client frenetically met with each other to see if they could change this client's decision, I asked one of the partners to approach this using their collective *NEXT* IQ. Initially, I encountered skepticism, but the rapidly dissolving hope of holding onto this client's business created a small crack in the firm's thinking. As one partner told me candidly, "we have nothing to lose at this point."

Although the partners who had historically worked for this client were considered the "best in the business" because of their individual and collective experience and expertise, each of them was using his old IQ to solve the problem. The attempt to shift from the RETRO IQ to THE *NEXT* IQ began with the partners thinking through whose relevant perspectives within the firm had not yet been sought or considered. It turned out that the partners had not sought out any perspectives other than their own. The partners were brilliant but not very inclusive. (Definitely using the RETRO IQ!)

We created a *NEXT* IQ strategy, and the partners began by making a list of everyone who had "touched" (come in direct contact with) the client in the last 12 months. They expected to come up with 10 to 12 people, but as they identified people and asked those people to identify yet more people, the list grew to over 40 individuals in the organization who had directly "touched" the client in the last 12 months!

The partners were surprised at the number of people on the list as well as the range of departments from marketing to accounting to different practice areas that were represented on the list. (As you will read later in this book, surprise is always a good indication that your NEXT IQ is activated and working!) They invited everyone on the list to an "all hands on deck" meeting where the relationship with the client was examined and analyzed. To their further surprise, the partners discovered that a specialist in their billing department had become good friends with one of the key managers in the client's corporate headquarters. The partners also discovered that the client had several concerns about the ways in which it was billed but had made the decision to not share the concerns with the partners because it was angry about it.

The partners were even more surprised to learn that a former employee now worked for the client, and several people in the firm were still very close to this person.

At the beginning of this "all hands" meeting, the partners talked a lot, but their talking slowly transitioned to asking questions and listening as they realized that their expertise on the subject matter did not translate into a complete expertise on the client relationship. When one of the partners solicited suggestions for next steps, the ideas flowed enthusiastically. From offers to make personal phone calls to strategically revising the billing framework, the individuals in the room stepped up with energy and creativity.

Final result? The firm did not get back all its previous work from the client, but it succeeded in rescuing and retaining about 60 percent of the work. The partners made it a point after this crisis to hold quarterly meetings with all the people in the firm who touched this client. The success of this "client retention" strategy led to this firm creating inclusive "client teams" for all its top-20 clients.

The RETRO IQ did not change in this situation. The brilliant experts were just as brilliant when they were about to lose the client as when they got the client back. What changed was THE NEXT IQ of the leaders. In order to lead, they had to shift from a stance of expertise to inclusive, actionable intelligence.

As you read the preceding example, it may have seemed unrealistic to you that a billing partner would not know all the facts about his client or perhaps it even felt crazy for senior partners to consult with billing clerks and administrative assistants to retain a major client. Yet, the reality was that the billing partner did not know all the facts, and the consultation with the billing clerks and administrative assistants provided more critical input into the service of the client than the partners had access to on their own. In most organizations, the more expertise someone has in a particular subject matter, the less he or she is expected to know about much else.

The hierarchical bent of the RETRO IQ (experts reign supreme over nonexperts) artificially raises the value of expertise and deflates the value of multiple perspectives. THE *NEXT* IQ feels awkward in these rigid hierarchies because what you are doing may not have been done before. Remember Carme Chacón, the pregnant minister of defense? The Chacón jolt of seeing something with our eyes that our brain cannot process based on our experiences is exactly what makes THE *NEXT* IQ powerful. THE *NEXT* IQ allows us to go beyond our own capabilities to create a collective intelligence that is not accessible to any one individual, and through that collective intelligence, THE *NEXT* IQ allows us to see new possibilities and solutions that look odd at first glance and simply profound when actualized.

THE *NEXT* IQ IN ACTION: OPINION VERSUS PERSPECTIVE

A large social service agency brought me in to work with its board of directors because the directors, although well-meaning, were having a difficult time approving a major renovation of the building that the agency's staff felt was critical to accomplishing the agency's mission.

The agency worked with children who had been sexually or physically abused, and the portions of the building that the staff wanted to renovate were the areas where the children were interviewed, where children ate and rested between interviews and examinations, and where the children waited for their caretakers to pick them up after they were done. The staff felt strongly that, as first responders for these children, they were unable to build connections with the children and get the information they needed from the interviews because the environment was not creating a place of comfort for the children.

The directors, many of whom were appointed by various political and legislative entities, felt that dipping into the budget for these renovations would weaken the organization's long-term fiscal viability. The staff countered with the argument that there was no point of being fiscally viable if they were not serving their primary mission of taking care of the children.

The conflict had been going on for about two years when I was brought in to facilitate a strategic planning decision to resolve this issue. I interviewed every staff member and director individually over the telephone and realized that this was a problem of "not seeing" as opposed to "not agreeing." In order to get people to "see more to agree more," I created a strategy focused on expanding perspectives instead of reconciling conflict.

I asked the board of directors to invite their children, grand-children, nieces, nephews, and godchildren between ages 6 and 10 to attend a "focus group on safety" at the interviewing facility. (The focus group was led by one of the staff psychologists, and it involved getting the children's perspectives on what made them feel safe and how they defined danger. The agency had written permission from each child's parent or guardian prior to the child's participation.) After much negotiating, cajoling, and promises of cookies and juice for the kids, a few of the directors agreed to invite their loved ones to attend this focus group.

About 15 children attended the "focus group." It was a 60-minute session in the interviewing area with a 15-minute break in the wait-ing area. After the official "focus group" was over, the directors were invited in to hear the children talk about the rooms. After hearing several versions of "it's creepy," "it's boring," "the books have missing pages," "the walls smell," "the bathroom is too far away," "the bath-room is nasty," "the TV doesn't work," and "it's cold" conveyed to them, the directors took their respective children home.

Next, I asked the staff to attend the budget meetings for the vari-ous legislative/political groups that had appointed the directors. After much negotiating, cajoling, and promises of cookies and juice for the adults, the staff agreed to attend these meetings. Over the next cou-ple of weeks, staff members split up and attended the various budget meetings/hearings for the entities that appointed the majority of the directors.

When the planning session at the social service agency got started, the mood in the room was far more subdued and far less combative than the informational session that I had initially conducted with them. For the first hour of the three-hour session, I asked that the directors make their strongest arguments FOR the renovation, and the staff make their strongest arguments AGAINST the renovation.

The following two hours of planning resulted in a strategic plan for a limited renovation. It was not a perfect plan by any means, and the details were far from being worked out; however, the staff and the directors were talking to each other in a way that they had never talked before. More importantly, the directors actually envisioned children in that space as they thought about the renovation, and the staff could now envision the pressures faced by the directors when they had to report the budget decisions that they were supporting.

Each director and each staff member could draw upon his or her own expertise, but the collective decision-making process was not dependent on this expertise. It was dependent on each person's ability to see beyond his or her own perspective.

THE *NEXT* IQ begins with the understanding that we all have opinions that are based on our perspectives, and our perspectives are based on what we have seen and what we have experienced. By agreeing to experiences that were outside of their comfort zone, both the directors and the staff allowed themselves to view the situation with a global mindset. By having to argue for "the other side's case," both the directors and the staff had to reach for perspectives that were different and contradictory to their own. The result was a planning process imbued with greater openness, empathy, and some agreement.

> The real voyage of discovery consists not in seeking new landscapes but in having new eyes.
>
> Marcel Proust (French novelist, critic, and essayist, 1871–1922)

THE *NEXT* IQ relies on multiple diverse perspectives to inform the expansion of one's intelligence, but it is not a "perspective gathering exercise" conducted simply to accumulate different takes on a particular subject. THE *NEXT* IQ makes intelligence intelligent when these various perspectives get integrated into the decision-making process of an individual leader or an organization to drive the process of creating action. THE *NEXT* IQ is about intelligence, but it is about intelligence that drives action and creates impact.

THE *NEXT* IQ INSIGHTS: CHAPTER 6

- Multiple sources of information and perspectives from different angles provide more intelligence with which to make decisions.

- An individual's intelligence is important, but it decreases in importance under time constraints, when information is incomplete, and when solutions require innovative thinking.
- Seeking and including diverse and contradictory perspectives requires the acceptance of "multiple rights," the ability to see that perspectives can differ and disagree and still be equally right.
- THE *NEXT* IQ is about intelligence, but it is about intelligence that leads to action and creates impact.

THE *NEXT* IQ ACTIONS: CHAPTER 6

- In the context of any problem that you are trying to solve, ask yourself what additional perspectives you can benefit from including. Try to think beyond the limits of hierarchy, job responsibilities, departmental divisions, and other perspective-limiting barriers. (See the Expertise versus Intelligence example in this chapter.)
- In the context of a disagreement that you are involved in or have a role in mediating, explore opportunities for each side to really "see" what the other side is seeing. Be open to creative ways in which you can truly take people out of their comfort zones in order to expand their perspectives whether it is the site of the next meeting, the roles people play, and so on. (See the Opinion versus Perspective example in this chapter.)

CHAPTER 7

The *Next* IQ MODELS FOR INDIVIDUALS AND ORGANIZATIONS

The *Next* IQ Model for Individuals

The *Next* IQ Model for Individuals (see figure) is built using four zones to illustrate the progression out of our closest comfort zones into zones where we can be open to and receive multiple perspectives. We can then create personal insights based on the collective knowledge of many instead of the limited information of one or a few. The shift from viewing our own intelligence as an independent process to viewing it as an interdependent process is best understood when seen as a progression from our point of greatest comfort to the point of greatest openness. This shift begins with the CORE global mindset of intellectual *courage* to embark on the journey, intellectual *openness* to welcome the unexpected, intellectual *reflection* to see how the unexpected can be integrated into the expected, and intellectual *empathy* to know that others on the same journey may see the very same things and experience them differently.

An individual's *Next* IQ is measured by the maturity of the individual's global mindset and how he or she exercises deliberate intelligence to seek and include contrasting points of view from diverse perspectives in order to create innovative high-impact solutions. Let's break that down, piece by piece.

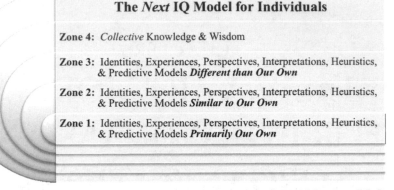

The *Next* IQ Model for Individuals

Zone 4: *Collective* Knowledge & Wisdom

Zone 3: Identities, Experiences, Perspectives, Interpretations, Heuristics, & Predictive Models *Different than Our Own*

Zone 2: Identities, Experiences, Perspectives, Interpretations, Heuristics, & Predictive Models *Similar to Our Own*

Zone 1: Identities, Experiences, Perspectives, Interpretations, Heuristics, & Predictive Models *Primarily Our Own*

Copyright © 2011 Nextions LLC.

In order to jumpstart and/or enhance your *NEXT* IQ, the first step is to actively solicit perspectives that are different than your own. Many of us have been taught that when we encounter different points of view we have to either tolerate the differences or resolve the conflict. Through the lens of THE *NEXT* IQ, contrasting points of view are instructional instead of burdensome, and different perspectives are knowledge to be gained instead of conflicts to be resolved.

> The belief that one's own view of reality is the only reality is the most dangerous of all delusions.
>
> Paul Watzlawick
> (psychologist and philosopher, 1921–2007)

When we view different perspectives this way, we think of differences in experiences, opinions, and thinking as beneficial to our personal ability to be intelligent thereby motivating us to actively seek these perspectives as part of our pursuit of excellence.

The process of actively seeking different perspectives often starts with the simple step of acknowledging the narrowness and limitedness of our own experiences and perspectives. No matter how much we know, "none of us is as smart as all of us."

Given our tendency to be most comfortable in what we know, the first foray out of our closest comfort zone is usually into the perspectives of others that most mirror our own. The new zone feels similar without being the same. The proactive journey through the zone of similarities into the zone of differences, however, is the journey that most of us avoid. It requires us to be uncomfortable, but just as getting muscles into shape requires stretching in order to strengthen them, we need to stretch our intellectual comfort zones in order to strengthen the intellect.

Part of that stretch is the acceptance that contradiction does not mean that one has to be right while another is wrong. Often, contradiction simply means contradictory right answers. THE *NEXT* IQ is the ability to hold as plausible that "right" from one perspective does not have to be at the expense of a contradictory perspective being "wrong." "Multiple rights" that are contradictory in nature can exist, and it is only when we can hold these "multiple rights" as concurrently feasible in our minds that our intelligence can grow to the level of being competitive and actionable in today's world.

Think back to the visual example of the 3, W, E, and M in Chapter 6. Every person around that table can be right even if each is directly contradicting the other. While the RETRO IQ mires us in trying to figure out who has the right answer, THE *NEXT* IQ asks us to reconceptualize what is on the table based on multiple rights.

"ALL OF THE ABOVE"

In working with a corporation headquartered in the "deep south," as it liked to tout, part of my assignment included revising its mission statement on diversity and inclusion. Inevitably, the corporation's task force and I began the thorny conversation of how to phrase the mission statement broadly enough so as to be inclusive of all employees but narrowly enough to not explicitly mention certain topics that were social and political hot buttons in the corporation, with gay and lesbian identities being at the top of the "do not mention" list.

I pushed to have gay, lesbian, bisexual, and transgender (GLBT) employees explicitly recognized as part of the fabric of the corporate culture, and many people on the task force pushed back that the corporation was not yet ready to deal with that issue. Interestingly, the corporation had an informal employee network group for gay and lesbian employees, and most people knew about this group. The group was informally accepted, but the corporation did not want explicit mention of the issue or the group in any formal corporate communications and/or marketing materials.

I suggested that we take the topic off the table, but I asked the task force members to hypothetically consider what the mission statement *could* look like if GLBT employees were directly recognized as part of the corporation's culture. The conversation about this hypothetical statement was discombobulated and confusing with some people referring to people's sexual preferences while others referred to sexual orientation and a few grumbled that what people did in their personal lives should not be brought into the workplace. As we dug deeper into the dialog, one member of the task force mentioned that there were people in the corporation who could not support the active inclusion of gays and lesbians because homosexuality was against their religion. GLBT inclusion, in their eyes, would result in the exclusion of others who had specific religious beliefs about this issue.

After several conversations on this topic (work on the mission statement continued on a separate track), I realized that these theoretical conversations were driving the members of the task force farther apart instead of bringing them closer together, so I set off in search of personal stories that could shift the conversation. I started with the few openly gay people in the corporation and learned more about how they negotiated the religious and cultural expectations in this particular community. I talked with church leaders in the area and asked them to help me understand the religious views on this topic. No matter how hard I tried to find common ground between these two worldviews, I primarily found entrenched perspectives that saw an either/or proposition. One view had to be wrong for the other view to be right.

Without any personal narratives in the community to bridge the warring views, I suggested that each member of the task force read Mary Cheney's *Now It's My Turn: A Daughter's Chronicle of Political Life* (2006). A candid autobiography by former Vice President Dick Cheney's daughter on her life as a lesbian, Mary Cheney's story takes the reader through her journey of being a lesbian in the anti-gay conservative movement, of her silent opposition to the Federal Marriage Amendment that reserved marriage only for heterosexual couples, and her work on her father's political team, which supported an anti-gay agenda, while she simultaneously worked to bring greater acceptance of gays and lesbians into the Republican party. Mary Cheney's life didn't make sense under the rules of any one perspective, but she embodied the "all of the above" principles that agree with both conflicting views while fitting into neither.

Discussing a biography would not have been my ideal way to introduce the "all of the above" thinking to this sensitive and difficult discussion, but the book opened up a dialog about the sadness that Mary Cheney must have felt when she heard her political party talk about who she was in a way that excluded her participation even though she was one of the key leaders of the 2004 Bush/Cheney reelection campaign. The group also discussed how conflicted Mary's parents must have felt, and how the family had to make sense of their lives in the public domain without privacy.

The task force—without prompting from me—invited members of the informal GLBT employee group to join them in a discussion of the book. They used Mary Cheney's story as the gateway through which the difficult dialog could begin and continue. After this joint meeting, one task force member commented to me that it felt much harder to take sides on an issue when a real live human being is involved. A personal narrative always adds dimensions to our perspectives because our lives rarely take place in any one dimension.

As of the writing of this book, this corporation still does not have sexual orientation integrated into its inclusion mission statement, but it now has domestic partner benefits and adoption leave. It also has a copy of Mary Cheney's autobiography in its main library.

Once we solicit the different and contradictory perspectives that inform and enhance our full intelligence capacities, THE NEXT IQ requires us to move into the next zone, where we include, engage, and integrate those diverse perspectives into the way we think, the data we analyze, and the problem-solving tools we utilize. The different perspectives we solicit cannot be gathered and viewed in isolation with our own beliefs and views. It is in the ability to allow our own perspectives to blend with contradictory perspectives that we can tap into the collective knowledge and wisdom that is necessary for us to thrive in the 21st century.

> I've always felt that a person's intelligence is directly reflected by the number of conflicting points of view he can entertain simultaneously on the same topic.
>
> Abigail Adams (wife of John Adams and mother of John Quincy Adams, 1744–1818)

Your NEXT IQ hinges on your ability to understand the "and" between your perspectives *and* the different perspectives that expand upon and perhaps contradict your own. It relies upon your eagerness to learn from those around you, especially those whose different experiences, perspectives, and insights inform what you know and how you think. By learning from others, you are able to know what you need to know when you need to know it even if your own experiences didn't have the opportunity to teach it to you. As writer and futurist Alvin Toffler opined, "[the] illiterate of the 21st century will not be those who cannot read or write, but those who cannot learn, unlearn and relearn."[1]

> You think that because you understand "one," you must understand "two," because one and one make two. But you must also understand "and."
>
> Sufi Wisdom

THE *NEXT* IQ is that openness to learn from others, unlearn what you thought you knew, and relearn what you now see from your new perspective.

The journey from Zone 1, staying within the comfort zone of your own identity and perspectives, to Zone 4, where you actively seek input to create collective wisdom, is a journey in which we constantly fight the pull to go back to the familiar, easy, and predictable. Upcoming chapters will deal with these zones of comfort in greater detail, but it is important to note at this juncture that getting directions, taking the journey, and staying on the journey all take sustained effort that may be difficult but is definitely worthwhile.

THE *NEXT* IQ MODEL FOR ORGANIZATIONS

THE *NEXT* IQ Model for Organizations (see figure) is based on three zones that explore both the people in the organization whose actions impact that zone and the nature of the impact that occurs in that zone. Similar to the Model for Individuals, the Model for Organizations follows the path of phased integration with a different way of thinking that builds on mission and values and leads to collaboration with competitors.

> Albrecht's Law:
> Intelligent people, when assembled into an organization, will tend toward collective stupidity.
>
> Karl Albrecht (German entrepreneur, founder of discount supermarket chain Aldi)

Similar to an individual's *NEXT* IQ, an organization's *NEXT* IQ is

The *Next* IQ Model for Organizations

Zone 3 Impact: Collaborative Efforts with Market Forces
Zone 3 People: Creative Two-Way Communications with Constituents & Competitors

Zone 2 Impact: Diverse Workplace with Inclusive Structures & Culture
Zone 2 People: Diverse Workforce with High Individual Inclusion Quotients

Zone 1 Impact: Inclusive Organizational Mission & Values
Zone 1 People: Diverse AND Inclusive Leaders with High Individual Inclusion Quotients

the collective mindset and capability of individuals within the organization to actively solicit, include, engage, and integrate different and contrasting points of view from diverse perspectives in order to create innovative high-impact solutions. As with anything else in organizations, the ability to activate and accelerate an organization's NEXT IQ begins with its leaders. A high organizational NEXT IQ begins with leaders personally and institutionally developing, executing, and stressing the mission and value of the collective intelligence that is generated from all individuals actively soliciting different perspectives to inform and enhance their own points of view. Furthermore, without clear leadership on the mission and intent to prioritize collective intelligence above individual expertise, many organizations and teams within organizations default into "group think" models that can, to invoke Karl Albrecht's words, veer toward collective stupidity.

Internally, leaders can raise THE NEXT IQ of their organizations by first ensuring that the organization's mission and values are aligned with prioritizing collective intelligence above individual talent or expertise. By embodying this priority through their own behaviors and leading with this priority in macro and micro actions, leaders can shift the structures and the culture of their organizations. Input into THE NEXT IQ begins with hiring a diverse workforce and developing inclusion competencies for that workforce. Once the organizational soil is primed for diverse perspectives and inclusive actions, the focus can shift to the output of THE NEXT IQ—the business results.

In leading the development of THE *NEXT* IQ in organizations, it is critical to not focus on tolerance of differences or even celebration of differences. Tolerance and celebration are vocabulary vestiges from the RETRO IQ that treat diverse perspectives as something that require sympathy. If someone offered you the opportunity to become smarter, would you offer your sympathies? Tolerate them? Celebrate with them? Or would you thank the heck out of them and dig into the opportunity to maximize your ability to extract all you can from the opportunity? That's the shift from the RETRO IQ to THE *NEXT* IQ, and that is the cultural change that leaders must lead.

Let's pause for a second to digest what this shift really means. This is the point in understanding THE *NEXT* IQ where skepticism usually rears its curious head and raises its eyebrows in doubt. The RETRO IQ is working fine for now, so what added value will THE *NEXT* IQ provide? Will THE *NEXT* IQ actually change our output for the better?

Margaret A. Neale, professor of organization and dispute resolution at Stanford Graduate Business School, states that "the worst kind of group for an organization that wants to be innovative and creative is one in which everyone is alike and gets along too well."[2] In fact, when everyone gets along, people on the team may feel better but actually perform worse. For example, when new members of a team are similar to the previous members, the team reports a high level of satisfaction with the group's productivity, but they perform the worst on a group problem-solving task. When the new members are different from the previous members, the group's satisfaction with its productivity goes down, but its performance actually rises significantly.[3] Neale stresses that what "feels good may not always reflect the performance of the team . . . In fact, teams with a very stable membership deteriorate in performance over time. . . ."[4]

It turns out, according to Neale, that "the mere presence of diversity you can see, such as a person's race or gender, actually cues a team in that there's likely to be differences of opinion. That cuing turns out to enhance the team's ability to handle conflict, because members expect it and are not surprised when it surfaces."[5] Productive conflict (conflict along the lines of intellectual conflict and a debate on ideas) makes teams perform better, but when differences lead to destructive conflict (conflict along identity lines that prevent/distort communication), the team's performance suffers; furthermore, the more diversity there is in a group, the more positive impact the differences will have.[6] The difference between productive conflict and destructive conflict: inclusive leadership.

In the 21st century, innovation is the key to competitive success, and the intelligence required to be innovative flows from differences in identities, interpretations, perspectives, and problem-solving modes, but these differences can quickly transition from productivity enhancers to productivity detractors if leaders do not have the competencies to lead inclusively.

Once an organization's leaders are committed and able to increase their NEXT IQ by setting a mission and values for the organization that is consistent with encouraging and empowering everyone to align their actions with inclusive intelligence, Zone 2 can be reached. In Zone 2 all individuals are held accountable for these behaviors in order to create a truly inclusive work environment.

Google, for example, is consistently evaluated by its employees to be one of the top five workplaces in America (and some Google employees insist that Google is one of the top workplaces in the world!). In fact, news reports of the gourmet food, the Ping-Pong tables, and the "work is play" culture as some of the key reasons for the happiness of Google employees are numerous. The perks are great, but the amazing retention of employees and the unmatched number of resumes that Google receives every day are due to a workplace culture that explicitly and implicitly communicates on a consistent basis that individual differences matter because collective wisdom matters.

> At Google, being yourself is a job requirement. When we encourage Googlers to express themselves, we really mean it. In fact, we count on it. Intellectual curiosity and diverse perspectives drive our policies, our work environment, our perks and our profits. It's through the amazing diversity of all us, where we come from, how we think, our functions, that allows us to do extraordinary things.[7]

Imagine if your organization identified individuality at this level as a job requirement! Google started with its leadership embodying these principles and then built them into the core foundation of what is important to the organization: "Everybody's searching for something different. Our success hinges on our ability to understand the needs of millions of Google users."[8] From the corporate mission and values that support multiple perspectives as an intelligence advantage, Google can move on to recruiting and hiring people who are not only ready to bring their individual perspectives into the Google team, but are equally ready to contribute to and benefit from a collective wisdom that is greater than their own unique skill set. This is not to suggest that Google is a utopistic workplace! Google suffers from its share of people not listening to each other or working well together; the focus on intellectual courage and openness as competencies instead of as niceties is a structural accelerator for how people think and learn and lead in a rapidly changing global industry.

Once an organization is on its way to increasing the collective impact of each individual's *NEXT* IQ, the competencies used to generate debate and ideas internally can also be used to import intelligence into the organization through collaborative interactions with external constituents, business partners, and even competitors (Zone 3).

Movie rentals illustrate what Zone 3 looks like in one corporation. In the last 10 years, the market for video rental has changed so dramatically that it barely resembles the "go to Blockbuster and rent a movie that needs to be returned two days later" model that dominated the 1990s and early 2000s. Now, you can order movies online from Netflix, have them delivered to your door, and return them when you feel like it without late fees, or you can just download whatever movie you want to see from Netflix or Amazon or iTunes and watch it on your computer or iPad. Or you can pick up a movie at a Redbox kiosk when you are out shopping for groceries or just stream a movie or a television show from Netflix or Amazon directly into your high-definition television. All these choices generated in the last 10 years slowly drove Blockbuster to file for bankruptcy in 2010.[9]

Amid these many options, Netflix continues to dominate the market. In 2011, Netflix became the "largest single source of internet traffic in North America,"[10] showing that it has become the dominant player in providing movie and television entertainment to people when and where they want it.

As competition in this area heated up in the last decade, Netflix very quickly learned to depend on a collective and collaborative intelligence model that enhanced the individual capacities it had hired internally.

What it had realized early on in its existence is that customers loved having future entertainment recommended to them based on their previous choices, and it focused on enhancing that feature to a point where customers became loyal to Netflix partly because they relied on the accuracy of these recommendations. Netflix could have hired brilliant minds to improve the recommendation algorithms internally, but that could have taken a long time, and the company would have been dependent only on the individual expertise of Netflix's internal experts. So, Netflix moved beyond its organizational walls to collaborate with the world.

COMPETITIVE COLLABORATION = $1 MILLION

In October 2006, Netflix announced a competition that would reward anyone who could substantially improve its movie recommendation system through advanced predictive modeling with $1 million.

In July 2009, two teams appeared to be left standing in the $1 million race, Bellkor's Pragmatic Chaos and Ensemble. On the surface, it looked like two teams had outperformed all the other competitors, but a closer analysis reveals that the two teams were actually amalgamated collections of many of the teams that had initially entered the competition. Each team was a collaboration of competitors.

As the *New York Times* reported on July 28, 2009, "[t]he biggest lesson learned, according to members of the two top teams, was the power of collaboration. It was not a single insight, algorithm, or concept that allowed both teams to surpass the goal . . . Instead, they say, the formula for success was to bring together people with complementary skills and combine different methods of problem-solving."[11]

Bellkor's Pragmatic Chaos was a seven-member collection of other teams who hailed from varying technical backgrounds and many countries. Ensemble was an international consortium of 30 members representing many rival teams.

On September 21, 2009, Netflix announced that Bellkor's Pragmatic Chaos had won the contest in a dead heat. Netflix congratulated the winner, awarded the $1 million prize, and quickly announced the next competition.

The Netflix competition is a great example of THE NEXT IQ model—by creating conditions outside of its organizational boundaries to actively seek, engage, and integrate external perspectives into its collective business intelligence, Netflix expanded its intelligence pool to all corners of the globe. Through its efforts, it not only high-lighted how it could benefit from multiple perspectives, but it also helped additional teams of brilliant experts realize that the more eyes they had on the problem, the more solvable the problem became.

THE *NEXT* IQ for organizations is about having the leadership, the structures, the culture, and the individual competencies in place to maximize the intelligence that inclusion brings even if inclusion sometimes means working with competitors. This level of expansive inclusion begins with each individual, but it does need to be executed on an organizational level in order to make organizations organically innovative.

So, if we know that inclusive thinking leads to innovation, and we know that innovation is a necessity if we want to succeed in the 21st-century marketplace, why do so many individuals and organizations revert back to their RETRO IQs when they know that they will be more successful using their *NEXT* IQs? Simply put, the RETRO IQ feels easier.

CHANGE IS ALSO A VERB

Individual Strategies to Prime for Change

Organizations can definitely do a lot to prime people to change, but individuals have tremendous power to enact changes in small ways that build up those change muscles into tools for innovation. We recommend our clients start working their change muscles by making the following small changes.

1. Once a year, attend a conference that has nothing to do with your area of expertise or your industry. Pay close attention to what people are discussing at the conference and try to find one way that you can use what you have learned in your own objectives at work. This is a great way to break out of the tunnel vision that results from focusing on the same area of expertise and/or the same industry.

2. Once a quarter, check out a book from your public library (or buy a book if that's your preference) on a different country, a differ-ent culture, a different religion, or any other subject that really feels different to you. Read the book and try to discover at least five ways in which people in this different country, culture, race, ethnicity, religion, and so on, are different from you and at least

five ways in which they are similar to you. This is a great exercise to help you expand your ways of seeing the world and the people around you.

3. Once a month, take a different route to work. If you usually drive, take the train. If you usually take the train, take a bus. Get off at an earlier stop and walk the remainder of the way. Whatever you do, make it different. Then, observe. Notice the changes in scenery, the people who are sharing your commute on the train, the highway, the bus, or the sidewalk. This is a good exercise to interrupt your unconscious from taking over when you do the same thing in the same way over and over.

4. Once a week, initiate a conversation with someone you have never spoken with before in your workplace, with a customer, at a client site, or in any other professional scenario.

5. Once a day, when you are trying to analyze a situation or solve a problem, ask at least three people the same question to see how different people respond before you solidify your own perspective. This is a good exercise to help you see the different ways in which people understand information and solve problems.

CHANGE IS ALSO A VERB

Organizational Strategies to Prime for Change

In almost every organization for which I've conducted assessments on the culture, the communication processes, leadership, and/or overall employee engagement, I have found the following to be true:

> People want change (the noun) but they
> don't want to change (the verb).

In order to prime any organization to start using THE *NEXT* IQ at an individual and collective level, the first step has to be to get people to prepare *to change*, not just *for change*. Fortunately, our change muscles can be exercised and strengthened regularly so that when they are called upon to act, they are strong enough to do so. The following strategies allow people to exercise and strengthen their individual and collective change muscles.

1. Use Dr. Edward de Bono's Six Thinking Hats[12] process to encourage people to think outside of their comfort zones. Each of the six hats focuses on a specific way of thinking. Assigning "a hat" to

each individual in a meeting and asking people to only speak in the voice of their assigned hats allows people to train their brains *to change* the way they think about issues.

White Hat:	Focus on facts, information, research data
Red Hat:	Focus on feelings, emotions, intuition
Black Hat:	Focus on caution, risk aversion, deliberation
Yellow Hat:	Focus on being positive, optimistic, and idealistic
Green Hat:	Focus on new ideas, innovation, outside-the-box thinking
Blue Hat:	Focus on the big picture, the long-term perspective

2. Encourage people to find one contradictory opinion before they present their perspective. The conversations that occur in a person's search for a contradictory opinion alone dramatically change the way a person thinks about his or her own idea and perspective.
3. Urge people to have lunch with someone from a different function, practice, role, department, and so on at least once a quarter. Ask people to use those conversations in the way they think about the organization and the way they think about their own roles.
4. Foster "creative conversations" where meetings are held for no other purpose than to brainstorm all possible questions, answers, challenges, and solutions to a particular issue. These meetings should be free from the pressure of having to make decisions or reach conclusions.
5. Embolden people to think of their jobs and their workplaces as positively anticipating of change because change means better, not harder. Communicate examples of change making things easier in order to drive this point home.

THE *NEXT* IQ INSIGHTS: CHAPTER 7

- THE *NEXT* IQ Model for Individuals explores the four sequential zones that an individual journeys in order to travel beyond the limitations of the RETRO IQ to the intelligence available in the collective wisdom of THE *NEXT* IQ.
- THE *NEXT* IQ Model for Organizations explores the three sequential zones that an organization has to journey to achieve the next level of organizational intelligence. The three zones in this model cover both what individuals, especially the organization's leaders,

have to do in each zone as well as the impact of those actions on the whole organization.

- The Netflix competition example provides an illustration of how an organization can become more intelligent by not limiting where and how it gets its intelligence and also by viewing competitors as collaborators.

- Although the majority of individuals and organizations want positive change, they resist the act of changing. The Change Is Also a Verb exercises for individuals and organizations offer concrete tools to prime for change (the verb).

THE *NEXT* IQ ACTIONS: CHAPTER 7

- Implement the Change Is Also a Verb exercises for individuals and note what happens to your attention levels, your observation skills, and your thought patterns, especially as you implement the daily and weekly suggestions.

- Explore the Change Is Also a Verb exercises for organizations and note what happens to team dynamics, interpersonal relationships, and collective problem-solving strategies. Are people learning new things about each other? Do different people speak up in different contexts? Have informal "water cooler" conversations shifted?

CHAPTER 8

THE COMFORT
OF THE RETRO IQ

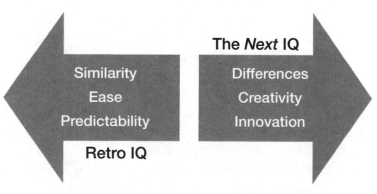

The RETRO IQ is comfortable because it relies on (1) similarity, (2) ease, and (3) predictability. In a complex interaction between unconscious patterns and conscious choices, human beings generally veer toward the similar, opting to remain in their closest comfort zone. These sources of comfort are well served through the RETRO IQ because looking to the past provides predictability, but it also enables us to thrive only in conditions identical to those in the past. For this reason, the RETRO IQ may work well for those who need to discharge routine tasks and responsibilities on a daily basis, but it is extremely ineffective for leaders who should be visionaries, creating a strategy for the unexpected and leading a culture of critical and innovative thinking.

Choosing between the RETRO IQ and THE *NEXT* IQ is much like choosing between driving in cruise control mode and driving actively with full control of the vehicle. Cruise control is a popular feature, and car manufacturers consistently entice consumers with their "smarter" cruise control systems. Cruise control feels active because you have to get the car up to a particular speed before setting the cruise control. You also feel engaged because you have to continue to watch the road and be ready to brake in an emergency. That said, cruise control is less tiring than full control driving because it is easier (you can take your foot off the pedals to relax your leg muscles) and more predictable (the car's speed stays consistent, and the car adjusts automatically for slight variations in incline and decline of the road).

Cruise control sounds great, except that research from the Federal Highway Administration and the National Highway Traffic Safety Administration[1] demonstrates that cruise control is fine unless the road surface is wet, slippery, or rough and you are not driving at night or in medium to heavy traffic. Therefore, unless you are driving on a smooth dry road in daylight with little traffic, cruise control can actually be quite dangerous. Cruise control feels active, but it is an illusion of engagement that comforts us while making us vulnerable to a slow response in an emergency.

The RETRO IQ is much like cruise control in that it is less tiring and feels more predictable; however, if the environmental factors are anything but consistently ideal, the RETRO IQ can actually cause leaders and organizations to make dangerous decisions. Remember the Circuit City example in the Introduction? Circuit City's RETRO IQ led its leaders to rely on cost-cutting instead of perspective-expanding measures, which led to bankruptcy very quickly. When leaders are not actively driving, sudden changes such as an economic disruption or shift in consumer purchasing patterns can lead to reactive decision making much like a person slamming on the brakes when she hits a patch of water while cruising.

Enron's collapse in 2002 was due to many complex, unethical, and even illegal machinations, but there is also a RETRO IQ element to Enron's demise that Dennis Moberg, Wilkinson Professor of Management and Ethics at Santa Clara University, described in a forum at that school's Markkula Center for Applied Ethics.[2] Moberg discussed Jeffrey Skilling, the former president of Enron Corporation, who was convicted in 2006 of multiple felony charges related to Enron's financial collapse. He commented on how Skilling not only had an inflated perspective of his own expertise and capacity (Skilling: "I've never not been successful at business or work . . . ever!"), but he also eschewed questions or comments from any different perspective than the one he advanced (Skilling to a reporter: "The people who ask questions don't understand the company."). In his analysis of the collapse, Moberg also found that "[m]anagers at Enron's divisions grew arrogant, thinking themselves invincible. We see this insular tendency of the company to seal itself off from forces on the outside. They had something called a rank-and-yank performance appraisal system . . . that took care of anyone who might potentially disagree."[3] Moberg advocated for reforms that prevented individual leaders as well as organizational structures from settling into familiar and easy cronyism that repelled differences in perspectives and cognitive complexity. He closed his comments with this observation: "Jeffrey Skilling, Andrew Fastow [former CFO of Enron], and Kenneth Lay [former CEO and chairman of Enron] all live in the same gated community in Houston, which I think is a great metaphor for what happened at Enron."[4]

When you compare the strategies of inclusive intelligence demonstrated by Starbucks (MyStarbucksIdea.com) and Netflix (competition for innovation) with the self-limiting intelligence models of Circuit City and Enron, you begin to see how the RETRO IQ allows leaders and organizations to cruise until circumstances suddenly change and require the leaders to drive actively again. The problem with cruise control is that when you get comfortable with cruising, you may not react in time to really drive when a change in circumstances requires you to do so, or you may overreact in unpredictable and potentially dangerous ways.

Unlike the RETRO IQ, THE *NEXT* IQ requires that you stay in active driving mode so that you can plan for shifts in the environment before you are shocked into doing so. Yes, active driving can take more effort and be more tiring than cruising, but you are far more likely to get to where you want to go without getting into accidents along the way. The examples I present in this book represent just the tip of the connection between THE *NEXT* IQ and success.

So, if leaders and organizations know that diversity in perspectives, cognitive creativity, and deliberate change create more successful organizations, why don't more leaders and organizations employ THE

Next IQ instead of staying stuck in the Retro IQ? The shift from the Retro IQ to The *Next* IQ is a difficult one, not because people don't want to or know how to make the transition, but because the Retro IQ operates in a way that doesn't allow you to realize that you are, in fact, stuck in it. Getting unstuck requires seeing beyond what is visible and actively seeking alternative perspectives that are different from yours even if you feel that everything is working just fine.

Let's explore the circular sticky logic of the Retro IQ a little further.

WHO'S ON FIRST? (comedy routine performed by Abbott & Costello)

Abbott: I say Who's on first, What's on second, I Don't Know's on third.
Costello: Are you the manager?
Abbott: Yes.
Costello: You gonna be the coach too?
Abbott: Yes.
Costello: And you don't know the fellows' names?
Abbott: Well I should.
Costello: Well then who's on first?
Abbott: Yes.
Costello: I mean the fellow's name.
Abbott: Who.
Costello: The guy on first.
Abbott: Who.
Costello: The first baseman.
Abbott: Who.
Costello: The guy playing . . .
Abbott: Who is on first!
Costello: I'm asking YOU who's on first.
Abbott: That's the man's name.
Costello: That's who's name?
Abbott: Yes.
Costello: Well go ahead and tell me.
Abbott: That's it.
Costello: That's who?

Abbott:	Yes.
Costello:	Look, you gotta first baseman?
Abbott:	Certainly.
Costello:	Who's playing first?
Abbott:	That's right.
Costello:	When you pay off the first baseman every month, who gets the money?
Abbott:	Every dollar of it.
Costello:	All I'm trying to find out is the fellow's name on first base.
Abbott:	Who.
Costello:	The guy that gets . . .
Abbott:	That's it.
Costello:	Who gets the money . . .
Abbott:	He does, every dollar. Sometimes his wife comes down and collects it.
Costello:	Whose wife?
Abbott:	Yes.

Without a doubt, the "Who's on First?" bit is a classical and perennially funny comedy routine. The clever play on words aside, what we find funny about this dialog is that, as the audience, we see the two characters talking past each other and continuing to get increasingly frustrated. In this bit, the characters are frustrated not because they disagree but because they don't understand why they are not being understood when, in their minds, they are being abundantly simple, clear, and insistent.

The RETRO IQ is very much like this dialog. When we are using our RETRO IQ—the IQ that looks back to look ahead—we are using the right words and forming the right sentences, but there is a nuance to the meaning of the conversation that we are missing. There is a logic to the RETRO IQ that sticks us to the past and makes us sound illogical as we progress in the conversation because we don't invite in additional perspectives that can suggest things like "maybe the man is named Who." Instead, we assume that we are right and the other person is daft, so we continue to try and push through our perspective. Lest we relegate this purely to the comedic realm, let's examine the sticky illogic of the RETRO IQ in the context of women's purses in Wimbledon.

Until 2007, women's championship purses for Wimbledon were set at a lesser amount than men's championship purses. The amount of prize money has historically been and continues to be decided by the Wimbledon Committee of the All-England Club. For several decades, former Wimbledon champion Billie Jean King and other female tennis players had been lobbying tirelessly for equal pay for women in this revered tournament. Venus Williams punctuated this long battle with an open letter in 2006 to the All-England Club published in *The Times* (of London) that directly chastised the continued pay inequities: "Wimbledon's stance devalues the principle of meritocracy and diminishes the years of hard work that women on the tour have put into becoming professional tennis players."[5] Venus's letter brought forth the endorsements of then Prime Minister Tony Blair and several prominent members of Parliament. For several months after Williams's letter was published, the back and forth on equal pay at Wimbledon went something like this:

For:	Men get paid more than women at Wimbledon!
Against:	Do women want to get paid the same as men?
For:	Of course they do!
Against:	So, why don't they?
For:	Because it's not up to them. The Wimbledon Committee decides.
Against:	So, they should just ask the Committee for more pay.
For:	They have asked. The Committee said no.
Against:	Why did they say no?
For:	They said it's because women play less than men. Three sets versus five sets.
Against:	That makes sense. If you play less, you should get paid less.
For:	No. Women would play five sets if given the chance.
Against:	Well, why don't they just play five sets?
For:	The Committee said no.
Against:	Because women can't handle playing five sets?
For:	No, because a long time ago, a woman playing in a full-length dress and a corset fainted while playing.

Against:	Why would a woman play in a full-length dress and a corset?
For:	Because the Committee said so.
Against:	Then, it makes sense that they would make women play less. It's ridiculous to try and play five sets in a full-length dress and a corset.
For:	But women didn't want to wear a full-length dress and a corset!
Against:	Did they tell the Committee that?
For:	Of course they did.
Against:	Looks like the Committee listened. Women wear what they want to now, right?
For:	Yes, but this is about pay, not what they wear!
Against:	So, why did you bring up what they wear?
For:	Because it had to do with how many sets women play.
Against:	Okay. So, how many sets do women want to play?
For:	Five!
Against:	But, why would they want to play five sets when they are only getting paid for three?[6]

The RETRO IQ logic is difficult to combat because it requires any vision of the future to reflect the image of the past. That would be fine if we did not want to see change in our future. Reliance on the past to forecast the future usually brings you a future that looks a lot like the past. A conversation on change has to find its logic in imagination, not history. Similarly, a conversation on including what has historically been excluded or not fully included cannot logically line up with the past. While the RETRO IQ logic stubbornly sticks to the past, THE NEXT IQ uses the past as an appropriate reference point and uses imagination to see and create something that does not yet exist.

Tightly packed into the RETRO IQ are many dynamics that keep it stuck to the past. These dynamics favor similarities: bias, stereotypes, prejudices, discrimination, and privilege, preferring cognitive ease (it is easier to think in concrete terms of what has happened as opposed to imagining what could happen), and veering toward predictable results (repetition is more predictable than change). These powerful winds impact the conscious and unconscious directions of our lives, but they are neither inevitable nor untamable.

THE *NEXT* IQ focuses on the active recognition and interaction with these dynamics to decrease their impact on the choices we make. Shifting from the RETRO IQ to THE *NEXT* IQ requires us to become comfortable navigating these dynamics. We cannot actively solicit different perspectives to grow our intelligence until we know the winds that are impacting us. Shifting requires us to get out of cruise control.

THE *NEXT* IQ INSIGHTS: CHAPTER 8

- The RETRO IQ is comfortable because it relies on similarity, ease, and predictability.
- The RETRO IQ is akin to driving a car on cruise control, a less tiring and more predictable way of driving that works well only in ideal driving conditions. Thinking in "cruise control" results in intellectually risky processes just as cruise control driving results in greater risk of accidents.
- Shifting from the RETRO IQ to THE *NEXT* IQ is difficult because the former often operates in a way that doesn't allow you to realize that you are stuck in it. The pull of similarity, ease, and predictability is strong.
- The RETRO IQ also is illogical if you try to apply it to change and innovation (see the Wimbledon example).

THE *NEXT* IQ ACTIONS: CHAPTER 8

For a quick and fun reminder that there is always more to life than what immediately meets the eye, take a few seconds to study each of the pictures below.

- Try to count how many legs the elephant has. Feeling a little frustrated? Your brain is trying to count the legs based on the elephant's feet. If you cover up the feet, you can see the four legs clearly.
- Look at the picture on the right carefully. Do you see a young woman or an old woman? Can you see both? (The young woman's chin is the old woman's nose. The young woman's necklace is the old woman's mouth.)[7]

CHAPTER 9

THE COMFORT OF SIMILARITY: WE SEE WHAT WE KNOW, WE BECOME WHAT WE SEE

WE *SEE* WHAT WE *KNOW*

Given the amount of research that validates the intellectual benefits of including more and different perspectives in our thinking, why are we not more proactively engaged in seeking different perspectives? We can contemplate logistical barriers like lack of time, lack of resources, and lack of organizational support—all legitimate obstacles—but none of those barriers are as powerful as the ones in our own heads. We think that we are already including when we are not; we think we are engaging with new ideas when we are really moving back to our comfort zones. This chapter will uncover some ways in which we only see what we already know and offer some tools to break through our own vision blockers so that we can see what is actually in front of us.

> We do not see things as they are, we see things as we are.
>
> Anaïs Nin (French-Cuban author, 1903–1977)

As social creatures, it is in our DNA to differentiate ourselves from others and to categorize people, animals, objects, knowledge, and events in order to survive and thrive. This talent for differentiation is a powerful assistant when we need to sense danger or distinguish quickly between friend and foe, but it has also led us to irrelevant differentiations that are based more on how we have been socialized and how we now define friend and foe.

For example, the ability to differentiate between tribes was a critical trait when geographically proximal tribes warred against each other, but those tribal instincts hold us back when we are trying to identify similarities and understandings across cultural and national boundaries in a borderless global marketplace. Our history with differences has geared us to default to "different equals dangerous." THE *NEXT* IQ is about thanking that instinct for getting us through history and letting it go so that it doesn't impede our progress. So, let's dive into the ways in which we see what we think instead of what is actually in front of us—biases, stereotypes, prejudices, discriminations, and privileges.

Biases are the proclivities we carry to believe one thing over another. For a simple example, if I asked you whether a man who is 5'3" or one who is 7'9" is more likely to have played in the NBA, most people (80–90 percent in our studies) select the 7'9" man. This innocuous question actually gets at two biases: (1) the taller someone is, the more likely people are to believe that he has played in the NBA (you may have guessed that bias already!), and (2) people assume that the NBA means "all professional basketball players," not just ones that play in the United States (you may not have been aware of this bias at work as you pondered the question). The right answer to the question actually is that a 5'3" man is more likely to have played in the NBA (Tyrone "Mugsy" Bogues, point guard in the NBA for 14 years) because although there are a few 7'9" professional basketball players in the world (in China, Japan, North Korea, and Soviet Union) none of them have ever played in the NBA. The tallest athletes (as of this book's print date) to play in the NBA are both 7'7" (Manute Bol and Gheorghe Mureşan).

Using this introduction to bias in the United States leads to very interesting discussions about bias because in America we have a cultural bias toward African American men having the greatest probability of being the tallest men around and the tallest men in basketball. Yet, the tallest professional basketball players have not been African

American—they have been Chinese, North Korean, and Japanese—and the tallest basketball players in the world have not played in the NBA. Yasutaka Okamaya—a Japanese man—is actually the tallest man to ever have been drafted into the NBA, but he opted to play in his home country instead.

Biases, stereotypes, prejudices, and discrimination are most often triggered by visual differentiators of identity such as gender, race, ethnicity, age, physical appearance, and physical ability. Triggers can also include visible indicators for invisible identities such as head scarves for Muslim women (religion) and hearing aids (physical abilities). Visible triggers signal our brains in ways that we cannot always control leading us to think we "know" things when we simply just think them. For example:

- "When shown photographs of people of the same height, evaluators overestimated the heights of male subjects and underestimated the heights of female subjects, even though a reference point, such as a doorway was provided."[1]
- "When shown photographs of men of similar height and build, evaluators rated the athletic ability of African American men higher than that of white men."[2]
- Evaluators' responses to one obese salesperson in a chain store were that (1) the store was not as successful as other stores, (2) store management had a lower effectiveness compared with other stores, and (3) the other sales associates were less than the best of the main company.[3]

Bias is that proclivity that we have to think one thing is truer than another because of socialization, past experiences, and a host of other factors, but *bias is not based solely on reality*. Biases can be conscious (being aware of our thoughts as we are thinking them) or unconscious (thinking we "know" something without realizing that we are predisposed to believe that thing is true). Furthermore, biases can be negative or positive. Although we colloquially tend to use bias in the negative sense (someone is biased against something), the majority of biases we have are actually "for" things. Preferences for certain characteristics in people is still a bias, a positive bias. In the NBA example, most people demonstrate both a negative bias against short people as probable

NBA players and a positive bias for tall people as probable NBA players. Additionally, the bias about height is often a more conscious bias for people but the bias about the NBA as the full (and perhaps only) universe of professional basketball players is usually an unconscious bias.

U.S. District Judge Bernice B. Donald of the Western District of Tennessee recounted a story about stereotypes in a recent article on implicit (unconscious) bias for the American Bar Association's Section of Litigation: "I remember selecting a jury once in a drug case . . . A public defender stepped up with her African-American defendant seated behind her at the table. She asked, 'How many of you know what a drug dealer looks like?' and the hands shot up. She didn't say anything else. Then, you could see the hands slowly go down as the people recognized what they were saying. The defendant sitting at the table looked like someone out of central casting. If she had asked them to describe a 'drug dealer,' they would have described her client."[4]

Stereotypes are the exaggerated group-based identities we build in our minds based on our biases. The jurors had biases as to what a drug dealer looked like, and those biases were captured in a distorted generalization about a particular group without much room for individual variation. Like biases, stereotypes can be positive or negative, and they can be conscious or unconscious. The defense attorney in Judge Donald's example quickly and creatively translated the juries' unconscious negative stereotypes into their conscious awareness so that she could deal with them more directly.

Prejudice is prejudgment of a group or its individual members because they belong to that group. Prejudices also can be positive or negative, but common usage of the term usually carries a negative connotation. Once stereotypes (exaggerated beliefs) solidify into prejudices (judgments about those exaggerated beliefs), we begin to form in-groups (groups in which we belong because of our similarities with other group members) and out-groups (groups of "others" based on what we see as different from ourselves).

Discrimination is behavior. It is the action we take in reference to an individual once an explicit or implicit bias has morphed from an image in our heads to an exaggerated belief about a group to a judgment about that group. In other words, most of our biases are latent until a situation causes us to use our biases instead of direct knowledge to make decisions. We discriminate using both positive and negative biases, and we tend to discriminate in favor of people who are in our in-group and against those who are in our out-groups.

Biases, stereotypes, prejudices, and discrimination are often used interchangeably to mean the same thing—the negative treatment of people based on the substitution of their identity traits for other characteristics (i.e., height equals basketball ability and lack of height equals basketball inability). It is important, however, to differentiate and understand each of these terms individually because the intervention mechanisms for each are different. Biases require awareness but may not always lend themselves to conscious choice whereas discrimination can often be corrected by conscious choice. We will get more into interventions in subsequent chapters, but while we are discussing bias, stereotypes, prejudice, and discrimination, let's take a look at one cutting-edge tool that is teaching us about our unconscious biases in a novel way.

The Implicit Association Test (IAT), developed by Anthony Greenwald, Debbie McGhee, and Jordan Schwartz,[5] is a social psychology tool used to measure a person's inherent "implicit association" between any identities, concepts, attributes, and visual images. The IAT evolved into a more expanded project entitled Project Implicit, which was cofounded by Anthony Greenwald, Mahzarin Banaji, and Brian Nosek. The theory behind the IAT is that the faster you can pair certain concepts such as black and white (in regards to racial identity) with attributes such as good and bad, the stronger your mental association between a pair of words. "Though the words and names aren't subliminal, they are presented so quickly that a subject's ability to make deliberate choices is diminished—allowing his or her underlying assumptions to show through."[6] In an analysis of over 900,000 responses on the black/white test, more than 70 percent of the respondents implicitly associated white with good and black with bad.[7]

Although the IAT has received a lot of attention for the aforementioned race study and its gender, sexual orientation, and other identity studies, it has quietly gained credibility as being able to measure not just our associations but also our behaviors. A recent IAT application with airline pilots found that the implicit attitudes that pilots have toward risky flight behaviors are more accurate in predicting their behaviors than traditional self-reported tests on attitude, personality, or behaviors.[8] In rapidly measuring the association that a person has between

two concepts, the IAT measures "introspectively unidentified (or inac-
curately identified traces of past experience that mediate favorable or
unfavorable feeling, thought or action toward social objects."[9] In other
words, the IAT measures what you really think, not what you think you
think. Try the test for yourself at www.projectimplicit.org.

When Mahzarin Banaji talks about the IAT, it is both a deeply
intellectual and a powerfully personal dialog. She talks about the validity of the test because of the now millions of people who have taken it,
and she discusses the impact of the results. But, she also talks about her
own shock of taking the test and finding that as much as she considers
herself to be a self-aware and nonbiased person, she discovered biases
on many fronts that she does not consciously realize, even after reflection and introspection. (After having taken several of these tests myself,
I understand her shock!)

The measurement of these implicit associations is critical because
"[m]ost fair-minded people strive to judge others according to their
merits, but our research shows how often people instead judge according to unconscious stereotypes and attitudes, or 'implicit prejudices.'"[10]
As Banaji explains, "[e]arly on, we learn to associate things that commonly go together and expect them to inevitably coexist: thunder and
rain . . . gray hair and old age . . . [W]e grow to trust them, and they can
blind us to those instances in which the associations are not accurate."[11]

The study of stereotypes has slowly evolved from studying the
explicit to identifying the implicit. As the first few lines of a *Psychology Today* article on implicit bias boldly declared, "[p]sychologists once
believed that only bigoted people used stereotypes. Now the study of
unconscious bias is revealing the unsettling truth: We all use stereotypes, all the time, without knowing it. We have met the enemy of
equality, and the enemy is us."[12]

INTERVIEWING INTELLIGENCE

In 2006, my firm ran private studies in two different large law firms
where we sat in on interviews for the incredibly competitive summer clerkship positions at the firms, and we evaluated the interviews
according to two primary criteria: (1) how much time the interviewer
talked versus how much time the interviewee talked, and (2) how
many personal things (such as family, hobbies, undergraduate alma
mater, etc.) were discussed in the interview versus how many things

directly related to the summer clerkship (law school alma mater, activities in law school, professional interests, previous work experience, etc.). After observing and recording the data from the interviews, we debriefed with the interviewers and interviewees on these additional considerations: (1) how well they thought the interview went, (2) how connected each person felt to the other, and (3) what general cues they used to arrive at conclusions about the other (i.e., body language, word choices, etc.).

Here are a few of the overall results:

- The more an interviewer talked during the interview, the more likely he or she was to like the candidate that was being interviewed. (Yes, you read that correctly. The more the person who was doing the interview talked, the more he loved the person being interviewed!)
- Many of the interviewers reported "having a gut feeling" that they were going to like the candidate before the candidate walked into the interview. The primary source of the "gut feeling" was the resume, specifically similarities that the interviewer spotted between himself or herself and the interviewee such as alma mater, extracurricular activities, and personal interests.
- The more the interviewer talked during the interview, the more likely personal issues were discussed more than job-related issues.
- The more the interviewer talked during the interview, the more likely the interviewer and interviewee were to rate the interview as a positive interview.

None of the interviewers felt that they were biased for or against any of the candidates, but when the interviewers "felt" that they would connect with the candidate, they spent more time talking in the interview, which led to them having a more favorable impression of the candidate.

Anecdotally, as I observed these interviews, I also noticed that the interviewer's interest in the candidate was immediately evident when he or she had that "gut feel" about a candidate. In these situations, the interviewers often had much greater eye contact with the candidate and seemed much more relaxed, which in turn created a greater ease for the candidate as well.

By the end of many of the interviews, there were certain candidates who definitely looked like they were more confident, charming, and intelligent; coincidentally, these candidates happen to have been in the interviews where the interviewers talked a lot.

In both firms, we found a high correlation between the candidates who "felt good" to the interviewers prior to the interview and the candidates who eventually received offers for the summer clerkship. The interviews were effectively irrelevant, so did the interviewers pick up something in the resume that they instinctively knew would net them a great candidate, or did the interviewers make great candidates through the way that they interviewed? It's difficult to say conclusively; however, the candidates that the interviewers connected with shared more visible identity characteristics with them than the candidates with whom the interviewers did not connect.

The type of "comfort zone" biases—where connections are made on similarities instead of differences—evident in the preceding case study is a primary cause of being stuck in the Retro IQ. While The *Next* IQ requires the active seeking of and engagement with different perspectives, the Retro IQ settles into comfortable patterns of seeking similarities. Not only does the Retro IQ mire decision-making processes in the muck of the status quo, it also prevents the different perspectives necessary to drive change, innovation, and forward thinking from entering the organization.

The law firms in our studies are quite typical of how the legal industry recruits and hires. Individual subjectivities of the interviewers have a disproportionate impact on the hiring process because there are no objective mechanisms to balance out the subjectivities. That said, law firms are not the only perpetrators of inserting unconscious bias into interviewing and hiring processes. Physical differences between individuals make a difference in how every profession interviews and hires, and the unconscious biases that we carry regarding differences and similarities results in statistics like the following:

- Malcolm Gladwell reports in his book, *Blink*, that "on average CEOs were just a shade under six feet. Given that the average American male is 5'9" that means that CEOs, as a group, have about three inches on the rest of their sex. But this statistic actually understates matters. In the U.S. population, about 14.5 percent of all men are six feet or over. Among CEOs of Fortune 500 companies, that number is 58 percent. Even more strikingly, in the general American population, 3.9 percent of adult men are

6'2" or taller. Among my CEO sample, 30 percent were 6'2" or taller."[13]

- In a study on the correlation between the particular type of name on a resume and the probability of getting called for an interview, Marianne Bertrand and Sendhil Mullainathan found that "White names receive 50 percent more callbacks for interviews. Callbacks are also more responsive to resume quality for White names than for African American ones. The racial gap is uniform across occupation, industry, and employer size . . . Equally importantly, applicants with African American names find it hard to overcome this hurdle in callbacks by improving their observable skills or credentials."[14]

- A study in England on the various accents within England and possible perceptions of intelligence connected with the accents found "speaking in a Birmingham accent gives a worse impression than saying nothing at all . . . [the study led by Dr. Lance Workman of Bath Spa University] compared the Yorkshire accent with those from Birmingham and with the clipped tone of what is known as Queen's English . . . [According to Dr. Workman] 'Surveys have shown that a lot of people associate Birmingham with criminal activity, and they associate criminal activity with low intelligence.'"[15]

- Several studies on people who weigh more than the norm have shown that obesity affects employment opportunities, advancement and promotion opportunities, as well as compensation, not due to deficiencies in qualification but perceptions that people who are obese are not hardworking, intelligent, self-disciplined, and/or trustworthy.[16] One study found that for women in the United States, an addition of 64 pounds above the average weight for women resulted in a 9 percent drop in wages, which roughly translates to about 1.5 years of education or 3 years of work experience.[17] A study conducted in the European Union found that a 10 percent increase in an individual's BMI (body mass index) decreased men's wages by 1.9 percent and women's wages by 3.3 percent.[18] These and other studies have shown that "overweight job applicants and employees were evaluated more negatively and had more negative employment outcomes compared to non-overweight applicants and employees."[19]

- A recent study demonstrated that when we have a choice, we will consistently sit next to someone who we feel looks similar to us.[20] As one of the primary researchers, Anne Wilson, summarizes, "[p]eople tend to think that someone who looks a little more like them is more likely to think like them . . . If you expect someone to be more like you, you might behave toward them in a more open and likeable way. And that kind of 'social lubrication' is a key ingredient in the foundation of a lasting relationship."[21]

The statistical sketches profiled above illustrate how our unconscious biases manifest without our explicit permission or even knowledge. When I've done assessments of workplaces and found very similar workplace and workforce patterns, I have rarely found conscious and deliberate efforts to select or promote or view positively an individual based on something like height or name or accent or body weight. Even when confronted with the statistical evidence within their organizations of bias along physical differentiators, most leaders quickly try to find specific reasons why individuals within a group may have not succeeded instead of acknowledging the reality of actions that are not conscious or deliberate.

> I used to say that whenever people heard my Southern accent, they always wanted to deduct 100 IQ points.
>
> Jeff Foxworthy (American comedian)

These patterns are not limited to physical attributes. We have done assessments in workplaces where we found unfounded correlations between neatness of work spaces and perceptions of analytical ability (direct correlation) and between the number of personal pictures displayed in offices and perceptions of friendliness (direct correlation). Our tendencies to see what we know allows us to quickly sort the world around us into preexisting categories, but when we do, we also lose the opportunity to see and learn something different from what we already know.

The RETRO IQ sticks to many of our workplaces because we have imbued these places with a false notion of meritocracy. When we are confronted with the possibility of concepts such as unconscious biases, subtle stereotypes, innate prejudices, or unintended discrimination, we defend our meritocracies instead of acknowledging their weaknesses.

Cultivating a global mindset requires the intellectual courage and intellectual openness to seek and include new perspectives and learn new ways to thrive in this changing world. In order to increase our individual and collective *NEXT* IQs, we have to open up to the possibility that though we may want to embrace new and different perspectives from people who are perceptibly different from us, we often unknowingly work to keep these perspectives out of our workplaces and our comfort zones.

We also have to open up to the possibility that the flip side to unconscious bias is unconscious privilege. Defined as a special advantage, immunity, permission, right, or benefit granted to or enjoyed by an individual, class, or caste,[22] there are individuals who benefit from unconscious privilege granted to them just as there are individuals who suffer from unconscious biases working against them.

In understanding privilege as the counterpoint to bias, it is critical to understand that when an individual or group benefits from one or many privileges, their lack of knowledge of the privilege(s) and/or their lack of affirmative permission to receive the privilege(s) do not negate the benefits that they enjoy. Furthermore, individuals who benefit from privilege cannot "give it back" just as those who are negatively impacted by bias cannot "opt out" of being perceived a particular way.

In our law firm studies, the candidates who benefited from the interviewers' higher degrees of comfort cannot "give back" that privilege even if they were to discover that other candidates had not been "connected with" in the same way. Taller men cannot "give back" whatever halo effect their height has on those around them. People with traditionally "white" names cannot "give back" the sense of trust and intelligence others feel when they see their name in contrast to the sense of foreignness felt when they see traditionally "African American names." And, people of average weight cannot "give back" the privilege of not being automatically viewed as lazy simply because their metabolism works differently than someone else's.

This is what makes the RETRO IQ so stubbornly sticky. People who benefit from certain identity privileges often feel that acknowledging the privileges that have advantaged them somehow minimizes the work that they have done and the challenges that they have overcome. Acknowledging privilege does not negate merit, but not acknowledging privilege does close out the ability to fully become aware of bias.

Without increasing awareness about bias, it is impossible to actively seek, include, and integrate the different perspectives necessary to increase your intelligence in the 21st century, especially as a leader.

WE BECOME WHAT WE SEE

Both unconscious biases and the privileges that they leave in their wake focus on the reactions and perceptions of external perspective; they reflect how one is perceived by others when biases, stereotypes, and prejudices get triggered. Stereotype threat and stereotype lift, on the other hand, are the internal reflections of external biases, stereotypes, and prejudices.

> It is not necessary to change. Survival is not mandatory.
>
> W. Edwards Deming
> (statistician, author, and consultant, 1900–1993)

Stereotype threat is the internalization of a negative stereotype about one's group as a natural or inevitable part of one's life or character.[23] The seminal studies in the field of stereotype threat "showed in several experiments that Black college freshmen and sophomores performed more poorly on standardized tests than White students when their race was emphasized. When race was not emphasized, however, Black students performed better and equivalently with White students. The results showed that performance in academic contexts can be harmed by the awareness that one's behavior might be viewed through the lens of racial stereotypes."[24] The impact of stereotype threat on THE NEXT IQ necessitates that leaders understand that the diverse perspectives they work to bring to their teams cannot always be maximized to full potential if the organization, culturally and structurally, cannot support that talent by fully understanding and including it.

As a leader, there are a few key dynamics of stereotype threats that are critical to understand if you are going to actively identify, seek, and integrate diverse perspectives into your own intelligence as well as the overall intelligence of your team:

1.   Individuals who belong to a group that is negatively stereotyped in any environment tend to disengage from that environment and tend to not feel high levels of commitment and/or invest-

ment in these organizations leading to lower morale, lower productivity, and higher attrition for those individuals.

2. Individuals who belong to a group that is negatively stereotyped show decreased performance[25] "on any task where a stereotype is invoked suggesting that members of some groups will perform more poorly than others."[26]

3. Individuals who belong to a group that is negatively stereotyped can often self-sabotage their own chances for success because they are forecasting that they will not be as successful as members of groups that are not negatively stereotyped.

4. Members of a negatively stereotyped group can suffer the consequences of stereotype threat in regards to what they believe about themselves and the goals to which they aspire. Thus such an individual is more likely to shift his or her career aspirations away from his or her true goals to fit the underrepresentation and negative stereotypes.

5. Stereotype threat is rarely a conscious process; however, emerging research is starting to show that we can actually measure what is happening in people's brains (e.g., increase in physiological stress,[27] disruptions in memory,[28] and increased anxiety[29]) that causes decreases in performance when stereotype threats are at work.

6. Stereotype threat can be reduced through several innovative techniques if leaders recognize the loss in talent that occurs through stereotype threat and invest in creating teams and organizations where stereotype threat does not minimize the input that underrepresented and/or negatively stereotyped people contribute to the team's and organization's overall output.

In order for a leader to actively seek and engage diverse perspectives, that leader must understand how stereotype threat impacts the ability of different people to contribute their best talents. Without this understanding, leaders can often underestimate the true talent of people who are part of negatively stereotyped groups. *Moreover, the flip side of stereotype threat—stereotype lift—can lead to the overestimation of the true talent of people who are not part of negatively stereotyped groups.*

Although social scientists have studied the consequences of negative stereotypes for decades, the focus on the consequences of not being stereotyped is relatively new. We have known for years that there are two aspects to IQ tests that decrease performance for some groups—potential bias in the test instruments and potential stereotype threat for the test taker. What we have not known until recently is whether there is a "stereotype lift" for those who belong to groups that are not negatively stereotyped. Research is starting to illustrate that "[w]hen a negative stereotype impugns the ability or worth of an outgroup, people may experience stereotype lift—a performance boost that occurs when downward comparisons are made with a denigrated outgroup . . . members of nonstereotyped groups were found to perform better when a negative stereotype about an outgroup was linked to an intellectual test than when it was not."[30]

One of the more fascinating aspects of stereotype lift is that individuals can benefit from being part of a group that is not negatively stereotyped regardless of whether the negative stereotypes of the outgroup are explicitly referenced or not. As long as you know that there are stereotypes about who does or does not do well in a particular situation or on a particular task, and you know that the negative stereotype does not apply to you, you will perform better than you would if there were no stereotypes attached to the situation.

As Gregory Walton, one of the primary researchers of stereotype lift, is quoted in an interview for an internal Yale communication, "Our evidence suggests that 'stereotype lift' improves the performance of white men on the Scholastic Aptitude Test (SAT) by, on average, 50 points—a performance boost that at the most selective colleges could make the difference between rejection and acceptance," Walton says. "Stereotype-inspired social comparisons may help alleviate the self-doubt, anxiety and fear of rejection that otherwise hamper performance on important intellectual tests."[31]

Stereotype threat and stereotype lift are the twin engines keeping the mechanism of self-fulfilling prophecies in motion. Philosopher and psychologist Paul Watzlawick, a trailblazer in understanding how we communicate explicitly, subtly, and even subconsciously, defined self-fulfilling prophecy as "an assumption or prediction that, purely as a result of having been made, cause the expected or predicted event to occur and thus confirms its own 'accuracy.'"[32] Self-fulfilling prophecies keep the Retro IQ cemented as the central framework of how we understand intelligence because we need the future to make sense with the past. THE *NEXT* IQ framework, however, recognizes that only in breaking these cycles of "what is becomes what can be" can we allow different perspectives to be strong enough to elevate our collective intelligence.

When I integrate the concepts of stereotype threat and stereotype lift into my work with clients on their talent management, leadership development, or innovation strategies, I see many "aha!" moments occur as leaders grapple with the potential consequences of these principles in their organizations. I also get this one question in almost every discussion: "Doesn't this assume that we are all working off the exact same stereotypes?" I answer this question with an exercise, so go ahead and quickly do the exercise that follows.

From each pair of words below, select the word that you feel is *generally* the *more powerful* of the two roles/identities in society.		
	Rich	Poor	
	High School Graduate	College Graduate	
	Male	Female	
	Thin	Obese	
	Homeowner	Renter	
	Child	Parent	
	Doctor	Nurse	
	African American	Caucasian	
	Heterosexual	Gay/Lesbian	
	Married	Divorced	
	Small Business	Fortune 500 Company	
	Urban	Rural	
	Citizen	Immigrant	
	Paralegal	Attorney	
	Landlord	Tenant	

We have run this exercise with hundreds of individuals across various industries and levels, and over 90 percent of the time the selections are: Rich, College Graduate, Male, Thin, Homeowner, Parent, Doctor, Caucasian, Heterosexual, Married, Fortune 500 Company, Urban, Citizen, Attorney, and Landlord. Depending on the audience and their personal experiences, we may get slightly higher numbers for Female over Male or Divorced over Married, but the exercise consistently arrives at very similar results.

How do individuals who don't know each other and who reside in different cities, industries, and hierarchical levels arrive at such consensus in analyzing such broad categories? Socialization. We are social creatures (even the introverts among us) and we are constantly being socialized into the norms of the social ties we have with the world around us. We learn behavioral norms and how to see others in our families, at work, on the streets, in restaurants, on the subway, in elevators, with our children, with our friends, and so on. We learn how to quickly scan the environment for cues on how to behave and what to say. Even if many of us choose to rebel again the norms or not abide with what is expected of us, we often do so after gaining insights into what we are supposed to do, so we know we are rebelling against the norms. In many ways this is the same thing as following the norms because in both instances, you are recognizing the norm and validating it before you choose to either adhere to or challenge it. Social norms are the basis of many of our stereotypes, and as we filter our surroundings through the media, our experiences, and our perceptions to identify norms, we are also taking in information about stereotypes and cultural biases.

We all scan a little differently, but if we are scruitinizing the same cultural data points, we arrive at eerily similar conclusions like the 90 percent plus agreement rate on which of the roles/characteristics generally had more power in society. Upon closer examination, we may decide that we don't agree with our own answers, but our answers are still our answers even if we choose to act in a divergent direction. And, these answers are what make stereotype threat and stereotype lift so pernicious. Since we know the categories, and we know how the categories stack up against each other, we also gauge how we stack up based on the categories in which we belong.

A DEEPER DIVE INTO THE COMFORT OF SIMILARITIES

Our biases are not conscious choices to think a particular way, rather they are the mental shortcuts we take before making decisions. These shortcuts, sometimes called heuristics, are the "rules of thumb" we use that we think are based on experiences but are just as often based on perceptions not at all rooted in observation or objective facts. The shortcuts we use in connection with seeing what we know instead of what is in front of us can be categorized as follows:

- **Stereotyping Bias**[33]—We use assumptions (consciously or unconsciously) to evaluate or assess a person instead of facts. Why do people do it? Because it is faster and easier to stereotype than to ask . . . unless you are wrong! We need to generalize for the sake of efficiency but THE *NEXT* IQ reminds us to question our generalizations for the sake of accuracy.

- **In-group Bias**[34]—There's the in-group—people who are similar in some way—and there's the out-group—people who don't share the relevant trait in common with the in-group. Imagine a group of people standing in a circle facing each other. That's the in-group—they see each other. Now, imagine a second group of people standing in a circle around that first circle. That's the out-group—they see some of the others in their circle, and they see the backs of the in-groupers. They also realize they have to go through the in-groupers in order to get to the circle. THE *NEXT* IQ reminds us to realize that we are often out-groupers in one situation and in-groupers in another. Knowing where we stand and how we see the situation is critical to understanding the situation.

- **Status Quo Bias/System Justification**[35]—We prefer the status quo that we know even if we believe that change could benefit us. So, we will lean toward the current situation in making our decisions even if we don't like the situation we are in. (We all say that change is good, but what we really mean is that change is good as long as we don't have to change!) THE *NEXT* IQ reminds us that our ability to change is the precursor to us creating any change. (See the Change Is Also a Verb exercises in Chapter 7.)

- **Illusory Correlation**[36]—We create a relationship between two things that doesn't really exist. Think about how we correlate cars, homes, or clothes to income, intelligence, and personality traits. Or an educational pedigree with future success. Or tattoos with character traits. This is very similar to the other shortcuts, but it offers a slightly different way of looking at the assumptions we make, especially around characteristics that are not identity traits. THE *NEXT* IQ reminds us that many of our correlations are accepted but unfounded.

Think of a time in your personal or professional life when you remember clearly not being included in a particular group. The group can be an informal clique, a formal club, an athletic team, a family unit, a professional association, a professional networking group, or any other group from which you perceived yourself to have been excluded. As you complete the following table, see if you can find examples of similarity biases that you perceived, observed, and/or experienced as an out-grouper.

COMMON COGNITIVE BIASES CONNECTED TO THE COMFORT OF SIMILARITY		
Bias	**Description**	**Your Examples**
Stereotyping Bias	We use assumptions (consciously or unconsciously) to evaluate or assess a person instead of facts.	
In-group Bias	The in-group members are similar in some way; the out-group members don't share the relevant trait in common with the in-group.	
Status Quo Bias/ System Justification	Even if we believe that change could benefit us, we will lean toward the current situation in making our decisions.	
Illusory Correlation	We create a relationship between two things that doesn't really exist.	

Now, think of a time in your personal or professional life when you felt you really achieved a high level of success. Who else belongs in this group of successful people? The group can be an informal clique, a formal club, an athletic team, a family unit, a professional association, a professional networking group, or any other group that includes peers who share your success. As you complete the following table, see if you can find examples of similarity biases that exist within this group of successful people. How does this group of people see those who don't fit within the group?

COMMON COGNITIVE BIASES CONNECTED TO THE COMFORT OF SIMILARITY		
Bias	**Description**	**Examples**
Stereotyping Bias	We use assumptions (consciously or unconsciously) to evaluate or assess a person instead of facts.	
In-group Bias	The in-group members are similar in some way; the out-group members don't share the relevant trait in common with the in-group.	
Status Quo Bias/ System Justification	Even if we believe that change could benefit us, we will lean toward the current situation in making our decisions.	
Illusory Correlation	We create a relationship between two things that doesn't really exist.	

Which set of examples did you have an easier time generating? Did it feel easier or harder to generate examples of similarity biases when you were part of the out-group or when you were part of the in-group? This is a powerful exercise that can be done with children as young as five and adults in any situation. The cognitive jump of thinking like an out-grouper and then switching to being an in-grouper can enable us to see that even our own perspectives shift as our perception of our identity shifts. The majority of people of any demographic that do this exercise find it easier to generate examples when they are the out-groupers.

Imagine you are at a concert sitting behind two tall people whose height makes it impossible for you to see the stage. You can hear the music so you know that the performer is on the stage, but you cannot see the performer. This sharp focus on the two people in front of you is the focus that out-groupers generally report. It is the wanting to see what is happening on stage but feeling like you are being blocked from it and not knowing how much of a right you really have to tell the people in front of you to move or bend down or lean to the side so that your line of sight clears. It would be much harder for the two tall people to understand the perspective of the person who could not see the stage, but the person who could not see the stage spends a considerable amount of time contemplating the lack of ability to see the stage, the two people who are blocking the stage, the amount of money spent on the concert tickets, and so on. In-groupers rarely have the perspective they need to understand what it is to be an in-grouper because they most often cannot even see the out-groupers, let alone access the experiences and perspectives of the out-groupers.

THE *NEXT* IQ BIAS BREAKERS

The word *bias* comes from the Old French word *biais*, which meant against the grain, slanted, or oblique. It was primarily used in connection with the game of bowls (similar to bocce) that used bowls weighted on one side in order to make their path more oblique than straight. Breaking through biases is about recognizing that we all have biases or slants that cause us to lean in a particular

> Everyone thinks of changing the world, but no one thinks of changing himself.
>
> Leo Tolstoy (Russian author, 1828–1910)

direction when we really intend to travel straight. We need to recognize that most biases cannot be eliminated, but they can be interrupted before they influence our actions. There is no doubt that there are many people who are intelligent in spite of their biases; THE *NEXT* IQ asks how much more intelligent that intelligence can get if the biases were interrupted so new information could seep in.

The following Bias Breakers© are generally useful to raise awareness of and interrupt all the various biases discussed in this and the next two chapters, but they are especially effective for breaking biases related to similarities in identity and other visible differentiators between people.

1. *Pay Attention to Surprise.*

    Our reaction of surprise is one of the best tools that we have to recognize and interrupt bias. Surprise is our brain's way of communicating to us that the reality in front of us is different than the expectation. Even if we are not fully aware of the expectations we hold in our mind, we are aware of our surprise. The essence of bias is that it causes us to create expectations about certain realities without actually experiencing those realities. Surprise is that difference between expectations and experience.

    - For one full day (one full week if you are ambitious), keep a written list of everything that surprises you. Here are just a few examples from some of our clients' Surprise Lists: *"I was not expecting her work product to be this good." "I was expecting him to handle that feedback much better than he did." "I didn't expect her to look like that." "I didn't expect this restaurant to have anything I would like." "I didn't expect the train to be crowded today."* Once you have your list, ask yourself why each of the surprises was, in fact, a surprise. *Why was I not expecting her work product to be this good?*

    - As you become more aware of what surprises you, start assessing the strength of your surprise. Rate your surprise from 1 to 10 with 1 being a very mild surprise to 10 being an utterly unexpected shock. The stronger your surprise, the deeper the bias.

Keeping a list of your surprises and assessing the strength of each surprise will raise your awareness of how often and by what you are surprised. Use this awareness of your surprise to people, events, and things to learn about your own expectations of the world around you. This is equally applicable to individuals, teams, or organizations. Doing this exercise as a team or an organization can be especially illuminating when you are creating a strategic partnership with a new organization, selecting vendors, or deciding how you plan to identify your organization's high performers.

Once you are aware of your own expectations, you are then in control of allowing that slant to impact your actions . . . or not.

2. *Oppose Yourself.*

A great way to activate our individual or organizational critical thinking skills is to deliberately challenge our own thinking. When you make a decision about a person, an event, or a thing (especially if you are able to arrive at that decision quickly, easily, or very comfortably), ask yourself to list all the reasons why you should decide to the contrary. Try this exercise in the reverse as well by actively listing all the reasons why you should choose an option that you easily or quickly rejected.

Sample decisions from our organizational clients where oppositional thinking actually led them to different decisions include hiring decisions, promotion decisions, vendor selections, technology selections, selections for event venues, and so on. Samples from our individual clients include selections of employers, decisions regarding resignation, choices on whether to/how to receive constructive feedback, and so on. With both organizations and individuals, we have seen the many "aha!" moments that occur when oppositional thinking is actively engaged.

Deliberately opposing your own decisions forces you to see beyond the "reasons for" something to actively consider the "reasons against" that same thing, or vice versa. This exercise interrupts our leaning to see only the positive in some things and only the negative in other things. Since our brains are weighted to see what we expect to see instead of what is actually in front of us, this exercise adds weight to the other side so our brain can actually evaluate all options equally critically.

3. *Ask One Question.*

For one day (or, again, for one week if you are ambitious), ask at least one question in each substantive conversation about something you already think you know. If you are in a meeting, challenge yourself to ask a question instead of offering your perspective. If you are mentoring someone, ask a question to get to know your mentee deeper instead of offering up advice. If there is someone in the workplace that you don't know especially well, ask a question to get a dialog started.

This can be especially illustrative in dealing with colleagues with whom you work frequently. Ask one question per conversation and see if the answers surprise you. If they do, then reread the section on using surprises as awareness tools!

One of our clients implemented the One-Question model in its senior leadership meetings by beginning each meeting with a round of each leader asking one question about the topic(s) in the agenda. Only when all the questions were asked did the meeting proceed with the actual agenda, and if the round of questions did not feel substantial enough, the group often agreed to do a second round of questions before they continued. The One-Question model is not powerful because of the answers that the questions can solicit, but because the questions themselves prime people for solving the problems by thinking about the issues from the angles of all the different questions asked.

4. *Focus on Behaviors.*

When you are in a situation (as an individual or an organization) to evaluate someone's potential, accomplishments, and/ or abilities, challenge yourself to focus only on evaluating his or her behaviors, not your impressions. This is equally important in both formal and informal evaluative situations since formal evaluations are usually the cumulative result of informal evaluations.

For every evaluative statement regarding someone's potential, think of least one behavior (ideally two or three behaviors) that supports your evaluation. If you cannot identify behaviors, the evaluation is more of an opinion than an assessment. Opinions are fraught with potential biases where evaluations of specific behaviors focus more on what you actually see instead of your expectations of what you think you should see.

One caveat to keep in mind about evaluating behaviors is that we don't perceive the same behaviors expressed by different people in the same way. So, an additional exercise in bias breaking can be to take the identified behaviors and ask yourself if you would evaluate the same behaviors if they were expressed by someone else who was very different.

THE *NEXT* IQ INSIGHTS: CHAPTER 9

- We default to what is comfortable, and one of our comfort zones is similarity in what we see. We default to similarity over difference, especially when the similarities or differences are visible.
- Biases, stereotypes, prejudices, and discrimination are often used interchangeably, but they mean very different things. Bias is leaning toward something, a stereotype is applying that leaning to a group of people, a prejudice is prejudging a person or a group based on a bias or a stereotype, and discrimination is the action an individual takes because of a bias, stereotype, or prejudice.
- The Implicit Association Test (projectimplicit.org) is a great way to test your own leanings in a private and reliable way.
- From height to names to accents to weight, studies have demonstrated that we all take mental shortcuts (mostly unconsciously) that prevent us from seeking and including different perspectives in the way we think.
- Bias is intrinsically connected to privilege, and together, they result in both stereotype threat and stereotype lift.
- The four primary mental shortcuts connected with our comfort with similarity are stereotyping bias, in-group bias, status quo/system justification bias, and illusory correlation bias.

THE *NEXT* IQ ACTIONS: CHAPTER 9

- Interrupt your biases! Although most biases are unconscious, they can be consciously and deliberately interrupted. They need to be interrupted in order for THE *NEXT* level of intelligence to enter and thrive. The four best Bias Breakers for visible similarities are (1) pay attention to surprise, (2) oppose yourself, (3) ask one question, and (4) focus on behaviors.
- Keep interrupting your biases! Biases don't disappear upon interruption. They need to be continuously interrupted in order to think, learn, and lead in new ways.

CHAPTER 10

THE COMFORT OF EASE: WE THINK WHAT WE KNOW, NOT WHAT WE THINK

Here's to the crazy ones. The misfits. The rebels. The troublemakers. The round pegs in the square holes. The ones who see things differently. They're not fond of rules.
And they have no respect for the status quo.

You can quote them, disagree with them, glorify or vilify them.

About the only thing you can't do is ignore them. Because they change things. They invent. They imagine. They heal. They explore. They create. They inspire. They push the human race forward.

Maybe they have to be crazy. How else can you stare at an empty canvas and see a work of art? Or sit in silence and hear a song that's never been written? Or gaze at a red planet and see a laboratory on wheels? We make tools for these kinds of people.

While some see them as the crazy ones, we see genius. Because the people who are crazy enough to think they can change the world, are the ones who do.

"Think Different" (Advertisement by Apple Inc., 1997)

Apple's "Think Different" ad won many awards including the 1998 Emmy Award for Best Commercial and the 2000 Grand Effie Award for the most effective campaign in America. The ad turned heads and inspired people globally, but the ad also clarified the subconscious understanding shared in our society that cognitive creativity—thinking—is difficult. If those who think differently are misfits, rebels, troublemakers, and crazy, thinking differently sounds great only if you strive to be labeled in this way. The underlying message in this ad is that most people don't think differently, thus those who do are likely to be seen as deviants from the norm, albeit deviants who will change the world.

This ad helps us understand that we want to think differently, but at the end of the day, we tend to prefer the ease of thinking in line with others because thinking differently is difficult, and it requires the courage to withstand being labeled a crazy misfit, rebel, or troublemaker.

The previous chapter dealt with biases, stereotypes (including stereotype threat and stereotype lift), prejudices, and discriminations based on our identities, especially visible social identities. We've explored how these social categories keep the RETRO IQ sticking to how we understand the world around us. We must remember, however, that diversity is a relative concept, not an absolute one. Nothing or no one is diverse by identity. We become (or don't become) diverse in relation to the people and things in a particular context.

From an identity or experience perspective, a woman adds gender diversity only if men are in the majority. There is no inherent diversity in being a woman. Thus, when we talk about differences, we can only talk about "different than" someone or something else. This "relativeness" attribute of diversity allows us to differentiate between people using visible identifiers such as gender, race, ethnicity, generation, ability, and so on, but the differences in how we think and how we prefer to solve problems can be as impactful in creating in-groups and out-groups as visible differences. More importantly, leaders who want to actively include and engage different perspectives in order to increase their own *NEXT* IQ as well as the overall *NEXT* IQ of their teams need to ensure that identity differences alone don't account for the contextual diversity. The ability to recognize, encourage, and value the expression of cognitive differences—differences in the way people think, analyze, and solve problems—is an essential component of increasing your *NEXT* IQ.

In 2009, the National Defense Authorization Act for Fiscal Year 2009, Section 596, Public Law 110-417, established the Department of Defense Military Leadership Diversity Commission (MLDC).[1] Although MLDC was specifically tasked by legislation to "conduct a comprehensive evaluation and assessment of policies that provide opportunities for the promotion and advancement of minority members of the Armed Forces, including minority members who are senior officers,"[2] one of the very first Issue Papers that the MLDC released was on the importance of cognitive diversity and the relationship between cognitive diversity and identity diversity.[3] Two of the primary conclusions from this Issue Paper were:

- "Diversity is often defined demographically, but it is also possible to define it more broadly in terms of cognitive traits . . . [and] Achieving diversity in this broader sense may improve the ability of the military to perform its wide variety of functions."
- "We conclude that efforts by the military to increase demographic diversity may also have the secondary effect of somewhat increasing cognitive diversity. However, given the modest sizes of many of these relationships and the importance of other factors involved in increasing cognitive diversity, we expect this secondary effect to be small."

Cognitive diversity describes the differences in how we think, and how we think is informed by (1) our perspectives (our points of view, the lessons we've extracted from our experiences, our values, our beliefs, our definition of truth, etc.), (2) our interpretations (how we take in the world around us, how we understand what we see, etc.), and (3) our heuristics (how we break down complex situations, how we solve problems, etc.). Our *perspectives* are the lens through which we see the world; our *interpretations* are the lens through which we take in information; and our *heuristics* are the ways in which we manage our perspectives and interpretations to make sense of the world around us.

As we mentioned in the previous chapter, heuristics are basically mental shortcuts or rules of thumb that we've adopted to solve problems quickly; heuristics allow us to bypass the analytical thought process and arrive at a conclusion as soon as we receive input. For example, if people see two similar products with one product priced considerably higher than the other, most of us conclude that the higher priced product is better in quality than the lower priced product. That assumption turns out to be true just enough in our experience that we will default to that conclusion without analyzing the situation. Another common heuristic is that the more effort something takes, the more we value it. Since we often have to work for things that we value, we have created a mental rule of thumb that if we have to work for something, it must be valuable. For example, if we earn $1,000, we value that money more than if $1,000 was gifted to us. We are more likely to spend the gifted money on luxuries and the earned money on necessities or put it into savings. Most of the time, heuristics help and they do save us time, but heuristics can also become cognitive liabilities as we will cover later in this chapter.

Since identity diversity is often visible, it quickly allows a group to predict that differences may be present even if the differences don't impact cognitive or behavioral diversity. Cognitive diversity, on the other hand, is invisible and is not triggered until differences are expressed. When these differences unexpectedly surface, cognitive diversity can create just as much tension as it does creativity and innovation. In order to capture the opportunity created by cognitive diversity, leaders have to better understand how to recognize and lead the impact of these differences.

OUR PERSPECTIVES

The IBM Jams and wisdom of crowds models discussed in earlier chapters reflect the growing body of research and business intelligence that demonstrates that multiple cognitive perspectives generate better ideas, insights, and solutions. IBM brings together diverse perspectives through its Jams to generate new ideas and even select new investments that the company will make. In the *Wisdom of Crowds*, James Surowiecki demonstrates through various examples how diversity of perspectives leads to collective intelligence, and he illustrates that the collective intelligence of a group of diverse perspectives is more intelligent than the highest intelligence level of any of the individuals in the group. Surowiecki advocates for aggregated intelligence over individual expertise and comments about the expertise hierarchies in many organizations: "Hierarchies have certain virtues—efficiency and speed—as a way of executing decisions. But they're outmoded as a way of making decisions, and they're ill-suited to the complex strategic landscapes that most companies now inhabit. Firms need to aggregate the collective wisdom instead."[4]

Michael Maubossin, in *Think Twice: Harnessing the Power of Counter-intuition*, reports on how James Surowiecki asserted in a presentation at Best Buy that "a relatively uninformed crowd could predict better than the firm's best seers"[5] and inspired Jeff Severts, the head of Best Buy's gift-card business, to experiment with collective wisdom in his business unit. When Severts asked about two hundred employees to predict gift-card sales for February 2005, the collective wisdom of the crowd was 99.5 percent accurate compared with Severts's team of experts who came in at about 95 percent accuracy.[6] Severts ran another experiment later that year and asked people in the organization to predict sales from Thanksgiving to end of the year. The three hundred random volunteers in the crowd came in at over 99 percent accuracy while the Best Buy internal experts came in at around 93 percent accuracy. Best Buy was convinced, and it created TagTrade, an internal prediction market that collects collective wisdom and has had a greater track record of forecasting sales and solving problems than the internal experts.

It seems like a no-brainer that individual leaders would create ample opportunity to gather and learn from diverse perspectives, but in reality many leaders feel more comfortable leading through easy consensus instead of productive conflict. "While many leaders pride themselves on their independence, research has consistently demonstrated that most people, including leaders, prefer conformity to controversy."[7]

Four primary stickers keep us spinning our wheels in the Retro IQ instead of thriving in the innovative possibilities of The Next IQ:

- *We value consensus over conflict*, especially when the leadership style guiding the discussion does not actively encourage productive disagreement and creative conflict. Even leaders who are open to this sort of conflict can sometimes be dissuaded by the overall culture of an organization or a team.
- *We value being an in-grouper and don't want to risk becoming an out-grouper.* We may see ourselves as having too much in common with the in-groupers to go against the grain of the majority opinion or we may not see ourselves as a true in-grouper, but we don't want to risk the in-groupers seeing us as out-groupers. As

the Apple advertisement at the beginning of the chapter reflects, being an out-grouper is difficult, and the ease of being an in-grouper can sometimes outweigh the value in opposing the majority opinion.

■ *We value established cognitive patterns over cognitive start-ups.* Most of us are all for innovation, but we value the ability to rely on ingrained thought patterns instead of thinking freshly about each new thing with which we are confronted. We even highly prize experience because we can rely on an experienced person's ability to provide the cognitive shortcuts needed to bypass having to think through everything.

■ *We value one right answer over multiple right answers.* Most of us are taught to identify something as "right" when it is opposed to a "wrong." This binary construction makes it uncomfortable for us to negotiate a situation where there are multiple right answers and no wrong answers. In these situations, leaders often tend to veer back toward finding the one "right" answer because it makes decision making easier when there is simply one right course of action.

What IBM Jams and Best Buy's TagTrade do is create organizational mechanisms that bypass individual leaders' tendencies toward consensus, in-groupness, and cognitive ease. These programs offer organized channels through which diverse perspectives are brought to bear on decisions without perceived conflict, loss of identity, or individual discomfort over cognitive complexity. Sharing a contrary opinion as part of a large crowd of opinions is easier than making a case for your perspective in the intimacy of a team meeting. That said, if leaders can recreate the wisdom of crowds in their teams by creating mini-jams and micro-trades, they can raise the overall intelligence of their teams.

OUR INTERPRETATIONS

Although facts are defined as objective pieces of information, the second we "understand" a fact, that fact becomes an interpretation. When we take in a fact through any one of our five senses, that fact travels through the filter of our own experiences, expectations, and beliefs before we "understand" it. These cultural and personal filters are presuppositions and presumptions that we "know to be true" in our minds.

Objective pieces of information that we perceive with our senses get filtered and interpreted in our minds and become "our facts." For example, words like *warm, cold, tall, short, funny,* and *boring* are relatively simple to classify as interpretive words because they derive their definitions through comparison to something else. Words such as *paper, computer, pen, table,* and *chair,* on the other hand, are assumed to be free of subjectivity because they do not derive their definitions through comparison to anything else; however, they have been filtered through our cultural and personal filters even though we may not realize it.

When my team does workshops on cognitive differences, we ask the group of individuals to identify five things in the room that can be objectively understood by everyone there. We usually end up with a list of things like paper, computer, pen, table, and chair. We then ask each participant to describe in detail what he or she meant by each word. When the participants are asked to read their descriptions of the items to the group, you can see surprise spread across the room as they realize that *paper* meant notepad, handouts, sticky notes, newspaper, and so on, and that *chair* was understood through filters of softness, height, seat material, and comfort. By the time we go through the descriptions of all five words, a quiet understanding has settled in the room that none of us can ever possibly be thinking the same thing no matter how clearcut we believe the object of our thoughts to be.

For example, think of the difficulty in explaining the color yellow to someone who cannot tell the difference between yellow and green. How would you explain which bananas are ripe and which are not? How would you describe tropical heat to someone who has always lived in perpetually cold climates like Alaska? Interpretation occurs both in terms of the sender who codes the message and the recipient who decodes the sent message. Therefore, by the time an objective piece of information has been interpreted, coded, sent, decoded, and reinterpreted, it is difficult to discern what is purely objective.

THE TRUTH, THE INTERPRETED TRUTH, AND NOTHING BUT WHAT YOU THINK IS THE TRUTH

Three youth are driving in a car. When they reach the intersection and see the stop sign, they come to a rolling stop and keep going instead of stopping fully. Two police officers see this rolling stop and pursue the car with their lights and siren on. The music in the car with the youth is so loud that they do not hear the police sirens. After a few blocks of pursuing the youth, the police officers pull up next to the car and signal that the car should pull over. The car does pull over. The police get out of their squad car and ask all the youth to get out of the car. The police officers search the car and find some drugs in the trunk.

- What time of day does this story take place?
- Does this story take place in an urban or rural setting?
- What race were the youth?
- What gender were the youth?
- What race were the police officers?
- What gender were the police officers?
- What kind of car were the youth driving?
- What kind of music was playing on the radio?
- What kind of drugs were found in the car?

I use this narrative and its related questions to illustrate how, as cultural beings, we are incapable of not seeing context, identity, and detail. When we are not provided the details needed in order to know how to interpret the information we are being given, we fill in the gaps with details from our own mind.

In this particular narrative, the majority of people see this scenario occurring in the evening in an urban setting with young African American or Hispanic men playing rap or hip-hop in a SUV or old car. The police offers are overwhelmingly male, but their races have been varied without any clear majority seeing any particular race. The drug was perceived by most to be either marijuana (loose in a baggie), marijuana (a joint), or methamphetamines (powder in a baggie).

Even people who profess to be colorblind admit that as they read the narrative, they have to picture the people as having some identity. It is impossible to see the word *youth* driving in a car or see the words *police officers* chasing them in a squad car. It is hard to hear the word *music*, and it hard to see the word *drugs*. We interpret these words, and we inject images that seem to make the most sense with what we know to be true based on our cultural and personal filters.

We have run this exercise with law enforcement officers, judges, prosecutors, defense attorneys, law students, and law professors with the same results. We see what we think should be, not always what is said.

Interestingly, when we have asked people in other countries to take this exercise, the answers vary greatly from the U.S. responses, but they fall in line with responses from other people in their own country. For example, race is interpreted differently in other countries as race/religion, race/nationality, race/tribe, and so on, but most people from France interpret race in the same way as other people from France, and so on.

What can this narrative teach us about our own interpretations? For each of the professional categories listed below, quickly identify the race/ethnicity/culture, gender, and socioeconomic status of the type of person who would most likely occupy that role.

	Race/ Ethnicity/ Culture	Gender	Socio- economic Status
1. Law Firm Lawyer			
2. Professional Athlete			
3. Teacher			
4. Nurse			
5. Cardiologist			
6. Babysitter			
7. Pilot			
8. United States Senator			
9. Astronaut			
10. Forest Ranger			

The ability to do this exercise is, in and of itself, an exercise in interpretation. Without our ability to filter and categorize, we would not be able to complete the exercise. The word *cardiologist*, for example, is a word that does not have identity characteristics attached to it. Yet, we cannot "see" that word without personifying it, and in order to personify the word, we have to socially categorize it because we don't "see" neutral human beings.

In this exercise, the visual representation of the presuppositions in our head—regardless of what the presuppositions are—allows us to be more aware that as soon as we "understand" something, it stops becoming purely objective.

Getting around our own presuppositions is a tall order, but it can be done, and when it is done correctly, our presuppositions are reflected back to us in glaring candor. Prior to the 1980s, major symphony orchestras were not only overwhelmingly male, but women were rarely even given the opportunity to compete because musical directors carefully selected who could audition and who would eventually win a seat in the orchestra. In the 1980s, orchestras realized how lopsided their gender representation was, and they opened up their auditions to include more women. Many more women applied and auditioned; however, female musicians were presumed to have "smaller techniques" and "poorer sound."[8] When symphony orchestras went one step further and adopted "blind screens" to hide a candidate's identity in a way where the candidate's music could be heard while his or her identity was concealed, the number of female musicians who were hired increased significantly. Research by Cecilia Rouse and Claudia Golden found that "[a]mong musicians who auditioned in both blind and non-blind auditions, about 28.6 percent of female musicians and 20.2 percent of male musicians advanced from the preliminary to the final round in blind auditions. When preliminary auditions were not blind, only 19.3 percent of the women advanced, along with 22.5 percent of the men."[9]

Similarly, when more than a hundred psychologists were asked to evaluate the same curriculum vitae with a male name versus a female name, the psychologists rated the male curriculum vitae as better for teaching, research, and service experience; further, the psychologists were more likely to hire the male applicant.[10] Keep in mind that the curriculum vitae was the exact same except for the change in the name! As the researchers discovered, "participants were four times as likely to write cautionary comments in the margins of the questionnaire if they had reviewed a female tenure candidate than if they had reviewed the male tenure candidate. The cautionary comments include[d] such comments as, 'We would have to see her job talk,' 'It is impossible to make such a judgment without teaching evaluations,' 'I would need to see evidence that she had gotten these grants and publications on her own.' Such cautionary comments on the male tenure candidate's vitae were quite rare."[11]

These are but a few of the examples that research has unearthed in showing us that our brains interpret facts based on context, and often, these interpretations are based on social biases that are not in our own or our organizations' best interests. If we know that we can't really hear music in the same way if we see a woman playing an instrument instead of a man, we need that screen in order to pick the best musician. If we know that we see qualifications differently when they come attached to a female name instead of a male name, we need to not see the name in order to evaluate the qualifications effectively.

We create cognitive shortcuts in our mind in order to make life easier for ourselves, and many of them are quite effective in saving us time and energy; however, the key to excelling as a leader or creating teams and organizations that are competitive in the 21st century is recognizing how to stop taking cognitive shortcuts and actually think more than we have become accustomed to thinking. Once we start thinking more, we realize that in order to think effectively, we have to have the input of diverse perspectives. When we stay in the comfort zone of cognitive ease based on our unchallenged interpretations, we don't see the need for diverse perspectives because we are barely using our own perspective.

As Alfred Korzybski—philosopher, scientist, and founder of the field of general semantics—once said, "the map is not the territory." In other words, no matter how exacting we think we are being in our details and descriptions, the map becomes our interpretation of the territory, and someone else viewing the territory from the exact same vantage point would still draw a different map.

OUR HEURISTICS

In our search for cognitive ease, we rely on the biases triggered by what our senses take in and the interpretations that our minds create with the input. When we put these perspectives and interpretations together and add some memories and past experiences, we arrive at heuristics—the rules of thumb or common sense we turn to when we don't care to reach a fully informed decision by analyzing a lot of data. Heuristics are the readily available, quickly employed techniques that we use to solve problems, and heuristics vary based on our perspective, interpretations, and experiences.

We use many heuristics every day that serve us quite well, but there are also heuristics that lead us astray and fool us into thinking we have solved problems when we have done no good and maybe have even done harm. My research and experiences have found the following heuristics to be the worst offenders in preventing leaders from actively seeking, engaging, and integrating the diverse perspectives they need in order to lead for maximum impact.

The Anchoring and Adjustment Heuristic

Without realizing it, human beings can often fixate on a particular anchor in the decision-making process and then make decisions adjusting for that anchor instead of solving problems or advancing toward a goal. Amos Tversky and Daniel Kahneman, pioneers in identifying and researching the anchoring heuristic, conducted a study where they asked individuals to guess the percentage of African nations that were members of the United Nations. They started one group off at 10 percent and asked them to adjust up or down to what they thought was the right answer. They started another group at 65 percent and asked them to adjust up or down to the right answer. The group with the 10 percent anchor, on average, guessed that 25 percent of African nations were members of the UN, and the group with the 65 percent anchor, on average, guessed that 45 percent of African nations were members of the UN.[12] Did the anchoring mechanism only work in this situation because people really did not know the right answer?

Let's take an experiment that Professor Dan Ariely conducted with postgraduate students at MIT. He auctioned off common items that the students would normally purchase such as computer equipment, bottles of wine, boxes of chocolates, and books. First, each of the students was asked to convert the last two digits of their Social Security number (SSN) into a dollar amount (for example 123-45-6789 would convert to $89), and each student was presented each item and asked if he or she would purchase that item for the SSN-derived dollar amount. After Ariely went through all the items with the SSN-derived dollar amount as an anchor, he told the students that the SSN-derived dollar amount was purely arbitrary and had no relevance. The students were then asked to bid on the items purely based on what they thought the items were worth and what they would want to pay for each item. The students who had the higher digits in their SSNs entered bids that were 60–120 percent higher than the bids submitted by students who had lower digits in their SSNs.[13]

THE ANCHORING AND ADJUSTING
HEURISTIC IN LEADERSHIP

The Compensation Conundrum

According to the National Association of Women Lawyers' 2010 National Survey on Retention and Promotion of Women in Law

Firms, female equity partners on average only get paid about 85 percent of what their male peers get paid.[14] That's definitely not a good statistic for law firms, at least not for the ones interested in increasing the percentage of women in their partnerships past the dismal current norm of 18–19 percent.

As with most partnership structures, law firms generally tend to determine compensation by committee. Many women's organizations and advocates have argued that the lack of female partners in general and the lack of female partners on compensation committees specifically is the culprit for the compensation differentials. Plenty of evidence suggests that this may, indeed, be true. There may also be an anchoring and adjusting heuristic at work that could be dragging down women's compensation.

I was brought into a large law firm a couple of years ago to analyze the gender differentials in its compensation distribution. After studying the numbers and interviewing all the members of the compensation committee, I found this firm's compensation process relatively objective and deliberate. I could not find any overt mechanisms of gender bias even though the committee was overwhelmingly male. In order to identify possible implicit biases in the compensation process, I observed several of the compensation committee's meetings.

The committee followed a very methodical protocol with each partner's portfolio. First, it looked at a partner's total compensation from the previous year. Then it reviewed the productivity reports from the current year. Then it discussed the partner's narrative about efforts expended and contributions made for that current year as well as the peer narratives and evaluations for that partner. Finally, the committee discussed the overall financial performance of the partner's practice group in relation to the partner's individual performance. After this full protocol was executed, it would give the partner an overall rating for that year, which, combined with a complex formula involving all the productivity numbers, would result in that partner's compensation amount for that year.

Once we had gone through about half of the partner portfolios, I asked if we could stop and see which of the factors correlated the strongest with a partner's rating. Interestingly, the strongest correlation was between a partner's previous compensation and his or her current year's rating. Partners who were similarly situated in regards to productivity for the current year would still be more likely to be ranked in accordance with the previous year's salary instead of this year's productivity. There were a few exceptions where extremely high or extremely low productivity stood out on their own merit, but the majority of ratings were being anchored by the initial discussion of how much the partner made the previous year.

When I pointed this out to the committee, it tried an experiment and analyzed the next 20 partners by putting the overall average partner compensation from the previous year on a flip chart and jumping into the evaluation of each partner without consideration of how much that partner was compensated the previous year. After the committee rated these 20 partners, we went back and tried to correlate the inputs with the rating and found that these ratings correlated more closely with the current year's productivity than they did with last year's compensation.

After this exercise, this law firm explored other arenas such as associate evaluations, associate compensation, and recruiting/hiring to see how anchors were playing a role in preventing fresh starts. The firm discovered what the Roman philosopher Seneca opined centuries ago: "Every new beginning comes from some other beginning's end." The anchoring and adjusting heuristic can feel like it's saving time, but if leaders want to create change, they do have to pull up those anchors that are keeping them moored to the past.

A recent research study found that when job candidates who were interviewing for positions joked around about extremely high salaries, they were offered higher salaries than those who threw out reasonable salary numbers.[15] The initial number, even in the context of a joke, anchored the potential future employers to think bigger in regards to initial salary offerings. Another study found that first offers in real estate transactions made by sellers resulted in higher sale prices than first offers made by buyers; the initial higher price in the negotiation anchors the price at a higher point.[16]

Anchors make a difference, but the differences are masked in the shortcuts that our brain is taking. Asking ourselves if numbers in our mind are anchored to numbers that we did not intentionally hitch them to frees us up to think analytically instead of assuming we are thinking when we are just anchoring.

The Availability Heuristic

The availability heuristic is a bit like the anchor heuristic in that the ways in which we learn and make decisions are more bound by what we know than we realize. As we become more aware that what we already know plays a role in what we will get to know, we become better at making heuristics work for us instead of against us.

The more that people can quickly, easily, and vividly recall something, the more likely they are to assume that the "something" will occur again with frequency regardless of the actual probability of its occurrence.[17] Particularly unusual, emotional, or graphic memories tend to be recalled easier than more mundane memories. This fact makes the unusual memories more "available" to people thereby causing people to think these unusual things are more likely to happen than their actual probability.

For example, when asked to name the cancer that they feel causes the greatest number of deaths for women, the majority of women's response is breast cancer. Yet, lung cancer kills almost twice as many women as breast cancer does every year. The media coverage of cancer in women, however, consists overwhelmingly of breast cancer coverage including individual stories, fund-raisers, and mortality statistics. For women, information on breast cancer is more readily available in their minds (think pink ribbon, and when was the last time you saw a ribbon of any kind for lung cancer?), so they overestimate the likelihood of deaths caused by breast cancer.[18]

Another similar example is the discrepancy between what parents worry will harm their children versus what actually is most likely to harm their children.[19] The top five worries that plague parents in this regard are:

1. kidnapping,
2. school sniper,
3. terrorists,
4. dangerous strangers, and
5. drugs.

Compare that with the top five things that actually cause harm and/or kill children:

1. car accidents,
2. homicide (usually committed by someone known to the child),
3. abuse,

4. suicide, and

5. drowning.

So, why do most parents fret more about stranger danger than buckling up in the car? The information about kidnappings is more available in parents' minds than fatalities of unrestrained children in automobile accidents. Information about what strangers do to harm children is more available than what friends and family do to children even though the chances of a stranger harming a child is far less likely. The availability heuristic allows us to think we are making smart decisions based on our perception of the probabilities of various events, but those probabilities are tainted by the immediate availability of particular memories and the usualness of other memories.

THE AVAILABILITY HEURISTIC IN LEADERSHIP

Once Seen, Twice Remembered: The Overvisibility of Underrepresented Groups

In the late 1970s Rosabeth Moss Kanter studied how tokens—members of underrepresented groups—in the workplace were perceived and treated. She concluded that "[T]okens are, ironically, both highly visible as people who are different and yet not permitted the individuality of their own unique, non-stereotypical characteristics."[20] Since then, multiple studies have reified and reinforced Kanter's findings that the visibility of individuals from underrepresented groups makes them and their actions unnaturally visible.[21]

So, how does the hypervisibility of being a "token" translate into the underside of the availability heuristic? When someone is underrepresented in the workplace to the point of being hypervisible (the one Asian woman, the only African American man, the only Arab, etc.), everything that he or she does is noted. And the memories of his or her mistakes are readily available for leaders to draw upon quickly when the person is being evaluated, being considered for advancement, or generally being discussed in a conversation.

Whereas a mistake made by someone who is adequately represented feels usual, a mistake made by an individual from an underrepresented group feels memorable and important because that mistake becomes a data point by which you view the whole group.

When we recently executed an attrition analysis for a Fortune 500 company's senior leadership ranks, almost everyone we interviewed could tell us every African American and Hispanic person who had been there in the last 10 to 15 years. The leaders could also tell us why they left and where they went. When I asked them to give me the same level of detail on white men who had left, they recalled a few, but not all, and the details were not as readily available to them for recall at a moment's notice.

If individuals from underrepresented groups are hypervisible in organizations, doesn't that work in their favor if they excel? Don't people notice their successes as pointedly as they remember their errors? They do, but an interesting phenomenon called the "ultimate attribution error"[22] takes place through which people attribute negative behaviors by people in an out-group to natural characteristics for people in that out-group and positive behaviors by people in an out-group to luck or as exceptions to the rule. In other words, out-groupers' failures are the rule, and their successes are the exception.

The availability heuristic explains why individuals who are underrepresented are more visible since they are deviants to the norm and unusual in the landscape, and when the availability heuristic is blended with the ultimate attribution error, we have highly visible failures that are attributed to the individual and highly visible successes that are attributed to serendipity. Without understanding and short-circuiting this heuristic, decisions that seem intuitively right become inherently wrong.

The Recognition Heuristic

Daniel Goldstein and Gerd Gigerenzer, psychologists who believe that the recognition heuristic is a critical tool for human beings, discuss this heuristic in the following way: "Consider the task of inferring which of two objects has a higher value on some criterion (e.g., which is faster, higher, stronger). The recognition heuristic for such tasks is simply stated: *If one of two objects is recognized and the other is not, then infer that the recognized object has the higher value.*"[23] Daniel Oppenheimer, another psychologist who perceives this heuristic as having the capacity to do both harm and good in decision making, defines it this way: "According to the recognition heuristic, when an individual only recognizes one of two items, the individual will judge the recognized item to be greater in whatever dimensions are positively correlated with recognition."[24] The difference between the two definitions is subtle yet significant.

Goldstein and Gigerenzer's take on the recognition heuristic is that your mind will automatically recognize the item that is of higher value, and you should trust your brain's ability to do that. Oppenheimer's take suggests that your brain will automatically give higher value to the item it recognizes, and you shouldn't always trust your brain's ability to value two items because it will value them based on what it recognizes, not on a full evaluation of both items. The differences seem semantic until you contextualize them concretely.

In 1995, Gigerenzer did a study where he asked Germans to identify whether San Antonio or San Diego was the larger city by population. The Germans were quite accurate in guessing that San Diego was the larger city, and Gigerenzer argued that this was the recognition heuristic working well because San Diego was more recognizable precisely because it was the larger city (e.g., it was covered more by the media and was discussed more generally because it was the larger city). Gigerenzer qualified the findings by stressing that the recognition heuristic only works well when you connect things that can be correlated with recognition such as size, popularity, and so on.

Oppenheimer's perspective, on the other hand, is that when there is a change in the facts, the recognition heuristic doesn't always catch up. In the case of San Antonio and San Diego, although the Germans guessed the larger city correctly, San Diego's population growth was not accelerating as quickly as San Antonio's, so 10 years after the study, San Antonio was actually larger than San Diego even though San Diego continues to get about 33 percent more coverage in the media nationally and internationally.[25] The recognition heuristic may work from time to time, but it is neither reliable nor consistent in its ability to act as an accurate surrogate for full information.

The recognition heuristic works if, of the available options, you recognize one option over the other(s) in a context where the recognition is connected to the shortcut you are creating (e.g., larger cities get more attention, which means that you are more likely to recognize the larger city intuitively). Most importantly, the purpose that the recognition heuristic serves is to bypass the active thinking process and use a cognitive shortcut. Recognition (shortcut) is different than recollection (thinking) in the same way that selecting an answer on a multiple-choice question is different than responding in detail to an essay question. Recognition is triggered by your options, and recollection is the active search and seizure of memories you have created.

WHAT'S IN A NAME?

The recognition heuristic is often as simple as actually recognizing someone by face and name. This is easier said than done in large organizations where people are spread out over several floors or across several buildings in a campus or even scattered across different cities and countries.

Sam Walton expressed his understanding of the power of recognition when he required all Wal-Mart employees to wear name tags with their first names so that customers had an instant connection with them. In 2008, the Wal-Mart in Dearborn, Michigan, took Sam Walton's "instant recognition" idea one step further by including the languages spoken by multilingual associates on their name tags. Customers now had more than one point of recognition with the associates, and the greater the recognition, the higher the trust. The higher the trust, the more loyal the customer.

Many retail organizations quickly followed Wal-Mart's lead by requiring customer-facing employees to wear name tags; however, the benefits of name and face recognition within organizations where customer/client contact was infrequent or nonexistent have not been fully expressed or realized.

Stuart A. Miller, CEO of Lennar Corporation (a Fortune 500 company recognized by *Forbes* as one of "America's Best Managed Companies"), has embraced the benefits of name recognition to the point of integrating name badges as part of the Lennar culture:

> A very special part of the Lennar Culture is our Name Badge. Our Name Badge is an outward sign of an inner accomplishment, a powerful statement, announcing to everyone that we work for one of America's top homebuilders. Our Name Badge is a badge of honor. It displays pride in ourselves and pride in our Company . . . The prominence of our Name Badges invites our Customers, our Business Partners, our personal acquaintances and friends, and even our own Associates to ask about it. What a great opportunity! Once someone asks about our Name Badge, we have a chance to tell the Lennar story. Our Name Badge is our Family Crest and represents our pride in our Company and

its successful five-decade history . . . Our Name Badge helps our Customers feel at ease. Introductions are often a stressful event for people. Our Name Badge provides our customers with an easy reminder of our names. They will not have to feel awkward about asking our name after they have toured our models. Instead they can feel comfortable about asking questions about our homes.[26]

We have recommended and implemented "name badge" strategies in organizations where our assessments have found noninclusive behaviors by leaders that reduce the willingness of personnel to fully bring forth their perspectives, interpretations, and ideas into the workplace. The name badges often act like vision correctors for leaders who have developed organizational myopia where they only consistently see the people in their inner circle, and the people are in their inner circle because the leaders was more likely to see them initially.

In many organizational cultures, the initial reaction to the idea of name badges is skeptical at best if not wholly negative. In one law firm (where the partners were adamantly opposed to the idea), we convinced them to implement one week per quarter where everyone wore name badges. The recognition levels increased exponentially during those weeks as people connected names and faces in the elevators, the hallways, and even in the parking garage.

In a large corporation with offices in multiple countries, we recommended that they tweak their internal email systems to show the sender's picture as well as the current time and weather where he or she was located. Just those details alone created deeper connections immediately even over email as people responded to the senders with comments about how late/early it was for them or remarks about the weather. As recognition levels increased, people commented that they felt they were emailing "to people" instead of "about things."

The recognition heuristic creates cognitive ease for us because it allows us to bypass thinking about things by simply attaching greater value to the things we recognize over the things we don't. In isolated situations where there is a clear relationship between what we are trying to analyze and why we may recognize one thing over another, this heuristic is indeed a good shortcut. However, in most situations—especially those involving leaders who are responsible for teams of people—the recognition heuristic eases the way by limiting our vision thereby also limiting the ability of our *NEXT* IQ to grow and thrive.

The Fluency Heuristic

Whereas the recognition heuristic is the preference for the option that you recognize over the option that you don't recognize, the fluency heuristic is the preference for the option that you recognize more fluently when you recognize both available options. Framed another way, the fluency heuristic is the cognitive ease of identifying which option you prefer when you have to select between recognized and recognized: "If two objects, *a* and *b*, are recognized, and one of two objects is more fluently retrieved, then infer that this object has the higher value with respect to the criterion."[27] The fluency heuristic allows us to "feel" like we are thinking because of the fluency of the context instead of forcing us to actually think.

Query: How many animals of each kind did Moses take on the ark?

If you took less than two seconds to read and answer the question, you probably answered "two." If you took more than two seconds to read and answer the question, you probably arrived at the right answer, which is "none" because Moses never took any animals on the ark; Noah did. In his book, *On Second Thought*, Wray Herbert talks about the Moses Illusion and other fluency tricks our brain plays to bypass conscious thought and deliberate analysis.[28] The Moses Illusion, aptly named, would not work if the query inquired how many animals Michael Jackson or Jennifer Lopez took on the ark. The illusion works because Moses and Noah are close enough—both players in the Old Testament, both older bearded men—that our brain reads what it thinks should be there instead of what is actually there. The appearance of Jennifer Lopez in a question about animals and an ark would alert the brain that there is incongruence present with what it knows to be true, but Moses slips in because he is close enough to Noah for our brains to read the question as fluent even though it is not.

Read the following paragraph to the best of your ability:

The phaonmneal pweor of the hmuan mnid, aoccdrnig to rschee-arch at Cmabrigde Uinervtisy, is that it dseno't mtaetr in waht oerdr the ltteres in a wrod are, the olny iproamtnt tihng is taht the frsit and lsat ltteer be in the rghit pclae. The rset can be a taotl mses and you can sitll raed it whotuit a pboerlm. Tihs is bcuseae the huamn mnid deos not raed ervey lteter by istlef, but the wrod as a wlohe. Azanmig huh? So mcuh for slpeling bineg ipmorantt![29]

This is the power of the fluency heuristic. Your mind will figure out a way to make sense of the gibberish especially if the gibberish gives you any reason to keep believing that it is not gibberish. As each word made sense, and a sentence seemed to be starting to form, you kept reading, and you kept making it make sense. That's the fluency heuristic at work!

Now, take a look at the following paragraph and see if you have the same patience to activate your fluency heuristic:

> *The phaonmneal pweor of the hmuan mnid, aoccdrnig to rscheearch at Cmabrigde Uinervtisy, is that it dseno't mtaetr in waht oerdr the ltteres in a wrod are, the olny iproamtnt tihng is taht the frsit and lsat ltteer be in the rghit pclae. The rset can be a taotl mses and you can sitll raed it whotuit a pboerlm. Tihs is bcuseae the huamn mnid deos not raed ervey lteter by istlef, but the wrod as a wlohe. Azanmig huh? So mcuh for slpeling bineg ipmorantt![30]*

If you became quickly dissuaded from deciphering the text, you are not alone. The complexity of the font reduces the likelihood of your mind triggering the fluency heuristic because the font makes the words and their meanings feel not so fluent. The positive aspect to your mind not defaulting to its fluency heuristic is that the trick query regarding Moses is less likely to trick people if the question was presented in a complex font instead of a simple font.

Additional research has also found that bypassing the fluency heuristic through use of complex fonts that are difficult to read actually improves students' abilities to learn.[31] This research has demonstrated that "student retention of material across a wide range of subjects (science and humanities classes) and difficulty levels (regular, Honors and Advanced Placement) can be significantly improved in naturalistic settings by presenting reading material in a format that is slightly harder to read."[32] Easier fonts make it easy for us to think we know what we are reading thereby activating the fluency heuristic and allowing us to confuse Moses and Noah. Complex fonts force us to slow down and deactivate our fluency heuristic thereby allowing us to fully read and deliberately process what we are taking in instead of automating the process.

So, the less our mind has to work to figure something out, the more we trust it. Easier is more trustworthy as far as our brain is concerned. So, a statement like "what sobriety conceals, alcohol reveals" is perceived to be more truthful than "what sobriety conceals, alcohol unmasks."[33] The same is true for "life is strife" versus "life is mostly struggle" and "caution and measure will win you treasure" versus "caution and measure will win you riches." In other words, "rhyme, like repetition, affords statements an enhancement in processing fluency that can be misattributed to heightened conviction about their truthfulness."[34] Rhyming creates a fluency that translates into credibility. The iconic moment in the O.J. Simpson defense in his 1994–1995 murder trial came when his attorney, Johnny Cochran, pointed to O.J. Simpson with the gloves from the crime scene barely fitting on his large hands and fluently said to the jury, "[i]f they don't fit, you must acquit." Rhyming makes it easier for our brain to remember things, so the fluency heuristic allows us to default to what rhymes as what is true because it takes less work to recall a rhyme.

By understanding the fluency heuristic, we can create more fluent messages for people that resonate and stick, but if we don't actively analyze the ways in which the fluency heuristic is affecting our decision-making process without our knowledge and/or permission, we could be making decisions that are easy instead of right.

WHAT YOU SEE IS NOT ALWAYS WHAT YOU GET

Many models of understanding differences in learning styles have been postulated from Kolb's Experiential Learning Theory to Fleming's Visual/Audial/Kinesthetic Learning Preferences to Howard Gardner's Multiple Intelligences, but there is one constant among researchers who study how people think, learn, and work; that is that we all think, learn, and work differently. Very differently!

In our work on how people give and receive informal feedback as well as formal evaluations, we continue to observe that a supervisor's learning style gets reproduced in his or her subordinates unless that supervisor is made aware of his or her preferences. Supervisors need to understand how their learning style preferences can impact their abilities to teach, grow, and evaluate someone under them who may have a very different style of thinking, learning, and working.

There has been much dialog in professional development circles about the "Matthew Effect," which reprises the biblical warning that "To him who has shall be given more, and he shall have abundance: but from him who does not have, even that which he has shall be taken away." According to research on the Matthew Effect, supervisors create self-fulfilling prophecies by "teaching up" selected in-groupers to live up to high performance evaluations and "ignoring down" out-groupers to low performance evaluations.[35] In other words, supervisors hand out their verdicts and then select the evidence that will back up their verdicts.

The research on how in-groupers and out-groupers are treated by senior leaders in organizations is pretty clear about the "what"—in-groupers are evaluated better than out-groupers for the same work and same errors—but what the research has not yet shown decisively is *why* senior leaders show this disruptive streak in their leadership patterns. Is it due to racial/ethnic, gender, or other identity bias as some have articulated? Is it weak leadership skills as others have posited? Or is it a simple lack of awareness or a lack of prioritization?

When we have coached senior lawyers, consultants, executives, and other leaders, we have worked with individuals who score low on racial/ethnic, gender, and other identity bias criteria. They don't seem to distinguish based on what someone looks like or who they are, but when we dig deeper, we find that they do in fact differentiate based on people's learning and working styles.

We coached one senior executive who had a very strong preference for a visual learning and working style. He loved graphics, PowerPoint presentations, flip charts, and other visual learning tools in meetings. He encouraged his team to study the visuals and give him their suggestions on next steps and action items. He did not, however, discuss the visual aids to any great extent so anyone on his team who learned by discussing, talking, listening, and even debating were often left with a jumble of images that they couldn't really understand enough to integrate into their thinking and problem-solving mechanisms. The learners who were kinesthetic and needed to physically move around and interact with the materials tuned out halfway through the meeting as the presentations continued and the flip chart pages started papering the walls.

When we shared our assessment with him, he was shocked to discover how much he evaluated people on their ability to think and learn like him. He recalled instances of talented people who needed to talk through issues with him, and he realized that they had irritated him because he perceived the need to discuss as an inability to work independently. He remembered one person in particular who could not sit through the staff meetings without getting up and standing or pacing at the back of the room. The executive had deemed this person as distracted and had viewed much of this person's work from that filter. The executive eventually had all his team members' learning styles assessed fully, and he rotated the responsibility for setting agendas, flow, and even venue for the meetings so that everyone could experience the different styles of their colleagues. He also shifted to an evaluation system that allowed for greater input from self-evaluations.

The more people think and learn the way we do, the more fluently we are able to understand them and "see" their intelligence. In order to "see" intelligence that is presented to us in ways that doesn't feel fluent, we have to actively disrupt our automatic mental shortcuts and find ways to be comfortable with what feels disjointed because our disjointedness is someone else's fluency.

In the previous chapter we saw how biases triggered by visual similarities and differences can keep us stuck in the RETRO IQ even when we see the benefits of THE *NEXT* IQ and intend to move into a more inclusive intelligence. This chapter has explored how we veer toward the mentally easy through biases in the ways we think, learn, and lead, and how our preference for cognitive ease also keeps us stuck in the RETRO IQ though we want to engage our *NEXT* IQ. The differences in our perspectives and our interpretations combine with how certain heuristics bypass our active thinking process through cognitive shortcuts, and when we bypass our ability to proactively think, we default to our RETRO IQ.

Yes, THE *NEXT* IQ requires more cognitive effort, but the effort gets you to better results faster. The cognitively easy way makes you feel like you are moving forward when you are mostly recycling what you already know. The RETRO IQ, in addition to being easier, creates less tension because a lack of differences leads to a lack of disagreement, but by actively creating this tension at the intersection of differences, leaders activate the power of THE *NEXT* IQ in their teams.

A Deeper Dive into Cognitive Ease

We've covered the major heuristics that can, in the pursuit of cognitive ease, lead us down the path of stagnation instead of innovation. In this section you will find additional examples of cognitive biases that impede the process of creative thinking. To explore how some of these biases may be impacting you as a leader or your team collectively, have your team generate some examples for each of the biases.

> A great many people think they are thinking when they are merely rearranging their prejudices.
>
> William James (psychologist and philosopher, 1842–1910)

Common Cognitive Biases Connected to the Comfort of Ease

Bias	Description	Examples
Confirmation Bias[36]	Our preference for interpreting information in a way that confirms what we already think so we are more likely to believe something that is consistent with what we think instead of something that challenges our perceptions, beliefs or experiences.	
Overconfidence Bias[37]	Our extreme confidence in our own answers because our answers comport with our perspectives and experiences.	
Illusory Correlation[38]	Our tendency to see a relationship between two or more things when none exists because of prejudice, our own interpretations, or our inability to see conflicting information.	

Bias	Description	Examples
Semmelweis Reflex[39]	Named for Ignaz Semmelweis, a doctor who was soundly rejected by the medical community in the middle 1800s for saying that doctors could dramatically reduce deaths from puerperal fever by disinfecting their hands between treating patients, the phrase now refers to the rejection of new knowledge that contradicts established norms, beliefs and/ or paradigms.	
False Consensus Effect[40]	Our false overestimate of how much people really agree with us.	
Halo Effect[41]	Our tendency to attribute a positive (or negative) characteristic of a person in one area of life to other areas of that person's life.	

THE *NEXT* IQ BIAS BREAKERS©

Courage is indeed required to break away from the comforts of cognitive ease and to think critically by seeking and integrating multiple perspectives. Challenging the path of cognitive ease means disrupting norms and making it difficult for people to carry on business as usual, which is not always an easy path to travel, even if there is understanding that the path

> Clear thinking requires courage rather than intelligence.
>
> Thomas S. Szasz (Hungarian psychiatrist and author)

will lead to a better destination. The four Bias Breakers© covered in the previous chapter work equally well in breaking through the leanings explored in this chapter, and the following four Bias Breakers give you additional tools to correct for your tendencies to lean toward what you already expect to find.

1. *Create Constructive Conflict.*

   Although consensus seems like a positive aspiration, trying to make decisions by consensus can often drive us to artificially agree with points of view that don't actually reflect our true perspectives. Pushing for consensus creates a goal of agreement instead of a goal of finding the best answer(s).

   Create constructive conflict (in teams and organizations) by creating a workforce where different perspectives, problem-solving methods, and interpretations create organic conflict. When those different views don't organically exist, try assigning someone the role of actively and constructively disagreeing with both the process and the conclusions of decision-making processes. "Why did we choose to do it this way?" "Why did we rule out that option?" "What if we waited to make this decision?" "What if we accelerated this decision?" "What would be the opposite of what we are trying to do, and what are reasons to not do it the opposite way?"

   As individuals, we can generate constructive conflict in our lives by fostering relationships with people who have very different perspectives than us and talking with them about decisions that we want to make. If we look at our lives and realize that we are primarily associated with people who agree with us, we can ask a few of them to serve as constructive conflict creators for us by playing the role of a dissenter.

   This tool does require an initial reflection on constructive conflict (conflict that produces better communication) versus destructive conflict (conflict that disrupts communication). One primary way to stay with the former and avoid the latter is to create conflict around ideas or concepts instead of individuals or personalities.

2. *Experiment with Being an Out-grouper.*

   If it takes courage to be a voice for constructive conflict, it takes sheer bravado to actively become an out-grouper. When you are in a position of leadership, it usually means that you have penetrated some in-group enough to advance into leadership. The more comfortable you feel when you walk into a situation, the more of an in-grouper you have become. One way to see beyond the comfort of being an in-grouper is to actively become an out-grouper periodically in order to remember what it feels like to not be part of the in-group—to not know the informal rules, to doubt your skill set, to wonder if you will fit in. Even if we wouldn't necessarily choose to become integrated into this out-group, the experience of being an out-grouper can stretch our minds beyond our comfort zones.

Join a running group (if you are not a runner), a knitting circle (if you are not a knitter), a golf clinic (if you have never played golf), or take part in other such benign activities where you will experience the sense of being on the outside looking in. Take those perspectives that you acquire into understanding the ways in which out-groupers in your organization may be perceiving their daily work lives.

3. *Disrupt Your Patterns.*
   We all have regular patterns from the foods we eat to the routes we travel to and from work to how we unwind at the end of the day. Our routines form a solid foundation into which we can lean when we are tired, but they also limit the ways in which our brain will think because it is easier for the brain to default to habit than to think of a new way to do something.

   Challenge yourself to disrupt your patterns maybe just once a day to start. Change what you eat for breakfast. Change how you get to work. Change what news sites you visit to get your news. Any change you make to a pattern in your life will translate into an opening for your mind to think differently. As Marshall McLuhan, the philosopher who coined the phrase "global village," noted: "The mark of our time is the revulsion against imposed patterns."[42] The 21st century will eventually create new patterns, but for now, it definitely requires the breaking of old patterns, individual, collective, and organizational.

4. *Generate Multiple Right Answers.*

We live in a culture where we still depend on that one singular right answer to resolve any question or challenge at hand. Dr. Arash Naeim, an oncologist at UCLA's Jonsson Comprehensive Cancer Center, concludes in his research that patients should always "[a]sk for alternatives. There is no one right answer and there are multiple options."[43]

Take that approach to any problem and challenge yourself, your team, or your organization to generate multiple right answers to any question. If you are looking for only one right answer, then you will stop the critical thinking process at the first right answer you find. If, by chance, you do generate more than one right answer, then, the "only one right answer" model forces you to choose the answer that is "more right." If the model actually shifted to "more than one right answer," and decisions actually required more than one right answer, then the next action you undertake becomes a choice of which right answer you will try first.

For every question you ask yourself, don't stop thinking until you come up with at least two right answers. Sometimes multiple right answers will be similar to each other, and sometimes they may even contradict each other. Either way, multiple right answers will allow you to think about a problem more inclusively than the search for that one right answer.

Needless to say, the more diverse perspectives that are represented in the answer generation process, the easier it will be to come up with multiple right answers.

The *Next* IQ Insights: Chapter 10

- Cognitive diversity—ways in which we perceive, interpret, and analyze the world—is as critical to The *Next* IQ as visible differences in identity. Leaders who want to maximize their individual intelligence and the intelligence levels of their teams will focus on cognitive diversity as much as they do visual diversity.
- Generally, we tend to value consensus over conflict, in-groupness over out-groupness, established cognitive patterns over cognitive

start-ups, and one right answer over multiple right answers. This tendency reduces our ability to think beyond what we know.

- Our perspectives are our points of view based on our own experiences, our interpretations are how we use our perspectives to make sense of new data, and our heuristics are the ways in which we choose to analyze and solve problems using mental shortcuts based on our perspectives and interpretations.
- The anchoring and adjustment heuristic, the availability heuristic, the recognition heuristic, and the fluency heuristic all tend to limit our thinking to past thoughts.
- The confirmation bias, the overconfidence bias, the illusory correlation, the Semmelweis Reflex, the false consensus effect, and the halo effect are common cognitive biases.

THE *NEXT* IQ ACTIONS: CHAPTER 10

- Anchors Aweigh! Reduce the effects of anchors and biases in the way you think by using the following techniques: (1) create constructive conflict, (2) experiment with being an out-grouper, (3) disrupt your patterns, and (4) generate multiple right answers.
- Keep pulling up your anchors and interrupting your biases! Biases don't disappear upon interruption, and anchors don't always stay up. Attention needs to be paid constantly to both biases and anchors in order to think, learn, and lead in new ways.

CHAPTER 11

THE COMFORT OF PREDICTABILITY: WE DON'T DO WHAT WE DON'T KNOW

We love the comfort zones of similarity (based on what we see) and of ease (based on how we think). Rounding out our list of RETRO IQ comfort zones is the comfort of predictability (based on what we do). Human beings have a strong need for predictability, partly resulting from our ability to think abstractly, which allows us to contemplate the future (and anticipate and try to avoid adversity),[1] and partly from our deeply engrained belief that predictability leads to security.[2] If that is true, then unpredictability leads to uncertainty. Facing uncertainty leads to feelings of insecurity, or a "fear of the unknown," which we try to reduce by rejecting the thing or event causing the unpredictability.[3] Basically, we need to know what will happen if we do something before we actually do it. If there is a new behavior that we can execute, unless we have some certainty about the results, we will default to old behaviors regardless of how attractive the consequence of that new behavior is.

This chapter is about how we choose conscious behaviors based on the predictability of the outcomes. For the purposes of understanding conscious behavior in the context of predictability, a behavior is defined as any action that you choose including actions that you choose to not take. Whereas the two previous chapters focused on the more or less unconscious comforts of similarity and cognitive ease, this chapter focuses on conscious actions, behaviors that we are far more capable of tuning into and changing than we are of changing our implicit associations, interpretations, or heuristics.

When we think about our behaviors—the actions that we choose to take—it is important to note that we can only choose to do something new once. After that, the choice we make is to "repeat" or "not repeat," not "do" or "don't do." It sounds merely semantic, but in regards to how we think about actions, the difference is quite significant. The first time we choose to do something, we make the decision based on an abstract notion of what *could happen*. Once we do something for the first time, we have a concrete memory of what *did happen*, and our future actions are based on what we think *will happen* based on what *did happen*.

Our memories of consequences from previous actions become the blueprints for our future actions, and when we follow the blueprints with enough frequency, we skip the blueprints and react from memory. When we react to the same stimuli with enough frequency, our actions bypass even our conscious memory and become automated. Actions (conscious behaviors of choice) slowly become reactions (conscious behaviors of habit), which eventually become reflexes (unconscious behaviors).

For example, try and remember the very first time you traveled to work whether you did so by car, train, bus, or foot. When the destination is new, the route has to be planned and executed very consciously and very deliberately. You pay attention to visual and audial cues, and you are conscious of each decision you make at each turn. Everything is a choice that you are making for the first time. The second time you traveled that route, your memory checked in to ask if you wanted to replay the memory you created the previous day. You probably answered in the affirmative, and you followed your steps from the previous day. The third time you travel that route, your memory may check in again, but by the fourth or fifth time, your memory stops checking in and assumes that given a particular set of stimuli—it's morning, it's a weekday, you have to go to work, and so on—you will take that route to work. (These are the times when you leave home and arrive at work with absolutely no conscious memory of how you got there!) Your conscious thought is no longer necessary and doesn't get reactivated unless there is a significant disturbance to the memory—there is a major traffic jam, the train isn't working that day, and so on—causing you to plan a new route.

Once your memory reflex has been interrupted, you have a choice to create a new pattern or fall back into the previous pattern. The majority of us fall back into the previous pattern, and the memory reflex absorbs the disruption and becomes automated once more.

The "route to work" example is one that many of us can recognize even if it has been relegated to that of an unconscious reflex. Other actions that fall into this category are those actions that we execute by habit and reflex every day such as brushing our teeth, showering, getting dressed, and driving. It is relatively easy to see how these actions evolve from conscious actions to habits to unconscious reflexes, but there are other examples that are just as pervasive in our lives that we tend to overlook.

Some of the most powerful examples of this reflex in the workplace are the relationships that we create and maintain with colleagues. Many of our relationships follow the action-reaction-reflex trajectory without us being fully aware of what is occurring. As illustrated in the two previous chapters, our initial actions may be conscious, but they are informed and guided by many unconscious processes such as implicit associations, unconscious biases, interpretations of events, and heuristic shortcuts, so our initial actions toward building relationships are going to default to what feels the most similar and easy. Once we get these relationships activated, our penchant for predictability keeps us from straying too far from the relationships that have become reflexes because a lack of familiarity and a perception of complexity suggest a level of unpredictability that we will not risk unless there is a compelling reason to do so.

There is a necessary tension between appreciating the human need for predictability and pushing the business need for innovation. For instance, in 1995, *Harvard Business Review* published an article called "The Power of Predictability" in which Howard H. Stevenson and Mihnea C. Moldoveanu argued that "predictability [in organizations] built the trust that allowed people to synchronize their actions in mutually productive ways."[4] Twelve years later, in 2007, the *Gallup Management Journal* published an article entitled "The Four Drivers of Innovation," in which Gallup chairman and CEO Jim Clifton observes that "[i]n the past, most businesses have focused on continuous improvement of their products and services to maintain a competitive edge. But in today's economy, that's not always enough . . . *Better* doesn't work anymore. *Different* does."[5]

In the Gallup study mentioned above, the researchers found that "[w]orkplace friendships play a significant role among engaged employees when it comes to setting the stage for [new] idea creation and refinement."[6] Across the various companies surveyed in this study, employees focused on the number and quality of relationships in their workplaces as sources of engagement and innovation. We may crave predictability, but we perform our best when we have many authentic relationships in the workplace. In other words, we have to step out of our comfort zones in order to step into our innovation zones.

Barry Conchie, a leadership consultant at Gallup, summarized Gallup's findings by stressing that innovation begins where relationships thrive: "An emotional commitment of one person to another makes a difference. But the control a manager has to enhance or limit [an employee's] contribution to innovation is the most powerful factor . . . It's important that [relationships are] cultivated from manager to manager and employee to employee. But we know that the [quality of the] relationship between a manager and an employee affects the ability to leverage that relationship. A bad relationship is a sure-fire way to kill innovation."[7]

Vibram Five Fingers shoes look like meshed gloves for your feet. They challenge everything we think we know about what a shoe should look and feel like and their odd appearance has resulted in them being called the "Next Ugly Shoe"[8] and the "creepy running shoes that look like fluorescent feet."[9] According to Vibram's website, "[i]n 1936, Vitale Bramani, an academic of the Italian Alpine Club, returning from a tragic alpine climb, had the intuition to apply the technique Pirelli used on automobile tires on shoe soles. Applying rubber under his mountain boots, he created the first vulcanized rubber soles and revolutionized the practice of mountain climbing."[10] Approximately 70 years later, Bramani's grandson, Marco Bramani, worked with industrial designer Robert Fliri to create what he thought would be shoes that revolutionized how boaters and water sport enthusiasts thought about footwear. Vibram's reputation as a shoemaker for mountain climbers raised eyebrows—mountain shoe people shouldn't be making water shoes, should they? The predictable thing to do would have been to make a better mountain shoe.

Within a year of release of the Five Fingers shoes, it wasn't just the skeptical market that was surprised. Vibram itself was shocked to discover that while sailors were mildly accepting of the oddly shaped shoes, runners were buying up the shoes so quickly that Vibram couldn't keep up with the demand. Between being celebrated in Christopher McDougall's bestseller *Born to Run* and being named as one of *Time* magazine's best health inventions in 2007, it is no surprise that in spite of not being that popular with sailors, Five Fingers went from $430,000 in sales in 2006 to about $11 million in 2009 and over $50 million in 2010.

Vibram's Five Fingers shoes are a case study in unpredictability for everyone involved, from the market that wondered who would ever buy the "ugly shoes" to runners who had no idea that the next best thing to happen in running would actually be intended for sailors and for Vibram, who quickly realized that business intelligence lies in getting your product to the people who want it regardless of who your initial target market was. Our default for what is predictable could have prevented us from seeing footwear that can help runners because it is in the aisle for sailors and it could have prevented Vibram from capitalizing on a tidal wave of demand for its shoes because the wave came from an unexpected direction.

As Michael Hammer and James Champy wrote in their groundbreaking book, *Reengineering the Corporation: A Manifesto for Business Revolution*, "The changes that will put a company out of business are those that happen outside the light of its current expectations."[11] We want predictability, but our success lies in what happens beyond our scope of expectations in the space outside of our comfort zones.

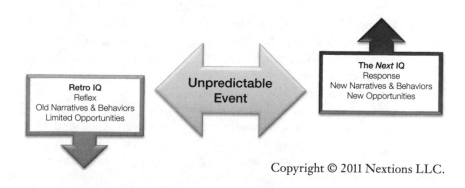

USING THE UNPREDICTABLE TO CREATE UNDERSTANDING

I was retained by the senior Human Resources executive in a large company to create "harmony in hell," as he phrased it, in his leadership team. The executive was a relatively new addition to the senior leadership team of this company, and he realized very quickly that not only was there no inclusion on behalf of the directors who reported up to him, but in many instances, there was active and explicit exclusion. The directors on his team (and by proxy the managers and employees below the directors) valued turf over trust, control over collaboration, and insolence over inclusion. In one meeting, I noticed that when any one director stood up to present on his or her department, many of the other directors would quickly start typing away on their Blackberries. In a strategic planning session, the director who volunteered to advance the slides for the presentations kept advancing the slides faster than the other directors wanted so that the presentations were unnaturally and rudely accelerated.

When the executive and I sat down to plan an inclusion strategy for his leadership team, I commented on how comfortable everyone on the team had grown with the high level of detachment and rudeness. I also noted that it was difficult to ascertain if the behaviors I had observed were truly personality/character traits of the leaders or if these communication patterns had cemented over time as reflexive behaviors of this team. The executive planned a full-day off-site retreat for his team to either "pull it together" or "break it apart for good."

The first exercise we did at the retreat (held at a modern art museum to kick-start the unpredictability) was to brainstorm everything that was predictable about the team from where individuals sat in meetings to who interrupted whom to agenda items to who argued with whom to who debriefed together after meetings to when and where meetings took place. This session lasted almost 2 hours, and we came up with a list of over 150 things that the team could easily predict about each other. There were some hurt feelings, some anger, and some frustration as people initially pointed out the predictable patterns of others, but there was also laughter and agreement as the list grew to include everyone in the room.

After a short break, I challenged them to go through each predictable item on the list and identify one way to actively break up the predictability. This session also lasted about 2 hours, and the team identified "predictability breakers" such as rotating seating assignments, a "mute" button that could be passed to an individual to silence him or her in a moment when the person was most likely to argue, a "speak" button that could be passed to an individual to encourage him or her to enter a conversation that the person normally would not enter, rotating the responsibility for creating the agenda and running the meeting, a list of venues to shake up where they held their meetings, and so on.

The last session of the day was a business session, but the executive ran the session with a few of the "predictability breakers" in place. The session looked and felt very different from their previous meetings. As the executive said to me at the end of the day: "It wasn't yet harmony, but at least it wasn't hell."

Our intrinsic need for predictability keeps us chained to unproductive behaviors that eventually morph into reflexes that prevent us from crafting deliberate and intelligent responses to information, events, and people. This is the RETRO IQ model where we see our capabilities and intelligences as inherent immutable characteristics instead of competencies that can be enhanced or reduced by our thoughts and actions. Even the most intelligent person per an IQ test can get derailed by the stickiness of unexamined biases, unproductive cognitive patterns, and entrenched behaviors.

A DEEPER DIVE INTO PREDICTABILITY

We crave predictability even if change carries great promise. We will work twice as hard to maintain a predictable environment that makes us miserable than we will work to create change that has the potential to make us happy. The amount of misery and pain that we will endure before deciding to give up predictability for change is truly remarkable, and it is truly a cornerstone of the RETRO IQ. THE NEXT IQ prioritizes change over predictability because all aspects of the world are already changing, so shifting our vision,

> Without change there is no innovation, creativity, or incentive for improvement. Those who initiate change will have a better opportunity to manage the change that is inevitable.
>
> William Pollard (physicist and Episcopal priest, 1911–1989)

our thinking, and our behaviors to meet the needs of the changing world is a necessity, not a choice. That said, the RETRO IQ is very effective at hanging on until the necessity becomes a severe emergency. The following chart gives an overview of three common biases that implicitly veer us toward predictability to our detriment. See if you can come up with some examples from your personal and/or professional lives where you have explicitly or implicitly made decisions along these biases. Then see if you can come up with organizational examples that you have observed in your workplace or other organization with which you are intimately familiar.

COMMON COGNITIVE BIASES CONNECTED TO THE COMFORT OF PREDICTABILITY		
Bias	**Description**	**Examples**
Status Quo Bias[12]	We have the proclivity to favor perspectives, decisions, and actions that will keep things relatively the same. We prefer existing relationships and realities over any potential change in spite of evidence that change may be personally beneficial.	
System Justification Bias[13]	We tend to justify the existing system (in organizations, politics, families, etc.) because systems provide certainty, stability, and safety; individuals who enjoy higher levels of social roles/ categories adopt a belief that the system is fair and works well because it enhances their self-esteem (wealthy people who attribute their wealth to their own competency who then support the system as meritocratic); individuals who suffer the lower levels of social roles/categories adopt an even higher attachment to the system because they believe the system is the only way to transcend their limited roles/categories (poor people tend to believe in the meritocratic fairness of systems because they see the system as their only hope to make their lives better).	

Bias	Description	Examples
Loss Aversion Bias[14]	We have a propensity to see our losses as greater than our gains of the same amount, which causes us to work harder to avoid losses than we would to acquire gains of the same amount (we will put twice as much money to recoup money that we have lost on a particular stock than we would to buy different stock that can make us twice as much money); losses are often two times as powerful as gains of the same amount in regards to meaning for individuals; there is a greater likelihood that we will take risks to minimize losses than we would to maximize gains (we would spend more time and energy trying to recover $100 that we lost than using that same amount of time and energy to gain $200).	

In bullfighting there is a term called *querencia*. The *querencia* is the spot in the ring to which the bull returns. Each bull has a different *querencia*, but as the bullfight continues, and the animal becomes more threatened, it returns more and more often to his spot. As he returns to his *querencia*, he becomes more **predictable**. And so, in the end, the matador is able to kill the bull because instead of trying something new, the bull returns to what is familiar. His comfort zone.

Carly Fiorina (former CEO of Hewlett-Packard)

THE *NEXT* IQ BIAS BREAKERS©

The gravity pull of predictability draws us into doing the same things over and over because we prioritize the predictability of the consequences instead of the success of the consequences.

Predictability leads to failure.

T. Boone Pickens (Texas oil and gas tycoon)

Breaking our addiction to probability can be achieved by using one or more of the tools presented in the previous two chapters, and this chapter provides a couple of extra tools to hone in order to break the addiction to predictability.

Predictability, by definition, means the ability to foretell the future based on reasonable information related to the past. We label weather, stock markets, human behavior, and political trends as unpredictable because we are comparing them to a very specific pattern in the past with which the current reality is not aligned. So, if the comfort of predictability is anchored to past experiences, breaking the addiction to predictability is connected to severing the present and the future from the past in a constructive way.

1. *Forecast the Possible.*
    In order to usher in the unpredictable, you have to focus on what is possible, not predictable. Possibility draws on the imagination while predictability draws on history. Create goals for yourself, your team, and your organization around what is possible, not predictable. In some organizations (and perhaps some individuals), this requires a dramatic shift in how you think about the future and its relationship to the present.

    I worked with a mid-size company where the average age of the senior leadership team exceeded 40 but the average age of the frequent consumer was below 35. The leaders were not operating on the same past as the company's consumers. Without the diverse perspectives of the younger generations on decision-making teams, the desire for predictability among the leaders was setting the stage for failure. It was not enough to try importing the perspectives of the younger generation via focus group reports or anecdotal examples. As we worked through what the leaders wanted in regard to predictability, they realized that their addiction to predictability was impairing their organization from being prepared for the 21st century. Knowing that they would not shift their perspectives overnight, they implemented a simple solution: they focused more on what the company *should* look like in 10 years than on what they thought the company *could* look like in 10 years. Their shift in how they made decisions is equivalent to being in a car going 30 miles per hour and asking "how fast do we need to go to get to where we want to be in 2 hours" versus "if we keep going this fast, where will we most likely end up in 2 hours."

Forecast the possible, not the predictable, and see how your perspective shifts.

2. *Create Micro Unpredictability.*

   While unpredictability at the macro level can cause destructive disruptions, unpredictability at the micro level can catalyze creativity and critical thinking. Of course, the more diverse perspectives you have in any context, the greater the levels of micro unpredictability will be, but any individual, team, or organization can actively create micro unpredictability to get beyond the comfortable.

   Micro unpredictability is the collective effort of small changes that you can make that keep things new and prevent people from operating purely by habit. Small and unexpected changes in routine, agendas, venues, meeting leaders, communication patterns, expectations, and so on can collectively amount to substantive shifts in how people think, learn, and lead.

THE *NEXT* IQ INSIGHTS: CHAPTER 11

- Our desire for predictable consequences to our actions works with our need for comfort for similarity and ease to keep the RETRO IQ in place even when we need to and want to transition to THE *NEXT* IQ.
- Our behaviors are a complex pattern of choice (the first time we do something) to reaction (we try and replicate or avoid the consequences from our initial choice) to habit (we do something without thinking). The more conscious we are that the majority of our actions are actually reactions and habits, the more we can consciously act in ways that are beneficial to us.
- Some of the biases that most affect our behaviors are the status quo bias, the system justification bias, and the loss aversion bias.

THE *NEXT* IQ ACTIONS: CHAPTER 11

- Act, don't react. THE *NEXT* IQ relies on our abilities to act anew in critical situations. When we default to our reactive and habitual behaviors, we replicate past consequences instead of creating new solutions. We must learn to (1) forecast the possible and (2) create micro unpredictability.
- Identify one thing that you do the same way every day at work. Now, change it. What changed because of your change?

CHAPTER 12

THE STUFF THAT MAKES THE Retro IQ REALLY STICKY

STUFF: Stress, Time Constraints, Uncertainty, Fatigue, and Fear

In October 2010, *Science* magazine published an article on a research study conducted by researchers from Carnegie Mellon University, Massachusetts Institute of Technology, and Union College in New York that showed that the collective intelligence of groups was significantly higher than the sum of the individual intelligence levels of each group member.[1] In other words 1 + 1 + 1 = 5, not 3. The study divided 699 people into random groups of 2 to 5 and gave them a wide array of challenging tests. The researchers found that the group's average IQ (based on individual IQ tests taken by the group members) had no correlation with the group's collective output, even if a group had an individual with an exceptionally high IQ. They also found three group dynamics that correlated with successful output:

1. Social Sensitivity in the Groups—the more people in a group asked questions of each other, listened to each other, and were empathetic to each other's emotions, the higher their collective intelligence.

2. Turn Taking—the more people in a group took turns speaking, resisted dominating a conversation, and asked each other to contribute, the higher the collective intelligence.
3. Female Members—simply put, the more women there were in any group, the more intelligent the group. The researchers noted that in individual social sensitivity tests, women scored higher than men. They believed that the presence of women raised the likelihood of the group being more socially sensitive and led to more turn taking in the group, thereby raising the probability of higher intellectual output.

Dr. Anita Williams Woolley, one of the study's researchers, "speculate[s] that one particularly important behavior that many women display is the willingness to admit what they don't know, and ask if anyone else in the group has better expertise ... Men seem less likely to reveal such deficits."[2] She further explains that, as the global marketplace grows increasingly complex, "more and more of our problems will have solutions that lie at the intersection of individuals with specialties, so they need to be able to collaborate."[3]

One area of the global marketplace where we see Dr. Woolley's prediction manifesting is in patents. Not only has the number of inventors per successful patent application increased dramatically over the last couple of decades, but the number of cross-national teams filing for patents has also increased significantly.[4] In 2010, patents issued in the United States had an average of 2.7 inventors per patent, with 68 percent of the patents having multiple inventors and 13 percent having 5 or more inventors.[5] The majority of issued patents in 1990, in comparison, had only 1 inventor. In regards to cross-national filings in 2010, 8 percent of patents issued in the United States had at least one inventor from another country listed; this was true of 20 percent of patents issued in Germany, 26 percent in Canada and in France, 36 percent in the United Kingdom, 38 percent in China, and 48 percent in Switzerland. The United States had the highest probability of being the country of origin for co-inventors for these international patents.[6]

So, if we know that the global marketplace is really becoming more seamless, and working in diverse groups makes us far more intelligent than working by ourselves, no matter how brilliant we are, why aren't we all clamoring to create diverse groups where productive conflict and collective intelligence dynamics elevate us to higher intellectual output?

In the previous three chapters, we discussed the strong pull of our comfort zones. The comforts of similarity, ease, and predictability keep us stuck in the RETRO IQ even though we want to actively engage with our *NEXT* IQ. Revisiting our cruise control versus active driving metaphor, we want to actively drive because we know we can maximize our ride, but we slip back into cruise control because it just takes less effort. We are especially susceptible to reverting back to our RETRO IQ when STUFF© happens—Stress, Time Constraints, Uncertainty, Fatigue, and Fear. Even when we recognize our need to shift from cruise control back to active drive, the STUFF of life and work keeps us in cruise control because it feels like it takes less work.

Stress

Richard Carlson, bestselling author of the *Don't Sweat the Small Stuff* books, once said that "[s]tress is nothing more than a socially acceptable form of mental illness."[7] The quote is funny until you really think about it and realize that stress can be quite debilitating to our cognitive abilities. In the context of how we activate and engage our intellectual capacities, a high level of negative stress can chain people to the RETRO IQ even when they want to break free and move toward a more innovative way to think, learn, and lead.

Chronic stress measurably affects almost every aspect of our cognitive abilities from memory retention to analytical problem-solving skills to decision-making capacities. (In discussing stress, it is important to note acute stress—stress created in an emergency—is not the same as chronic stress—a high stress level that becomes the normal state of being.) When people are in states of high chronic stress, they move into a rapid analysis mode (often unconsciously), deciding whether something is necessary/unnecessary, good/bad, or safe/unsafe.[8] This rapid analysis mode feels like a "do or die" moment in which people don't feel like they have the time or resources to make thoughtful decisions, and the rapid analysis mode becomes the default mode of operation. Chronically elevated levels of stress actually reroute our cognitive resources away from the task at hand because we are using our resources to "stress out" instead of attending to the problem.[9] Chronic stress negatively impacts our cognitive abilities in specific ways:

- It blocks our ability to use our full range of taking in information, thereby creating a "tunnel vision" through which we fixate on certain information to the detriment of missing the larger picture.[10]
- It increases the likelihood that we will make decisions based on incomplete information.[11]
- It increases the likelihood that we will use heuristics and other cognitive shortcuts instead of fully thinking through what is in front of us.[12]
- It increases the probability that we will use habits instead of analysis to make our next decision.[13]
- It decreases our abilities to manipulate information, analyze complex situations, and solve problems.[14]
- It decreases overall accuracy in task completion and increases overall amount of time necessary to complete the task.[15]

As chronic stress narrows our range of vision, increases our dependency on heuristics, and decreases our ability to manage complex problems and layers of information, we become focused on surviving instead of thriving, on getting by instead of getting ahead. The irony, of course, is that the more we default to surviving, the easier it becomes to stay in that mode instead of stepping out of our comfort zones to actively solicit, include, engage, and integrate different and contrasting points of view in order to create high-impact solutions. Engaging THE *NEXT* IQ sounds overwhelming when you are under a heavy amount of stress, especially because chronic stress results in negative emotions, and the act of trying to decrease the stress without changing the present situation only results in more negative emotions. These emotions then impact how we see the world and what we believe about the world; these emotions also influence how we interpret cues from our environment and interact with our environment.[16]

The cycle of "context-stress-negative emotions-greater stress-inability to do anything about the context-more stress" is very common when the RETRO IQ is at work. Precisely because the RETRO IQ assumes that intelligence resides as expertise in each solitary individual, stress causes us to look inward to see if we can change the context that is causing our intelligence to be out of sync with our environment. If our knowledge and experiences don't give us a way to sync up with the environment, and we don't feel that we have the power or authority to change our environment, the stress continues to build with no release. We become even more out of harmony with expectations in the environment because we are now disabling ourselves from performing at our best.

It is important to note that not just individuals are prone to losing capability in high-stress situations. Organizations, as collectives of individuals, often develop chronically stressful cultures where the structures of the organization (and the people within those structures) are prone to defaulting to rapid analysis mode instead of critical thinking mode. When chronic stress is maintained at high levels in organizations, the following breakdowns are likely to occur:

- a decrease in overall communications and a decrease in the effectiveness of communications that do occur[17]
- an increase in "groupthink" where individuals in a group agree with each other without expressing individual perspectives and/or disagreements necessary to reach a good decision, not just a decision of consensus[18]
- a decrease in an individual's commitment to the team/organization and an increase in an individual's risk of detachment and attrition from the team/organization[19]

When chronic stress is high, it is harder to move into active drive, and it is easier to justify staying in cruise control even when the contexts and conditions require an active driver. Paradoxically, it is precisely in moments of chronic stress that shifting out of the RETRO IQ to THE NEXT IQ can infuse the individual and/or organization with the new ideas, innovative thinking, and creative leadership necessary to decrease the stress.

Time Constraints

Working under time constraints is a specific and narrow slice of the general stress we've just discussed that deserves to be explored and understood as a unique circumstance since working under time constraints has quickly become a component of competing and thriving in the 21st-century global marketplace. As a subset of stress, time constraints can lead to many of the decreases in cognitive abilities that general stress does, but when time constraints become really tight, people rely even more heavily on heuristics that lead to biases.[20] When we operate under the stress of time constraints, we are more likely to engage in stereotyping (especially racial/ethnic stereotyping) and anchoring (in ways that reinforce in-groups and out-groups).[21] When we see the clock ticking, we have difficulty remembering things that we would normally remember, and we have difficulty doing things that normally come naturally to us.

Time constraints push us into instinctive thinking that is automatic, implicit, heuristic, and biased without our awareness. While we think that time constraints merely make us reason through the necessary facts faster than we normally would, we are actually using completely different cognitive mechanisms with reason than we do with instinct.[22] Time constraints make us less likely to check that we have the available information to make well-informed decisions or that we have spent adequate time analyzing the situation before deciding on a course of action. As the global marketplace becomes more seamless, more of us are operating in a 24/7 day where time constraints are an unavoidable component of global competition. The Retro IQ is vulnerable to time constraints because individual stress impacts individual performance, but The *Next* IQ is less vulnerable because collective intelligence can diffuse the effects of stress across different minds while benefiting from the strengths of each individual mind.

Uncertainty

Human beings do not like uncertainty. We will pay dearly and often in order to reduce uncertainty even if the uncertainty portends potentially great results and the certainty that would take its place portends definite doom. No, we do not like uncertainty. So, when we are faced with uncertainty, we play mind games to reduce (or even erase) the uncertainty in order to make ourselves think that we have the information we need to make logical decisions when we really don't.[23] We tell ourselves that we know things we really don't know in order to manufacture certainty, and we default to a "preference fluency" that draws us into what is familiar when faced with uncertainty.[24]

A challenge with uncertainty is that we often confuse uncertainty with risk, and because we value and reward risk takers in many industries, we are loath to discuss uncertainty. One way to separate risk from uncertainty is to think of risk as choosing between options that have known outcome probabilities, whereas uncertainty means choosing between options where the outcome probabilities are unknown.[25] While taking risks, especially calculated ones, can be rooted in critical thinking, making decisions in uncertainty most often involves using heuristics.

Interestingly, new research is finding that while individuals tend to cooperate less in groups when there is certainty, they cooperate much more when uncertainty is introduced into the context.[26] The cooperation is a sign of seeking different perspectives when our own perspectives are evidently limited in allowing us to make decisions. The more uncertainty we deal with, the more we benefit from (and feel better with) diverse perspectives providing alternative courses of action in a world where uncertainty is often the new normal.

Fatigue

None of us needs a study to tell us that when we are tired, we don't think as clearly or as sharply. That said, there are researchers who have investigated the specifics of how our cognitive skills (such as reaction time, concentration, and memory[27]) are affected when we are fatigued, and analysis has shown that eight cognitive functions are specifically impacted when we are tired:[28]

- appreciating a complex situation while avoiding distraction
- keeping track of events and developing and updating strategies
- thinking laterally and being innovative
- assessing risk and anticipating range of consequences
- controlling mood and uninhibited behavior
- showing insight into own performance
- remembering "when" rather than "what"
- communicating effectively

For example, a study conducted on the cognitive and physical motor skills of surgical residents before and after their calls found that fatigue after a call caused a significant deterioration in the surgical residents' cognitive and physical motor skills.[29] Not only is our ability to pay attention decreased when we are fatigued,[30] but our perception of how we are performing and solving problems gets greatly compromised.[31]

In 2007, the National Transportation Safety Board (NTSB) asked the Federal Aviation Administration (FAA) and the National Air Traffic Controllers Association (NATCA) to collaborate to revise the schedules for air traffic controllers in order to reduce the number of controller-related aviation accidents.[32] As the American Society of Safety Engineers reported in 2007, "According to NTSB, the controller errors in each incursion incident were similar in nature and were consistent with the known effects of fatigue. 'In each case, critical information about the traffic situation was forgotten, resulting in the controller issuing a conflicting or inappropriate clearance,' NTSB explains."[33] Fatigue is not just an issue in professions where "high alertness" is a key requisite such as air traffic controllers, surgeons, or truck drivers; fatigue is now linked to lowered productivity in almost every profession.[34] A recent Society for Human Resources Management article reported that "81% of 820 HR leaders think that fatigue among workers is worse than in previous years" and that "cognitive fatigue affects alertness, perception, reasoning or learning [in the workplace]."[35]

Fear

Fear plays a predictable role in our conscious actions; we are less likely to do things when we are afraid, but the conscious predictability of what we may or may not do pales in comparison to what fear does to us unconsciously. Fear can be understood as having five main components—affective responses (facial, vocal, or physical expressions), physiological responses (increased heart rate, shallow breath, etc.), perceptive responses (actual perception of thing causing fear), cognitive responses (confusion, anxiety, avoidance, etc.), and behavioral responses (fight, flight, etc.).

For instance, when two groups—one group of people who were afraid of heights and another group who were not afraid of heights—were asked to estimate the distance from the ground to a second floor balcony, the acrophobic group far overestimated the height of the balcony in comparison to the other group.[36] We perceive the objects of our fear in exaggerated ways, and the exaggerated vision of what we fear makes us even more afraid.

This phenomenon helps us understand the impact of individual perceptions of individual fears, but the impact of collective perceptions is far more severe. Recent research reveals that "individuals from a racial group other than their own are more readily associated with an aversive stimulus [fear] than individuals for one's own race, among both white and black Americans."[37] This fear of "the other" manifests in an implicit fear that translates into affective, physiological, cognitive, perceptive, and behavioral responses just as a fear of heights does.[38]

In addition to the fear of "the other," people fear change and the unknown.[39] The status quo and familiarity biases discussed in previous chapters are consistent with fear of change. Fear of the unknown keeps people rooted to what they know even if what they know is no longer what they want. An interesting study involving children with Williams Syndrome (WS), a neurodevelopmental disorder in which there is abnormal activity in the amygdala where responses to social threats usually originate, found that not only are these children overly friendly to strangers, but they never develop negative attitudes about people from other races/ethnicities.[40] Much of our in-group versus out-group behaviors in the workplace relate more to our fears of "the other," "change," and "the unknown," than conscious distinctions that lead to active differentiation on our part.

> In the perspective of every person lies a lens through which we may better understand ourselves.
>
> Ellen J. Langer (professor of psychology, Harvard University)

THE *NEXT* IQ INSIGHTS: CHAPTER 12

- The resistance to change (discussed in Chapters 9–11) that makes the RETRO IQ sticky is exacerbated by the STUFF of life—Stress, Time constraints, Uncertainty, Fatigue, and Fear. The transition to THE *NEXT* IQ requires an understanding of how this STUFF makes us crave the comforts of similarity, ease, and predictability even more than we normally do.

- Stress, time constraints, uncertainty, fatigue, and fear reduce our overall cognitive and critical thinking abilities thereby making it more likely that we revert to reactive and habitual patterns that block out new ideas and keep us mired in the past.

The *Next* IQ Actions: Chapter 12

Many resources focus on how to deal with stress, time management, uncertainty, fatigue, and fear. I will not attempt to quickly and concisely summarize the wisdom of the material that already exists on these topics. The following are the "If I could just do one thing today to make it better, what would it be?" suggestions that I share with my clients on each of these topics.

- Stress: Stress is the difference between expectations and reality, so the one thing you can do immediately is decide whether it is easier for you to shift your expectations or your reality. Just making that decision will change your perspective on your stress.
- Time constraints: Focus on the next thing that you have to do. That's it. There is always time to do the very next thing.
- Uncertainty: Identify if what you are dealing with is risk (known probabilities) or uncertainty (unknown probabilities). Risk requires a calculated decision. Uncertainty requires a leap of faith, and leaps of faith cannot be proven or market-tested so don't bother trying.
- Fatigue: Sleep. Seriously, take a nap. There's plenty of research that now shows that short naps, long naps, vacations, and so on allow us to think better.
- Fear: Fear is a natural instinct that tells us that we need to be on alert, but fear should not cause you to stop moving; accept your fear as the very conservative companion on your journey that you have to listen to every once in a while.

CHAPTER 13

SHIFTING FROM THE Retro IQ TO The *Next* IQ

In his book *True North*, former Medtronic CEO Bill George observes that "[i]ntellectual intelligence, or IQ, has long been thought of as an essential characteristic for managers . . . Too many leaders believe that by being the smartest person in the room, they can use their intellect to carry the day. As a result, they overpower less forceful voices that may have the vital ideas, insights and answers they need to succeed."[1] This observation contains the essence of the shift from the Retro IQ to The *Next* IQ—the shift is not about helping someone else, it is about actively cultivating a global mindset and then deliberately seeking and including different perspectives in order to gain the answers that you need in order to succeed. The *Next* IQ is about being smarter by thinking differently about what smarter is.

Shifting from cruise control to active driving requires a shift in the way we think about both cruise control and active driving. Cruise control "feels" easier because it "seems" to take less effort, but the risks—slower response time and less control over how you choose to respond—far outweigh the benefits of not having to "work so hard" when you drive. There may be times (long straight stretches of road, great weather, light traffic, etc.) when cruise control can be utilized for a break, but the break should be the outlying experience, not the norm. As the previous chapters on heuristics and STUFF have illustrated, many of us default to cruise control because it "feels" familiar, easier, and more predictable; yet, the 21st century's global marketplace requires us to drive actively because our environment is anything but repetitive, simple, or routine. We need to drive if we are going to get to the right place at the right time and lead the right people there, and we need to shift out of cruise control in order to think, learn, and lead in these complex times.

In order to disengage cruise control and shift into drive, we need to

- shift from seeking information to seeking insight,
- shift from prioritizing aptitude to prioritizing action, and
- shift from being competitive to being collaborative.

SHIFTING FROM INFORMATION TO INSIGHT

In the global marketplace of the 21st century, information is everywhere, and it is available to everyone. Information is data; it can even be sorted and packaged and presented as knowledge. We need information, but information alone is no longer valuable because it is easily accessible by many. The value, then, is not the information itself but the insight that transforms information through critical analysis and is refined by relevant experience.

> In a world where facts are readily available, from multiple sources, basic information will be commoditized. But the explosion of sources will create a real burden for the consumers of information. Raw information will become not just a commodity, it will be a nuisance. In that world, consumers will value scarce, relevant insight over abundant facts.
>
> Brad Burnham (Union Square Ventures)[2]

The RETRO IQ continues to deal in informational intelligence while THE *NEXT* IQ deals with insight intelligence. The RETRO IQ focuses on the dots while THE *NEXT* IQ focuses on connecting the dots to reveal hidden patterns. Because individual insight cannot connect as many dots as multiple insights can, this shift from information to insight requires (1) diverse perspectives to analyze the information and (2) a clear context in which the information is translated into insight.

Research has definitely shown that "[c]ommunication ties which cut across demographic boundaries—and the different sets of information, experiences, and outlooks that such boundaries divide—enriches the research process and promotes greater productivity."[3] Research has also shown that stronger and denser communication links between individuals in a team make it more likely for these individuals to use differences to drive higher levels of productivity.[4] In other words, the stronger the communication networks within a team, the more likely team members will be to contribute their individual perspectives when solicited, especially if their perspectives are unique or differ from the norm.[5] Also, the more diverse the team, the more connections the team collectively has to external networks through which they can import additional perspectives and turn easily available information into valuable insight.

Once diverse perspectives are represented on a team, in order to shift from information to insight—whether the shift is to achieve an individual objective, solve an organizational problem, or create an innovative solution for a client—the following questions have to be explored, debated, and answered before you analyze any information:

> You can tell whether a man is clever by his answers.
> You can tell whether a man is wise by his questions.
>
> Naguib Mahfouz (winner of Nobel Prize for Literature, 1911–2006)

1. *What* is the objective?
2. *Why* is it important to achieve this objective?
3. *Who* needs to be included in the process of achieving this objective? Who needs to be consulted prior to moving forward with action? Who is the audience that will help us measure the effectiveness of our actions?
4. *How* will we know the objective has been achieved?

Information needs context in order to be transformed into insight, and the same information can lead to different insights in different contexts. For example, if we see that the ground is wet, our brain quickly and often without conscious thought tries to create the context necessary for that piece of information to become insight we can use. We scan for signs of rain or live sprinklers because rain will require a different action on our part than live sprinklers. The information about the ground being wet is not as important as the insight we need in order to drive our next action.

The what-why-who-how questions above create a consciously deliberate process of activating our brain's ability to shift from information to insight. To further examine the contextualization process that occurs when we are given the information that the ground is wet, we look for the source of the wetness, but we also arrive at different insights if we are driving instead of walking. The wet ground, the source of water, and the probability of an individual getting wet are all important information dots, and the context adds the "so what?" that is needed for us to make the information mean something. So what if the ground is wet? So what if the ground is wet from rain? So what if the ground is wet from rain, and I'm in a car? So what if the ground is wet from rain, and I'm in a car that has balding tires and bad brakes?

The more you "so what?" the information within the context of the objective that you are trying to achieve, the closer you drive that information to insight. And, here is where diversity of perspectives makes the difference—if you are "so what-ing" information in order to push it toward insight, the more different and even contradictory answers you can generate to each "so what," the more insights you will spark. The more insights you spark, the more intelligence you create for the individuals, teams, or organizations involved.

See the dots. Connect the dots. The process is relatively simple even when you add in the activities of setting the context and drilling into the information to extract insight. The key to successfully shifting from information to insight is *the ability to actively solicit, include, engage, and integrate different and contrasting points of view from diverse perspectives.* The integration of diverse perspectives requires both the active solicitation of these perspectives as well as the active willingness on behalf of others to contribute these perspectives, which is why the gathering and gelling of diverse perspectives is the critical first step to turning information into insight.

SHIFTING FROM APTITUDE TO ACTION

To understand the shift from aptitude to action, we need to better understand how aptitude differs from ability and how ability differs from action. Aptitudes are the inherent proclivities that make it easier for us to learn certain things over others. Abilities are the skills and knowledge that are acquired through study, experience, and practice. Abilities can be enhanced or atrophied based on various factors such as frequency of use. Actions are behaviors expressed by people and can be reflective of actions that were taken in the past (historical), ongoing actions (current), or actions that have not yet occurred (future).

> Never mistake motion for action.
>
> Ernest Hemingway
> (American author and journalist, 1899–1961)

Since the pull of the RETRO IQ relies on the compelling forces of similarity, ease, and predictability, the shift from the RETRO IQ to THE NEXT IQ requires the deliberate expression of action—the active solicitation, inclusion, engagement, and integration of different and contrasting points of view. Yet, in many of the organizations with which I work, I find that the people perceive aptitude or ability as the deficiency causing them to stick in their RETRO IQ. In fact, when I've done extensive cultural, leadership, communication, or inclusion assessments in organizations, I find that most individuals have the aptitude and the ability to express inclusive behaviors, but they do not always choose to act upon these aptitudes and abilities.

When the deficiency—in an individual or an organization—is aptitude or ability, the question is "how do we teach the skills necessary for people to act in a way that enhances intelligence?" When the deficiency, however, is action—in an individual or an organization—the question has to be "how do we inspire the use of existing aptitudes and abilities to enhance intelligence?"

In order to lead effectively in this new millennium, you need to be able to ask and answer both questions adequately. I've discussed many techniques and tips throughout this book on how to teach the skills necessary to increase inclusive intelligence. Next, I will spend some time discussing effective (and ineffective) ways to inspire action when aptitudes and abilities are already there.

1. *Model NEXT IQ behaviors at every level of leadership, not as an initiative or program but as personal investments by leaders in their own*

abilities to lead the organization. The shift from aptitude and ability to action has to first be visible in the behaviors of the leaders. How are leaders running their meetings? How do leaders evaluate performance? What behaviors get rewarded and what behaviors get put on notice for modification? As people in the organization see leaders focused on thinking, learning, and leading in a new way, they will be inspired to follow that example.

2. *Differentiate between the organizational value proposition for* THE NEXT *IQ and the individual proposition for* THE NEXT *IQ. And, do not call either value proposition a business case!* The organizational value proposition for THE *NEXT* IQ and the inclusive thinking it requires leans toward the increased productivity and innovation for the team and greater success for the organization. On the other hand, without first hearing the personal value proposition, it is difficult for individuals to fully be inspired by the organizational value proposition. The benefits of using THE *NEXT* IQ focuses on the increase in individual intelligence and excellence by thinking differently, not thinking more.

3. *Prime for change so that change is welcomed instead of feared.* Priming yourself, other individuals on your team, or an organization as a whole is the process of paving the path of change well before you expect anyone to travel on that path. The more change is framed in the context of individual value propositions, the more likely people are to be inspired to battle the pull of similarity, ease, and predictability to embrace and accept the change. Change has to feel like an "I want to," not an "I have to."

4. *Prioritize behaviors above commitment and intention. Measure the behaviors and hold people accountable for those behaviors.* No matter how persuasive the leadership is about the value of thinking, learning, and leading in a new way, individual and organizational behaviors will slowly get pulled back into old patterns if the new behaviors are not prioritized and measured. The belief in the benefit of multiple perspectives is very different than the action of actively seeking multiple perspectives. Dissect a project, a case, a deal, or a transaction into its micro components and ask how diverse perspectives can be infused into each micro component and hold people accountable for doing so.

Shifting from what you can do to what you actually do is where the rubber meets the road in the shift from the RETRO IQ to THE *NEXT* IQ. The ability to think and learn differently has no discernible impact in the lives of individuals or the success of organizations unless the actions are also different.

> Action is the real measure of intelligence.
>
> Napoleon Hill (American author, 1883–1970)

SHIFTING FROM COMPETITION TO COLLABORATION

Individuals and organizations generally have five different strategies for approaching problems.[6] Although each of these strategies may look distinct when employed by different individuals, teams, or organizations in different contexts, the general categories do effectively capture the ways in which we approach situations that require some form of action on our part.

- **Avoidance:** Direct or indirect denial of the problem to be solved; the refusal to take action; creating delays for the execution of action so as to not take the action. *All parties lose because the situation cannot get resolved.*
- **Accommodation:** Taking action fully in accordance with another party's requests or demands even though those requests or demands are contrary to one's own needs; accommodating external demands through inaction by allowing an unbeneficial circumstance to occur. *Accommodating party feels a loss and other party(ies) feel a win.*
- **Competition:** Adversarial interactions where both parties are fighting for their rights, needs, and demands with the purpose of having winners and losers. *One party wins, the other party(ies) lose.*
- **Compromise:** All parties agree to give up some of their rights, needs, and demands in order to secure other interests. *All parties win some and all parties lose some.*
- **Collaboration:** All parties work together to find a solution(s) where all parties feel that they have won. In a collaborative process, it's not that all parties get their rights, needs, and other

interests met. Instead, the collaborative process enables each party to see their interests as intertwined with the interests of the other party(ies) thereby making the solution feel like a win only when it is truly in the best interest of all involved. *All parties feel like they have won.*

The shift from the RETRO IQ to THE *NEXT* IQ is the shift from competition to collaboration. Since the RETRO IQ stresses individual intellect and expertise, it flows well into the competitive model because one individual's expertise has to be lesser than or more than another individual's expertise. One organization's expertise has to be better than or worse than another organization's expertise. This hierarchical perspective automatically activates the competitive mechanism and forces us to fight for success. When the fighting doesn't work or it becomes a protracted battle where the losses are quickly accumulating, the RETRO IQ defaults to the compromise strategy where the parties each give up something to secure something else in order to end the fight. The use of tools such as hostility, secrecy, and insults (among others) in fights usually prevents parties that have engaged in competition to transition into collaboration without extensive intervention. Competition results in either winners and losers or compromise, and compromise does not create new ideas or innovation.

The competitive model is a relic from the industrial economy when the world, the workplace, and individual lives were individualistic and mechanistic, where ideas could be traced to specific owners and communication controls were in the hands of a few powerful forces. In a global marketplace where social networks have more influence on people's lives than traditional media sources and the global economy is a necessity instead of an option for business success, using the competitive model is like using the fax machine. Yes, your document will eventually get to its intended recipient, but it will get there more slowly and in worse condition than if you send the document in a portable document format via the Web.

The 21st century demands collaboration for success, and collaboration requires full inclusion of multiple, diverse, and even contradictory perspectives. This shift into a collaborative mode is essential to activating THE *NEXT* IQ for individuals or organizations because including your competitors' perspectives as part of the solution is a key to thinking inclusively.

UNLIKELY PARTNERSHIPS

After decades of battles between environmental protection groups and companies with commercial truck fleets, each side had defined the other in negative, adversarial, and hostile terms. The environmental protection agencies were deemed to be radically anti-business, and companies that had trucking fleets out on the road were labeled as uncaring anti-environmentalists. Each side fought to mute the other with litigation, public relations campaigns, and legislative lobbying. The competitive model was in full effect: either the environmentalists would win and cripple the industry or industry would win and destroy the environment. As the competition heated up, the emissions from the transportation sector also increased,[7] as did the overall fuel expenditures for companies with truck fleets.[8]

In 2000, an unlikely collaboration between FedEx and the Environmental Defense Fund (EDF) changed how these two competing interests viewed not only themselves and their respective problems, but the industry as a whole. With fuel prices driving up the cost of doing business, FedEx was looking for innovative ways to reduce fuel expenses while increasing efficiencies. The EDF was urging trucking companies to reduce their emissions, but there weren't any alternatives (other than rail, which was not always feasible) that the organization could suggest to companies like FedEx.

When the EDF and FedEx teamed up in 2000, they realized that their collaboration needed to result in viable alternatives for industry that would reduce both fuel costs as well as fuel emissions. In other words, a joint interest was constructed that met the needs of both sides. They agreed to work together to create a "street-ready hybrid truck" that reduced soot emissions by 90 percent, increased fuel efficiency by 50 percent, offered the same functionality as a standard delivery truck, and would be cost competitive over the truck's lifetime.[9] This FedEx-EDF collaboration worked with "Eaton Corporation and Freightliner Custom Chassis Corporation to introduce the first available commercial hybrid delivery truck into service."[10]

As FedEx integrated these new hybrid trucks into its fleet, the FedEx-EDF collaboration worked together to entice more companies to replace their trucks with these new hybrid models. They also lobbied for government intervention and investment at all levels to make it easier for the new technology to continue to develop rapidly and to ease the cost of introducing the new trucks into companies that couldn't fully afford the initial investment. All the previous channels for battle were now channels for collaboration.

In 2005, WestStart-CALSTART, America's leading advanced transportation technologies consortium, recognized the FedEx-EDF collaboration with the Blue Sky Award for their "nearly single-handed placement of commercial hybrid trucks on the map for corporate America."[11]

According to the EDF's website: "As of 2010, FedEx operates one of the largest hybrid fleets in the industry, with more than 1,800 alternative energy vehicles worldwide, including the first all-electric parcel delivery trucks in the United States. Four electric FedEx trucks now operate in the Los Angeles area, home of smog. Their tailpipe emissions: zero."[12]

A glowing report for a commercial trucking fleet on the website of the Environmental Defense Fund? Absolutely. That's inclusive collaboration in action.

For those of you who may resist the notion of letting go of competition, collaboration is not the absence of competition. Collaboration can be very competitive, but the competition is over the ideas, not between people. If competition is focused on coming up with a better solution, a more innovative idea, or a simpler route to success, then individuals and organizations are incentivized to collaborate in order to compete at their best. Competition by itself cannot get anyone to think inclusively because it, by its nature, requires that you see yourself as against others. Collaboration, on the other hand, encourages you to think inclusively because different ideas allow you to compete better.

INSIGHT, ACTION, AND COLLABORATION IN THE *NEXT* IQ

In thinking about insight, action, and collaboration in THE *NEXT* IQ, certain questions often arise regarding the differences between insight and instinct, collective wisdom and groupthink, and crowdsourcing and inside experts. I'll comment on each of these issues in this section to further clarify what the shift to THE *NEXT* IQ fully entails.

THE NEXT *IQ in Focus: Informed Insight versus Reactive Instinct*

Shifting from information to insight requires a closer look at the difference between insight and instinct. While insight is information that has been processed by the intellect to become knowledge, instinct is often an intellect-bypassing shortcut.

In *Blink*, Malcolm Gladwell presents several case studies of situations where instinct led to a more positive outcome than deliberate intellectual reasoning.[13] Referring to these decision-making instincts as "thin slicing," Gladwell makes the argument that extremely thin slices of information can often result in the same outcomes as taking the time to analyze the full data. Our instincts are powerful tools we can use to quickly make decisions that may lead us to better outcomes than carefully packaged intellectual information. Yet, even as he touts the power of instincts, Gladwell warns that our socialized and contextual prejudices and stereotypes can often appear masked as instincts.

The example used by Gladwell of the J. Paul Getty Museum purchasing a kouros statue in the 1980s only to learn that it was a fantastically executed fake is referred to by many as evidence of the primacy of expert instincts. Although the Getty did a robust and thorough examination of the statue lasting over 18 months, it failed to discover what other experts immediately perceived within just a couple of seconds of viewing the kouros. The experts who saw the fake for what it was did indeed have excellent expert instincts, but Gladwell also points out that the people hired by the Getty to authenticate the sculpture were also experts. The Getty experts saw what they wanted to see because they were incentivized to see the statue as authentic. Therefore, even among experts, objective instincts are contextualized by people's internal incentives to believe what they want to believe instead of what is in front of them.

In understanding THE *NEXT* IQ, it is critical to understand the difference between *reactive instinct*, which relies on the narrowness of prejudices and stereotypes, and *informed insight*, which derives instinctive intelligence from experience and openness to input from diverse perspectives. As former Secretary of State Colin Powell proposes in his biography, *My American Journey*, "Dig up all the information you can, then go with your instincts. I use my intellect to form my instinct. Then I use my instinct to test all this data. Hey, instinct, does this sound right? Does it smell right, feel right, fit right?"[14] Informed insight is instinct that has been educated but not bound by intellect.

In *The Fifth Discipline*, Peter Senge notes that "[p]eople with high levels of personal mastery do not set out to integrate reason and intuition. Rather, they achieve it naturally—as a by-product of their commitment to use all the resources at their disposal. They cannot afford to choose between reason and intuition, or head and heart, any more than they would choose to walk on one leg or see with one eye."[15]

While intellect can learn from mistakes and solve problems through deliberation, intellect's reaction time can be much slower than instinct's. Intellect takes its time to really know if it is right or not. Instinct and intuition operate on what "feels right" even if they cannot point to the evidence that proves why they feel that way.

The informed insight aspect of THE *NEXT* IQ leverages the power of the instinct, but it filters an individual's instinct through an intellect that has been inspired by multiple perspectives from diverse sources. When instinct is filtered through an inclusive intelligence, the tendency to fall prey to false instincts like prejudices and stereotypes is significantly neutralized.

In Gladwell's example of the kouros, the experts who had the most intense instinctive reactions to the kouros were individuals who had actually experienced an archaeological dig before or had handled pieces of previously excavated kouros statues. Their insights were informed, not abstract. Similarly, the experts at the Getty also had informed instincts, but they were informed by the desire to see this kouros be the real thing, so they were led astray by what they wanted to see. If the Getty had created an initial screening mechanism that consisted of many different perspectives, it would not have fallen prey to the vulnerability of a few reactive instincts.

THE NEXT *IQ in Focus: Collective Wisdom versus Groupthink*

Shifting from aptitude to action sounds like a simple enough choice to make once you become aware of the need to make that choice; however, if you are part of a team and/or an organization where groupthink prevails, the ability to do something does not always translate into action. In his seminal works on groupthink in the 1970s, Irving Janis theorized that the "more amiability and esprit de corps there is among the members of a policy-making ingroup, the greater the danger that independent critical thinking will be replaced by groupthink, which is likely to result in irrational and dehumanizing actions against outgroups."[16] A group is especially vulnerable to groupthink when the group's members have homogeneous backgrounds and experiences, when the group is closed off to outside opinions, and when there is a high level of stress involved in the group's decision-making processes. Janis studied several critical decision-making moments in American history such as the failure to avoid the Japanese attack on Pearl Harbor in 1941 and the foiled Bay of Pigs invasion in 1961 to show how groupthink leads groups to (1) think too highly of their own capacities, (2) stereotype anybody not in the group as inferior, and (3) pressure people within the group to agree with the group by labeling disagreement as disloyalty.[17]

> When everyone thinks the same, nobody is thinking.
>
> Walter Lippmann (Pulitzer Prize–winning journalist, 1889–1974)

The need to differentiate between groupthink and collective wisdom is key to understanding the shift from aptitude to action that THE NEXT IQ requires. Groupthink happens when agreement is prioritized over the quality of thought and decision making in the group, which frequently results in keeping unpopular, minority, or new ideas from being expressed, heard, or accepted. As James Surowiecki illustrates so clearly in the *Wisdom of Crowds* with examples ranging from NASA's failure to prevent the *Columbia* shuttle disaster to the U.S. intelligence community's inability to prevent the 9/11 attacks, if a group does not have diversity of opinion, independence, and decentralized sources of information and networks, groupthink is not only probable, it is inevitable. Diversity (of identity, experience, thought, perspective, etc.) is critical for critical thinking, and engaging our NEXT IQ allows us to understand that encouraged disagreement may lead to better actions than unexamined agreement. As Mahatma Gandhi is quoted as saying—"Honest differences are often a healthy sign of progress."

The full intellectual aptitude and ability in a group is only maximized when diverse opinions are actively sought and integrated into the overall decision-making process. Without creating an opportunity for the full aptitude and ability of a group to be expressed, shifting from potential to action is challenging, if not impossible. When groupthink is confronted and neutralized, a group can benefit from its inherent capacity for collective wisdom, which is fundamentally more intelligent than the most intelligent individual in the group.

THE NEXT *IQ in Focus: Crowdsourcing versus Inside Experts*

Individuals can shift their focus from information to insight, and teams/organizations can shift their focus from groupthink to collective wisdom, but how do you get individuals from diverse backgrounds who are not part of any structured entity to collaborate in order to generate groundbreaking ideas and create innovative solutions for today's challenges? The global marketplace of the 21st century requires leaders that want to thrive in the modern economy to understand how to answer this question for themselves, their teams, and their organizations. The best ideas and solutions should no longer be presumed to originate within your organizations, but the best ideas and solutions are also not captured in the old model of "best practices research." Researching best practices is the process of analyzing the past, which has some limited value. This new information-driven millennium, however, requires that you generate new ideas and new solutions if you want to fully thrive. This is the core of THE *NEXT* IQ—that success today requires you to actively solicit, include, engage, and integrate different and even contradictory perspectives from diverse sources—and crowdsourcing is an incredibly effective model of creating collective centers of intelligence and expertise that benefit you but don't have to belong to you.

I have already explored examples like MyStarbucksIdea.com crowdsourcing for new ideas and Linux crowdsourcing for better software with fewer bugs, but crowdsourcing is developing an economic momentum that captures the power of THE *NEXT* IQ and uses it to change the way business gets done.

Take InnoCentive.com as an example. InnoCentive.com is the scientific innovation website to which major organizations such as Procter & Gamble, Lilly, NASA, and Accenture turn when they have complex problems that cannot be solved internally. So, who are these amazing problem solvers? Everyone. Anyone. Anyone can sign up to be a solver at InnoCentive.com. Organizations register challenges on the site along with what they are offering to a successful solver, and any solver can take a crack at solving the challenge. InnoCentive.com acts as the mediator and protects the intellectual property rights on both sides. Successful solvers get their promised rewards, and InnoCentive. com has negotiated another crowdsourcing success.

A 2007 study done by InnoCentive and professors from Harvard Business School and the Copenhagen Business School found that "the broadcast of problem information to outside scientists results in a 29.5% resolution rate for scientific problems that had previously remained unsolved inside the R&D laboratories of well-known science-driven firms. Problem solving success was associated with the ability to attract specialized scientists with diverse scientific interests. Furthermore, successful solvers created solutions to problems that were on the boundary or outside of their fields of expertise, showing that openness in science can trigger the transfer and transformation of knowledge from one scientific field to [an]other."[18]

With crowdsourcing, chemists can solve biology problems and biologists can solve math problems because our 20th-century workplaces are not yet organized to solve problems in a 21st-century way. InnoCentive.com also offers solvers the opportunity to create collaborative teams in Team Project Rooms (TPRs) to blend the best of crowdsourcing and collaboration. If you peek into InnoCentive.com's TPRs or scan their list of solvers, you see a sea of global faces from various countries, expertise, backgrounds, and languages.

Crowdsourcing can also lead to "emergent thinking," a critical thinking process that occurs when a group of people think together. Ideas emerge from the collective wisdom of crowds that bear no resemblance at all to the individual ideas of each of the people in the crowd.

A good example of an emergent property is the sweet taste of simple table sugar, or sucrose. At the elemental level, sugar is comprised of hydrogen, carbon, and oxygen. These basic chemicals combine in a unique way so that sugar is the result of this synthesis. However, none of the component parts of sugar possess the sweetness that is commonly known to be its distinguishing characteristic. Further, if one had no existing knowledge of the make-up of sucrose, one could not predict such a product of these elements combining. This is because the characteristics of sugar are not present in its component parts. In short, the sweetness emerges from the unique combination or synthesis of these basic elements.[19]

THE *NEXT* IQ INSIGHTS: CHAPTER 13

- The shift from the RETRO IQ to THE *NEXT* IQ is not about helping someone else or implementing a business case—it is about being the most intelligent that you can be in order to achieve the success you want to achieve.
- The shift from the RETRO IQ to THE *NEXT* IQ involves shifting your focus from information to insight, from aptitude to action, and from competition to collaboration.
- Informed insight is different than reactive instinct. The former is deliberately intelligent where the latter is unconsciously habitual. Similarly, collective wisdom is deliberate intelligence consisting of multiple perspectives while groupthink is many people thinking the same thing blindly. Crowdsourcing, like collective wisdom, is the deliberate intelligence of multiple voices creating new thought, where inside experts derive their expertise from information that is raw and lacks the insight created by multiple perspectives.

THE *NEXT* IQ ACTIONS: CHAPTER 13

- Actively shift from the RETRO IQ to THE *NEXT* IQ by focusing on insight as opposed to information. As you work on a project, ask yourself if you are applying information (available to all) or if you are applying insight (information processed by multiple perspectives).
- Identify two aptitudes (skills, talents, etc.) that you have that you currently do not translate into action at work. What could your workday look like if you acted on those two aptitudes on a regular basis?
- Shift from a competitive mindset to a collaborative mindset about something that you are in direct competition for right now. How are your competitors helping you seek new levels of insight and achievement? Can you see them as collaborators in your growth? Is it possible to team up with one or more competitor(s) in order to achieve your goals?

CONCLUSION

In my leadership workshops I administer a simple exercise to illustrate how shifting our thinking to integrate multiple perspectives can dramatically shift the trajectory and conclusion of a discussion. I organize participants into small groups and give each group the detailed annual budget of a fictitious family that wants to go on a very specific vacation. While each of the small groups gets the same description of the family and the same annual household budget, half the groups are instructed to evaluate the question "*Can* this family afford the vacation that it wants to take?" and the other half are instructed to evaluate the question "*How can* this family afford the vacation that it wants to take?"

The groups who work on the first set of instructions evaluate the budget to arrive at a yes-or-no response to the question "Can this family afford the vacation that it wants to take?" The question inevitably sends the groups down the path of finding the right answer between two possible answers, and these groups tend to become more argumentative, and they rarely reach consensus. When they report on their processes and conclusions, they usually discuss how people disagreed with each other and how they had to resort to a "majority rule" type of analysis in order to complete the exercise.

The groups who work on the second set of instructions evaluate the budget to create a solution. They discuss how this family can rearrange its budget in order to make its vacation a reality. They work to solve a problem instead of reacting to a set of limited possibilities. When these groups report on their processes and conclusions, they talk about how they shared their own personal strategies when faced with similar budgeting dilemmas, and they comment on what they learned from each other as they completed the exercise. Rarely does a group given this set of instructions come back with a yes-or-no answer. They return with a solution to a problem.

The difference between these two sets of instructions is one simple three-letter word: *how*. This one word shifts the way people think about the problem. With this one word present, the group dynamics shift from competition to collaboration, from finding the right answer to creating solutions.

This shift is the shift to THE *NEXT* IQ.

By changing *how* the question is asked, the dynamics of how people communicate, seek different perspectives, and solve problems is fundamentally changed. This shift is the shift that individual leaders and organizations can make deliberately if they employ the principles and tools discussed throughout this book.

In 2011, the world watched as the Arab Spring blazed a trail of revolution through Tunisia, Egypt, Syria, and Libya to name just a few countries. We rode the ups and downs of incredible volatility in the global financial markets. We waited to see what Greece would do to save itself from bankruptcy, and we watched the political debacle of the debt-ceiling talks in Washington, D.C. We watched countries try to recover from more natural disasters per annum than ever before in recorded history, and we watched riots and protests break out with such regularity that they became a staple of everyday news coverage. We announced our revenge against Osama bin Laden while we fretted about how many soldiers were still in Iraq and when the war in Afghanistan would end.

The common thread weaving all these events together was that all across the world, people were searching for leadership that was consistent with the needs of the world entering this volatile second decade of this new millennium. In a world of uncertainty, change, and volatility, we wanted leaders who could actively solve the problems of the day without getting mired in the binary arguments of right versus wrong. The less we received that leadership, the more the uncertainty and volatility increased.

The commonality in the political, economic, social, organizational, and personal volatility of the day is that we are seeking leaders who can think and lead in ways that make sense in today's world. The dissatisfaction that we feel toward our leaders is partially caused by our collective understanding that the way we used to do things can no longer work. THE *NEXT* IQ is the start of the conversation on how we need to think, learn, and lead differently in order to thrive in today's reality.

Leaders in all arenas around the globe today have to lead organizations and individuals in unprecedented conditions where easy answers are rare and the consequences of bad leadership are irreversible. (Think of the debt ceiling crisis in August 2011.) Leaders can stick to the RETRO IQ, the rules of intelligence with which they are comfortable, and they can force a zero sum game where people are seeking right versus wrong and yes versus no answers to questions that are far too complex to be reduced to binary simplicities. Leaders can cling to their individual constructs of intelligence where they focus on singular expertise and narrow definitions of knowledge. Leaders can do and do the above, and they may be fine temporarily, but they are risking their long-term success and their ultimate impact. It is the way of Enron and Circuit City, the way of short-term survival and long-term disaster.

Or, leaders can shift to THE *NEXT* IQ. This next level of intelligence requires more on the front end, and it delivers more in the long run. The leaders who shift to this new way of thinking realize that the way you think can dramatically shift how you think and what results from your thinking. It is the difference between "*Can* you do something?" and "*How can* you do something?" The former requires a yes or no, while the latter presumes a yes and looks to how the yes can be achieved.

This new paradigm of intelligence challenges those who are ready to think and solve problems at a higher level to understand that this next level of intelligence is delicately balanced at the intersection of intelligence, leadership, and inclusion—three different fields of inquiry that have coalesced into one cohesive new leadership strategy that is not only relevant but incredibly necessary for the realities of this new millennium. It begins with the understanding that leadership requires us to answer questions from a "yes, how" perspective, and it progresses to seeking the diverse perspectives to figure out the details of the how.

The reality that can be created when we focus on a "yes, how" framework can transform disagreements back to dialogs, and we can start to look for different perspectives as assets to be leveraged instead of differences to be neutralized.

In a world where change is inevitable but growth is optional, purposing to change the way you think is the critical choice you need to make in order to grow. THE *NEXT* IQ is that change from a parochial mindset to a global mindset, and it is the transformation of individual intelligence to insightful intelligence. With raw information no longer being as valuable as actionable knowledge, the only way to quickly gather and analyze necessary information is to have multiple diverse perspectives filter it to reveal all of its possibilities.

The ancient fable of the blind men and the elephant reminds us that each of us has the potential to either argue that our own perspective is more right than others or actively seek the other perspectives in order to inform and enhance our perspective. The fable reveals a lesson that is more relevant than ever today—each of us can be completely right with what we know and equally incomplete in how much our knowledge allows us to understand the totality of the situation. As the men fought about whose perspective best described an elephant that none of them had actually seen, the ability to view the perspective from a global mindset and deliberately create new intelligence shifted them from "which perspective is right" to "what does reality look like if each of our perspectives is right."

ENDNOTES

INTRODUCTION

1. Andy Serwer, "Starbucks Fix: Howard Schultz Spills the Beans on His Plans to Save the Company He Founded," *CNNMoney*, January 18, 2008, http://money.cnn.com/2008/01/17/news/newsmakers/starbucks .fortune/index.htm?postversion=2008011805.

2. Between March 19, 2008, and March 19, 2010, the Dow Jones Industrial Average fell 11.22 percent from $12,099.66 to $10,741.98; the S&P 500 fell 10.67 percent from 1298.42 to 1159.90; and the NASDAQ (where Starbucks is listed) rose 8.22 percent from 2209.96 to 2391.28.

3. Ben Elowitz and Charlene Li, "The World's Most Valuable Brands. Who's Most Engaged? ENGAGEMENTdb Ranking the Top 100 Global Brands," embedded in Erick Schonfeld, "The Most Engaged Brands on the Web," *TechCrunch*, July 20, 2009, http://bx.businessweek.com/ marketing-strategy-in-web-20-age/view?url=http%3A%2F%2Fwww .techcrunch.com%2F2009%2F07%2F20%2Fthe-most-engaged-brands-on-the-web%2F.

4. Mark Clothier, "Circuit City to Fire 3,400, Hire Less Costly Workers (Update8)," *Bloomberg*, March 28, 2007, http://www .bloomberg.com/apps/news?pid=newsarchive&sid=awBiOvPYHhgc.

5. Todd Sullivan, "Circuit City: How Can Shareholders Stand for This?" *Seeking Alpha*, December 25, 2007, http://seekingalpha.com/ article/58315-circuit-city-how-can-shareholders-stand-for-this.

CHAPTER 1

1. Esther Dyson, George Gilder, George Keyworth, and Alvin Toffler, "Cyberspace and the American Dream: A Magna Carta for the Knowledge Age," in *Future Insight 1.2* (Washington, DC: The Progress & Freedom Foundation, 1994).

2. Thomas L. Friedman, *The World Is Flat: A Brief History of the Twenty-First Century* (New York: Farrar, Straus and Giroux, 2005).

3. Steve Ballmer, *Brainy Quotes*, www.brainyquote.com/quotes/quotes/s/steveballm368857.html

4. James Turley, "The New Global Mindset," *BusinessWeek*, January 26, 2010, http://www.businessweek.com/managing/content/jan2010/ca20100126_437043.htm (accessed June 19, 2011).

5. Ibid.

6. Anil K. Gupta and Vijay Govindarajan, "Cultivating a Global Mindset," *The Academy of Management Executive (1993–2005)* 16, no. 1 (February 2002): 116–126.

7. Anne Nemer, "The New Manager—Developing a Global Mindset" (speech, AIMA 35th National Management Convention, 30 September–1 October, 2008, Regal Room, Trident Hotel, Mumbai), http://www.business.pitt.edu/katz/global/aima-speech.html.

8. C. George Boeree, *Intelligence and IQ*, http://webspace.ship.edu/cgboer/intelligence.html (Shippensburg, PA: Shippensburg University, 2003).

9. Tim O'Reilly, "What Is Web 2.0: Design Patterns and Business Models for the Next Generation of Software," *O'Reilly*, September 30, 2005, http://oreilly.com/web2/archive/what-is-web-20.html (accessed June 19, 2011).

CHAPTER 2

1. Anna T. Cianciolo and Robert J. Sternberg, *A Brief History of Intelligence* (Malden, MA: Blackwell, 2004).

2. "Intelligence and Achievement Testing: Is the Half-Full Glass Getting Fuller?" *American Psychological Association*, June 17, 2004, http://www.apa.org/research/action/intelligence-testing.aspx.

3. Walter Lippmann, "The Mental Age of Americans," *New Republic* 32, no. 412 (October 25, 1922): 213–215; no. 413 (November 1, 1922): 246–248; no. 414 (November 8, 1922): 275–277; no. 415 (November 15, 1922): 297–298; no. 416 (November 22, 1922): 328–330; no. 417 (November 29, 1922): 9–11.

4. James R. Flynn, "Massive IQ Gains in 14 Nations: What IQ Tests Really Measure," *Psychological Bulletin* 101, no. 2 (1987): 171–191; J. R. Flynn, "The Mean IQ of Americans: Massive Gains 1932 to 1978," *Psychological Bulletin* 95, no. 1 (1984): 29–51.

5. James R. Flynn, *What Is Intelligence?: Beyond the Flynn Effect* (London: Cambridge University Press, 2007).

6. James Surowiecki, *The Wisdom of Crowds* (New York: Anchor Books, 2005).

7. Katherine Shrader, "Over 3,600 Intelligence Professional Tapping into 'Intellipedia,'" *USA Today*, Inside Technology, November 2, 2006, http://www.usatoday.com/tech/news/techinnovations/2006-11-02-intellipedia_x.htm (accessed June 29, 2011).

8. Scott Shane, "Logged In and Sharing Gossip, er, Intelligence," *New York Times*, September 2, 2007, http://www.nytimes.com/2007/09/02/weekinreview/02shane.html (accessed June 29, 2011).

9. Robert Cardillo, "Remarks and Q&A by the Deputy Director for Analysis, Defense Intelligence Agency" (Transcripts from the 2007 Analytic Transformation Symposium, Office of the Director of National Intelligence, Chicago, Illinois, September 5, 2007–September 6, 2007), http://www.dni.gov/speeches/20070905_speech.pdf (accessed June 29, 2011).

10. Eric S. Raymond, *The Cathedral and the Bazaar* (Sebastopol, CA: O'Reilly Media, 1999).

11. *WordIQ*, s.v. "computer bug," http://www.wordiq.com/definition/Computer_bug (accessed September 10, 2011).

12. Excerpted from Eric S. Raymond, "The Cathedral and the Bazaar," version 3.0 (2000), http://catb.org/~esr/writings/homesteading/cathedral-bazaar/index.html. Rule 3 is a quote from Fred Brooks, *The*

Mythical Man-Month, Chapter 11. Rule 13 is a quote from Antoine de Saint-Exupéry.

13. David A. Wheeler, "Why Open Source Software/Free Software (OSS/FS, FLOSS, or FOSS)? Look at the Numbers!" last modified April 16, 2007, http://www.dwheeler.com/oss_fs_why.html (accessed June 19, 2011).

14. Ioannis Samoladas, Ioannis Stamelos, Lefteris Angelis, and Apostolos Oikonomou, "Open Source Software Development Should Strive for Even Greater Code Maintainability," *Communications of the ACM* 47, no. 10 (2004): 83–87.

15. Joe Clabby, "Linux—Enterprise Ready?" Research report (Bloor Research, London, January 9, 2003), http://www.bloorresearch.com/research/Research-Report/468/linux-enterprise-ready.html.

16. Helen D'Antoni, "Hurdles Aside, Open Source Wins Converts," *InformationWeek*, August 30, 2004, http://www.informationweek.com/news/42700016.

17. Scott E. Page, *The Difference: How the Power of Diversity Creates Better Groups, Firms, Schools, and Societies* (Princeton, NJ: Princeton University Press, 2007).

18. Ibid., 375.

19. James Turley, "The New Global Mindset," *BusinessWeek*, January 26, 2010, http://www.businessweek.com/managing/content/jan2010/ca20100126_437043.htm (accessed June 19, 2011).

20. Robert G. Lord, Roseanne J. Foti, and Christy L. De Vader, "A Test of Leadership Categorization Theory: Internal Structure, Information Processing, and Leadership Perceptions," *Organizational Behavior and Human Performance* 34, no. 3 (December 1984): 343–378.

21. Robert S. Rubin, Lynn K. Bartels, and William H. Bommer, "Are Leaders Smarter or Do They Just Seem That Way? Exploring Perceived Intellectual Competence and Leadership Emergence," *Social Behavior and Personality* 30, no. 2 (2002): 105–118.

22. Fred E. Fiedler, "The Curious Role of Cognitive Resources in Leadership," in *Multiple Intelligences and Leadership*, ed. R. E. Riggio, S. E. Murphy, and F. J. Pirozzolo, 91–104 (Mahwah, NJ: Erlbaum, 2002).

23. Lisa Abend, "Spain's Pregnant Defense Minister," *Time*, April 15, 2008, http://www.time.com/time/world/article/0,8599,1730927,00.html.

24. Helene Zuber, "Charming Carme: Spain's Defense Minister Makes Her Mark in a Macho World," *Spiegel Online International*, April 15, 2010, http://www.spiegel.de/international/europe/0,1518,688785-2,00.html.

CHAPTER 3

1. L. J. Kamin, "The Pioneers of IQ Testing," in *The Bell Curve Debate: History, Documents, Opinions*, ed. Russell Jacoby and Naomi Glauberman (New York: Times Books, 1995).

2. Ibid.

3. C. Spearman, "'General Intelligence,' Objectively Determined and Measured." *American Journal of Psychology* 15 (April 1904): 201–293.

4. Louis L. Thurstone, *Primary Mental Abilities* (Chicago: University of Chicago Press, 1938.)

5. Howard Gardner, *Frames of Mind: The Theory of Multiple Intelligence* (New York: Basic Books, 1983.)

6. Robert J. Sternberg, *Beyond IQ: A Triarchic Theory of Intelligence* (Cambridge, UK: Cambridge University Press, 1985.)

7. Ibid.

8. Peter Salovey and John Mayer, "Emotional Intelligence," *Imagination, Cognition, and Personality* 9, no. 3 (1990): 185–211.

9. Daniel Goleman, *Emotional Intelligence* (New York: Bantam, 1995).

10. Carol S. Dweck, *Mindset: The New Psychology of Success* (New York: Random House, 2007).

11. Lisa S. Blackwell, Kali H. Trzesniewski, and Carol S. Dweck, "Implicit Theories of Intelligence Predict Achievement Across an Adolescent Transition: A Longitudinal Study and an Intervention." *Child Development* 78, no. 1 (January–February 2007): 246–263.

12. Laura J. Kray and Michael P. Haselhuhn, "Implicit Negotiation Beliefs and Performance: Experimental and Longitudinal Evidence," *Journal of Personality and Social Psychology* 93, no. 1 (July 2007): 49–64.

13. Peter A. Heslin and Gary P. Latham, "The Effect of Implicit Person Theory on Performance Appraisals," *Journal of Applied Psychology* 90, no. 5 (September 2005): 842–856.

14. C. George Boeree, *Intelligence and IQ*, http://webspace.ship.edu/cgboer/intelligence.html (Shippensburg, PA: Shippensburg University, 2003).

15. Adapted from Eric S. Raymond, "The Cathedral and the Bazaar," version 3.0 (2000), http://catb.org/~esr/writings/homesteading/cathedral-bazaar/index.html.

CHAPTER 4

1. Max De Pree, *Leadership Jazz: The Essential Elements of a Great Leader* (New York: Doubleday, 1992), 5.

2. M. Rex Miller, *The Millennium Matrix: Reclaiming the Past, Reframing the Future of the Church* (San Francisco: Jossey-Bass, 2004), 110.

3. Thomas Carlyle, *On Heroes, Hero-Worship, and the Heroic History* (Boston: Houghton Mifflin, 1841).

4. J. Thomas Wren, *The Leader's Companion: Insights on Leadership Through the Ages* (New York: Free Press, 1995), 129–130.

5. K. Lewin and R. Lippitt, "An Experimental Approach to the Study of Autocracy and Democracy: A Preliminary Note," *Sociometry* 1, no. 3/4 (January–April 1938): 292–300.

6. D. Katz, Nathan Maccoby, Gerald Gurin, and Lucretia G. Floor, *Productivity, Supervision, and Morale among Railroad Workers* (Ann Arbor: Survey Research Center, Institute for Social Research, University of Michigan, 1951).

7. J. Woodward, *Management and Technology* (London: Her Majesty's Stationery Office, 1958).

8. Fred E. Fiedler, *A Theory of Leadership Effectiveness* (New York: McGraw-Hill, 1967).

9. Fred Dansereau, Jr., James Cashman, and George Graen, "Instrumentality Theory and Equity Theory as Complementary Approaches in Predicting the Relationship of Leadership and Turnover among Managers," *Organizational Behavior and Human Performance* 10, no. 2 (October 1973): 184–200; Fred Dansereau, Jr., George Graen, and William J. Haga, "A Vertical Dyad Linkage Approach to Leadership within Formal Organizations," *Organizational Behavior and Human Performance* 13, no. 1 (February 1975): 46–78.

10. George Graen, James Cashman, Steven Ginsburg, and William Schiemann, "Effects of Linking-Pin on the Quality of Working Life of Lower Participants," *Administrative Science Quarterly* 22, no. 3 (September 1977): 491–504; George Graen, Robert C. Liden, and William Hoel, "Role of Leadership in the Employee Withdrawal Process," *Journal of Applied Psychology* 67, no. 6 (December 1982): 868–872; George Graen, Michael A. Novak, and Patricia Sommerkamp, "The Effects of Leader-Member Exchange and Job Design on Productivity and Satisfaction: Testing a Dual Attachment Model," *Organizational Behavior and Human Performance* 30, no. 1 (August 1982): 109–131; George B. Graen and Terri A. Scandura, "Toward a Psychology of Dyadic Organizing," *Research in Organizational Behavior* 9 (1987): 175–208; George Graen and William Schiemann, "Leader-Member Agreement: A Vertical Dyad Linkage Approach," *Journal of Applied Psychology* 63, no. 2 (April 1978): 206–212; Mary Uhl-Bien, George Graen, and Terry Scandura, "Implications of Leader-Member Exchange (LMX) for Strategic Human Resource Management Systems: Relationships as Social Capital for Competitive Advantage," in *Research in Personnel and Human Resource Management*, ed. G. Ferris, vol. 18, 137–185 (Greenwich, CT: JAI Press, 2000).

11. Ursula Hess, Rainer Banse, and Arvid Kappas, "The Intensity of Facial Expression Is Determined by Underlying Affective States and Social Situations," *Journal of Personality and Social Psychology* 69, no. 2 (August 1995): 280–288.

12. Dov Eden and Uri Leviatan, "Implicit Leadership Theory as a Determinant of the Factor Structure Underlying Supervisory Behavior Scales," *Journal of Applied Psychology* 66, no. 6 (December 1975): 736–741.

13. Bernard M. Bass, *Transformational Leadership: Industrial, Military, and Educational Impact* (Mahwah, NJ: Erlbaum, 1998); B. M. Bass and B. J. Avolio, eds., *Improving Organizational Effectiveness through Transformational Leadership* (Thousand Oaks, CA: Sage, 1994).

14. C. Dean Pielstick, "The Transforming Leader: A Meta-Ethnographic Analysis," *Community College Review* 26, no. 3 (Winter 1998): 15–34; Beverly Alimo-Metcalfe and Robert J. Alban-Metcalfe, "The Development of a New Transformational Leadership Questionnaire," *The Journal of Occupational & Organizational Psychology* 74, no. 1 (March 2001): 1–27.

15. "What Is Servant Leadership?" Greenleaf Center for Servant Leadership, http://www.greenleaf.org/whatissl/ (accessed May 1, 2011).

16. Ken Wilber, *A Theory of Everything: An Integral Vision for Business, Politics, Science, and Spirituality* (Boston: Shambhala, 2001).

17. J. Antonakis, A. T. Cianciolo, and R. J. Sternberg, eds., *Leadership: Past, Present, and Future* (Thousand Oaks, CA: Sage, 2004).

18. Jonathan Martin, "Is Rick Perry Dumb?" *Politico*, August 29, 2011, http://www.politico.com/news/stories/0811/62214.html.

19. Douglas MacKinnon, "Was Barack Obama Smart Enough to Make It as an Air Force Pilot?" *The Washington Examiner*, August 30, 2011, http://washingtonexaminer.com/opinion/op-eds/2011/08/was-barack-obama-smart-enough-make-it-air-force-pilot.

CHAPTER 5

1. Eric Schnapper, "Affirmative Action and the Legislative History of the Fourteenth Amendment," *Virginia Law Review* 71 (June 1985): 753.

2. Sujit Raman, "Caste in Stone: Consequences of India's Affirmative Action Policies," *Harvard International Review* (September 22, 1999).

3. C. Seierstad and T. Opsahl, "For the Few Not the Many? The Effects of Affirmative Action on Presence, Prominence, and Social

Capital of Female Directors in Norway," *Scandinavian Journal of Management* 27, no. 1 (September 30, 2010): 44–54.

4. Richard Kahlenberg, "The French Twist on Affirmative Action," *The Chronicle of Higher Education*, July 7, 2010, http://chronicle.com/blogPost/The-French-Twist-on-Affirma/25340/.

5. Associated Press, "Pregnant Defense Minister a First in Spain," MSNBC.com, April 16, 2008, http://www.msnbc.msn.com/id/24162934/ns/world_news-europe/.

6. Brian S. Lowery, Miguel M. Unzueta, Eric D. Knowles, and Phillip Atiba Goff, "Concern for the In-Group and Opposition to Affirmative Action," *Journal of Personality and Social Psychology* 90, no. 6 (2006).

7. Ian Traynor, "'I Don't Hate Muslims. I Hate Islam' Says Holland's Rising Political Star," *The Observer*, February 17, 2008, http://www.guardian.co.uk/world/2008/feb/17/netherlands.islam.

8. Erik Hayden, "End Affirmative Action to Avoid White Backlash," *The Atlantic Wire*, August 2, 2010, http://www.theatlanticwire.com/politics/2010/08/end-affirmative-action-to-avoid-white-backlash/19230/.

9. Steven Erlanger, "Top French Schools, Asked to Diversify, Fear for Standards," *New York Times*, June 30, 2010, http://www.nytimes.com/2010/07/01/world/europe/01ecoles.html?ref=stevenerlanger.

10. "Business Case for Diversity," Chubb Group of Insurance Companies, http://www.chubb.com/diversity/chubb4450.html (accessed April 20, 2011).

11. Siemens Global Website, http://www.siemens.com/sustainability/en/core-topics/employees/diversity (accessed April 20, 2011).

12. Scott E. Page, "Making the Difference: Applying a Logic of Diversity," *Academy of Management Perspectives* (November 2007).

13. Ibid., 9.

14. McKinsey & Co., *Women Matter 3*, 2009, http://www.mckinsey.com/locations/paris/home/womenmatter/pdfs/Women_matter_dec2009_english.pdf (accessed April 21, 2011).

15. Anshuman Prasad, "Understanding Workplace Empowerment as Inclusion: A Historical Investigation of the Discourse of Difference in the United States," *Journal of Applied Behavioral Science* 37, no. 1 (March 2001): 51–69.

16. Herminia Ibarra, "Personal Networks of Women and Minorities in Management: A Conceptual Framework," *Academy of Management Review* 18, no. 1 (January 1993): 56–87; Michael E. Mor Barak, David

A. Cherin, and Sherry Berkman, "Organizational and Personal Dimensions in Diversity Climate," *Journal of Applied Behavioral Science* 34, no. 1 (March 1998): 82–104.

17. Candice Silverstone, "Women as the Next Smart Business Strategy," Deloitte Consulting (April 20, 2011), http://deloittesa.wordpress.com/2011/04/20/women-as-the-next-smart-business-strategy-tapping-female-talent-increases-the-bottom-line/ (accessed April 20, 2011).

18. Peter Hom, quoted in "Women and Minorities' High Quit Rates Make Corporate Diversity Difficult," Knowledge@W.P. Carey (April 25, 2007), http://knowledge.wpcarey.asu.edu/article.cfm?articleid=1404.

19. Lisa Hope Pelled, Gerald E. Ledford, Jr., and Susan Albers Mohrman, "Demographic Dissimilarity and Workplace Inclusion," *Journal of Management Studies* 36, no. 7 (December 1999): 1014.

20. Quinetta M. Roberson, "Disentangling the Meanings of Diversity and Inclusion" (CAHRS Working Paper #04-05, Center for Advanced Human Resource Studies Working Paper Series, Cornell University, Ithaca, NY, June 2004), http://digitalcommons.ilr.cornell.edu/cahrswp/12.

21. Ibid.

22. Frederick A. Miller and Judith H. Katz, *The Inclusion Breakthrough: Unleashing the Real Power of Diversity* (San Francisco: Berrett-Koehler, 2002).

23. Eric Davis, "Inclusion Measurement: Tracking the Intangible," *TrendWatcher* 504 (July 14, 2010), http://www.i4cp.com/trendwatchers/2010/07/14/inclusion-measurement-tracking-the-intangible (accessed June 11, 2011).

24. "Advancing Inclusiveness Model (AIM) for Excellence," The Center for Legal Inclusiveness, http://www.legalinclusiveness.org/clientuploads/pdf/aimmodel.pdf (accessed April 23, 2011).

25. See "Minorities and Women," National Association for Law Placement, http://www.nalp.org/minoritieswomen (accessed April 23, 2011) for additional details.

26. Calvert Investments, *Examining the Cracks in the Ceiling: A Survey of Corporate Diversity Practices of the S&P 100* (October 2010).

27. Alliance for Board Diversity, *Missing Pieces: Women and Minorities on Fortune 500 Boards* (2011).

28. Ibid., 4.

29. Calvert Investments, 4.

30. Brian D. Smedley, Adrienne Y. Stith, and Alan R. Nelson, eds., *Unequal Treatment: Racial and Ethnic Disparities in Health Care*, Institute of Medicine of the National Academies (Washington, DC: The National Academies Press, 2003).

31. Sullivan Commission, "Missing Persons: Minorities in the Health Professions: A Report of the Sullivan Commission on Diversity in the Healthcare Workforce" (2005), http://www.aacn.nche.edu/media/pdf/sullivanreport.pdf.

32. Ibid, i.

33. Samuel R. Sommers, "On Racial Diversity and Group Decision Making: Identifying Multiple Effects of Racial Composition on Jury Deliberations," *Journal of Personality and Social Psychology* 90, no. 4 (2006): 597–612.

34. Hassan Abolghasemi, Nasim S. Hosseini-Divkalauyi, and Fariba Seighali, "Blood Donor Incentives: A Step Forward or Backward," *Asian Journal Transfusion Science* 4, no. 1 (2010): 9–13.

35. Ibid.

36. Dan Ariely, Anat Bracha, and Stephan Meier, "Doing Good or Doing Well? Image Motivation and Monetary Incentives in Behaving Prosocially," *American Economic Review* 99, no. 1 (2009): 544–555.

CHAPTER 6

1. This idea was inspired by Anthony Pignataro's blog at http://anthonypignataro.blogspot.com/2009/02/same-story-different-headlines.html.

2. Sue Kirchhoff and Barbara Hagenbaugh, "Bernanke Sees Possible End to Recession in 2009," *USA Today*, February 25, 2009, http://www.usatoday.com/money/economy/2009-02-24-bernanke-economy_N.htm (accessed June 16, 2011).

3. Catherine Rampell and Jack Healy, "Fed Chairman Says Recession Will Extend through the Year," *New York Times*, February 24, 2009, http://www.nytimes.com/2009/02/25/business/economy/25econ.html?hp.

4. Chris Isidore, "Bernanke: Recovery Will Take Years," *CNNMoney*, February 24, 2009, http://money.cnn.com/2009/02/24/news/economy/bernanke/index.htm?postversion=2009022410.

5. Mark Felsenthal and Alister Bull, "Bernanke Says Recession to Linger but Banks Will Survive," *Reuters*, February 24, 2009, http://www.reuters.com/article/2009/02/24/us-usa-fed-bernanke-idUSTRE51L1SS20090224.

6. Testimony of Chairman Ben S. Bernanke—Semiannual Monetary Policy Report to the Congress, *Board Governors of the Federal Reserve System* (February 24, 2009), http://www.federalreserve.gov/newsevents/testimony/bernanke20090224a.htm.

7. Ernst & Young, "Winning in a Polycentric World: Globalization and the Changing World of Business," 2011, http://www.ey.com/GL/en/Issues/Business-environment/Winning-in-a-polycentric-world—globalization-and-the-changing-world-of-business—Responding-to-a-polycentric-world (accessed June 16, 2011).

8. Ibid.

9. Ibid.

10. John Jay Chapman, *Brainyquote.com*, http://www.brainyquote.com/.

11. Margaret J. Wheatley, *BrainyQuote*, http://brainyquote.com.

12. Steve Case, *BrainyQuote*, http://brainyquote.com.

13. Howard Winters, as quoted by Anne-Marie Cantwell, in "Howard Dalton Winters: In Memoriam" (unpublished paper, Midwest Archaeological Conference, Lexington, KY, 1994).

14. I received this graphic from a friend of mine several years ago and have been unable to find its origins.

15. Wayne Gretzky, *The Quotations Page*, http://www.quotationspage.com/quote/39110.html.

CHAPTER 7

1. Alvin Toffler, http://www.quotationspage.com/quotes/Alvin_Toffler/.

2. Marguerite Rigoglioso, "Diverse Backgrounds and Personalities Can Strengthen Groups," *Stanford Graduate School of Business News* (August 2006).

3. Katherine W. Phillips, Elizabeth A. Mannix, Margaret A. Neale, and Deborah H. Gruenfeld, "Diverse Groups and Information Sharing: The Effect of Congruent Ties," *Journal of Experimental Social Psychology* 40 (July 2004): 497–510.

4. Rigoglioso, "Diverse Backgrounds and Personalities Can Strengthen Groups."

5. Ibid.

6. Ibid.

7. Google, "Diversity in Our Culture and Workplace," http://www .google.com/diversity/culture.html (accessed June 16, 2011).

8. Google, "Users and Communities," http://www.google.com/ diversity/users.html (accessed June 16, 2011).

9. David Lieberman, "Blockbuster Files for Chapter 11 Bank-ruptcy, Will Reorganize," *USA Today*, September 23, 2010, http://www .usatoday.com/money/media/2010-09-23-blockbuster23_ST_N.htm.

10. Erick Schonfeld, "Netflix Now the Largest Single Source of Internet Traffic in North America," *TechCrunch*, May 17, 2011, http:// techcrunch.com/2011/05/17/netflix-largest-internet-traffic/; "Global Internet Phenomena Report: Spring 2011," *Sandvine Intelligent Broad-band Networks*, http://www.sandvine.com/news/global_broadband_ trends.asp (accessed June 18, 2011).

11. Steve Lohr, "Netflix Competitors Learn the Power of Teamwork," *New York Times*, July 28, 2009, http://www.nytimes.com/2009/07/28/ technology/internet/28netflix.html.

12. Edward De Bono, *Six Thinking Hats: An Essential Approach to Business Management* (New York: Little, Brown, 1985).

CHAPTER 8

1. U.S. Department of Transportation, Federal Highway Admin-istration, http://www.fhwa.dot.gov (accessed April 30, 2011), and the National Highway Traffic Safety Administration, http://www.nhtsa .gov (accessed April 30, 2011).

2. "What Really Went Wrong with Enron? A Culture of Evil?" Markkula Center for Applied Ethics, Santa Clara University, March 5, 2002, http://www.scu.edu/ethics/publications/ethicalperspectives/ enronpanel.html (accessed April 30, 2011).

3. Ibid.

4. Ibid.

5. Venus Williams, "Wimbledon Has Sent Me a Message: I'm Only a Second-Class Champion: The Time Has Come for It to Do the

Right Thing: Pay Men and Women Equal Prize Money," *The Sunday Times*, http://www.timesonline.co.uk/tol/sport/tennis/article679416.ece (accessed July 5, 2011).

6. Imagined dialog informed by National Public Radio, "Billie Jean King Cheers Equal Pay at Wimbledon: Interview with Rebecca Roberts," *All Things Considered, National Public Radio*, February 24, 2007, http://www.npr.org/templates/story/story.php?storyId=7590503 (accessed June 1, 2011).

7. E. G. Boring, "A New Ambiguous Figure," *American Journal of Psychology* 42 (1930): 444.

CHAPTER 9

1. Monica Biernat, Melvin Manis, and Thomas Nelson, "Stereotypes and Standards of Judgment," *Journal of Personality and Social Psychology* 60, no. 4 (April 1991): 5–20, excerpted from WISELI, "Benefits and Challenges of Diversity in Academic Settings," Women in Science & Engineering Leadership Institute, University of Wisconsin-Madison, 2010.

2. Monica Biernat and Melvin Manis, "Shifting Standards and Stereotype-based Judgments," *Journal of Personality and Social Psychology* 66 (1994): 5–20, excerpted from WISELI, "Benefits and Challenges of Diversity in Academic Settings."

3. D. Clayson, M. L. Klassen, and C. R. Jasper, "Perceived Effect of a Salesperson's Stigmatized Appearance on Store Image: An Experimental Study of Students' Perceptions," *The International Review of Retail, Distribution and Consumer Research* 6, no. 2 (1996): 216–224; *Academic Periodical Search* (October 26, 2003).

4. Mark A. Drummond, "Section of Litigation Tackles Implicit Bias: Implicit Bias Can Be Eliminated by Awareness," *American Bar Association, Litigation News* 36, no. 3 (February 1, 2011): 21.

5. Anthony G. Greenwald, Debbie E. McGhee, and Jordan L. K. Schwartz, "Measuring Individual Differences in Implicit Cognition: The Implicit Association Test," *Journal of Personality and Social Psychology* 74, no. 6 (June 1998): 1464–1480.

6. Annie Murphy Paul, "Where Bias Begins: The Truth about Stereotypes," *Psychology Today* (May 1, 1998), http://www.psychologytoday.com.

7. Project Implicit, "Archive for the 'Racial Attitudes and Stereotypes' Category," September 4, 2009, http://projectimplicit.wordpress.com/category/racial-attitudes-and-stereotypes/ (accessed May 1, 2011).

8. Brett Molesworth and Betty Chang, "Predicting Pilots' Risk-Taking Behavior through an Implicit Association Test," *Human Factors: The Journal of the Human Factors and Ergonomics Society* 51, no. 6 (February 23, 2010): 846–857.

9. Anthony G. Greenwald and Mahzarin R. Banaji, "Implicit Social Cognition: Attitudes, Self-Esteem, and Stereotypes," *Journal of Personality and Social Psychology* 102, no. 1 (January 1995): 4–27.

10. Mahzarin R. Banaji, Max H. Bazerman, and Dolly Chugh, "How (Un)Ethical Are You?" *Harvard Business Review* 81, no. 12 (December 2003): 3–10.

11. Ibid.

12. Murphy Paul, "Where Bias Begins."

13. Malcolm Gladwell, *Blink: The Power of Thinking without Thinking* (New York: Little, Brown, 2005).

14. Marianne Bertrand and Sendhil Mullainathan, "Are Emily and Greg More Employable Than Lakisha and Jamal? A Field Experiment on Labor Market Discrimination," *American Economic Review* 94 (September 4, 2004).

15. "Perceptions 'Affected by Accent': Accent Could Affect How Intelligent People Are Thought to Be, A New Study Suggests," *BBC News*, last updated April 3, 2008, http://news.bbc.co.uk/1/hi/uk/7329768.stm.

16. Rebecca M. Puhl and Chelsea A. Heuer, "The Stigma of Obesity: A Review and Update," *Obesity* 17, no. 5 (2009): 941–964. doi:10.1038/oby.2008.636.

17. John Cawley, "The Impact of Obesity on Wages," *Journal of Human Resources* 39, no. 2 (Spring 2004): 451–474.

18. Giorgio Brunello and Beatrice d'Hombres, "Does Body Weight Affect Wages? Evidence from Europe," *Economics & Human Biology* 5, no. 1 (March 2007): 1–19.

19. Puhl and Heuer, "The Stigma of Obesity."

20. Sean P. Mackinnon, Christian H. Jordan, and Anne E. Wilson, "Birds of a Feather Sit Together: Physical Similarity Predicts Seating Choice" (published online before print, April 5, 2011,

doi:10.1177/0146167211402094), *Personality and Social Psychology Bulletin* 37, no. 7 (July 2011): 879–892.

21. Adam Marcus, "Pull Up a Chair: We Tend to Move Closer to Those Who Share Our Physical Traits," *Scientific American Mind* (September–October 2011): 10.

22. The Free Dictionary, s.v. "Privilege," www.freedictionary.com.

23. Claude M. Steele and Joshua Aronson, "Stereotype Threat and the Intellectual Test Performance of African-Americans," *Journal of Personality and Social Psychology* 69, no. 5 (November 1995): 797–811.

24. ReducingStereotypeThreat.org, "What Is Stereotype Threat?" http://reducingstereotypethreat.org/definition.html (accessed June 17, 2011).

25. Barbara Cole, Kimberly Matheson, and Hymie Anisman, "The Moderating Role of Ethnic Identity and Social Support on Relations Between Well-being and Academic Performance," *Journal of Applied Social Psychology* 37 (March 7, 2007): 592–615; Patricia M. Gonzales, Hart Blanton, and Kevin J. Williams, "The Effects of Stereotype Threat and Double-Minority Status on the Test Performance of Latino Women," *Personality and Social Psychology Bulletin* 28 (May 2002): 659–670; Catherine Good, Joshua Aronson, and Jayne Ann Harder, "Problems in the Pipeline: Stereotype Threat and Women's Achievement in High-Level Math Courses," *Journal of Applied Developmental Psychology* 29, no. 1 (January–February 2008): 17–28.

26. http://www.reducingstereotypethreat.org (accessed June 17, 2011).

27. Toni Schmader, Michael Johns, and Chad Forbes, "An Integrated Process Model of Stereotype Threat Effects on Performance," *Psychological Review* 115, no. 2 (April 2008): 336–356.

28. Toni Schmader and Michael Johns, "Converging Evidence That Stereotype Threat Reduces Working Memory Capacity," *Journal of Personality and Social Psychology* 85 (2003): 440–452.

29. David M. Marx and Diederik A. Stapel, "It's All in the Timing: Measuring Emotional Reactions to Stereotype Threat Before and After Taking a Test," *European Journal of Social Psychology* 36 (2006): 687–698; D. M. Marx, D. A. Stapel, and D. Muller, "We Can Do It: The Interplay of Construal Orientation and Social Comparison under Threat," *Journal of Personality and Social Psychology* 88 (2005): 432–446.

30. Gregory M. Walton and Geoffrey L. Cohen, "Stereotype Lift" (Department of Psychology, Yale University, New Haven, CT, October 9, 2002).

31. Ibid.

32. Paul Watzlawick, *Brainy Quotes*, http://www.brainyquote.com/quotes/quotes/p/paulwatzla242493.html.

33. See Charles E. Hurst, *Social Inequality: Forms, Causes, and Consequences*, 6th ed. (Boston: Pearson, 2007); Marilynn B. Brewer, "In-Group Bias in the Minimal Intergroup Situation: A Cognitive-Motivational Analysis," *Psychological Bulletin* 86, no. 2 (1979): 307–324.

34. See Itesh Sachdev and Richard Y. Bourhis, "Status Differentials and Intergroup Behavior," *European Journal of Social Psychology* 17, no. 3 (July–September 1987): 277–293; Isabel R. Pinto, Jose M. Marques, John M. Levine, and Dominic Abrams, "Membership Status and Subjective Group Dynamics: Who Triggers the Black Sheep Effect?" *Journal of Personality and Social Psychology* 99, no. 1 (June 2010): 107–119; Patricia W. Linville and Edward E. Jones, "Polarized Appraisals of Out-Group Members," *Journal of Personality and Social Psychology* 38, no. 5 (May 1980): 689–703.

35. See William Samuelson and Richard Zeckhauser, "Status Quo Bias in Decision Making," *Journal of Risk and Uncertainty* 1 (1988): 7–59; Daniel Kahneman, Jack L. Knetsch, and Richard H. Thaler, "Anomalies: The Endowment Effect, Loss Aversion, and Status Quo Bias," *Journal of Economic Perspectives* 5, no. 1 (Winter 1991): 193–206.

36. See Jane L. Risen, Thomas Gilovich, and David Dunning, "One-Shot Illusory Correlations and Stereotype Formation," *Personality and Social Psychology Bulletin* 33, no. 11 (August 24, 2007): 1492–1502; David L. Hamilton and Robert K. Gifford, "Illusory Correlation in Interpersonal Perception: A Cognitive Basis of Stereotypic Judgments," *Journal of Experimental Social Psychology* 12, no. 4 (1976): 392–407.

CHAPTER 10

1. Military Leadership Diversity Commission, http://mldc.whs.mil/ (accessed June 15, 2011).

2. Military Leadership Diversity Commission, "About the Military Leadership Diversity Commission," http://mldc.whs.mil/index.php/about (accessed June 15, 2011).

3. "What Is the Relationship between Demographic Diversity and Cognitive Diversity?" (MLDC Issue Paper #4, December 2009), http://mldc.whs.mil/download/documents/Issue%20Papers/4_Cognitive_Diversity.pdf.

4. James Surowiecki, "Smarter Than the CEO," *Wired* 12.06 (June 2004), http://www.wired.com/wired/archive/12.06/view.html?pg=2.

5. James Surowiecki, *Wisdom of Crowds* (New York: Anchor Books, 2004).

6. Michael Mauboussin, *Think Twice: Harnessing the Power of Counterintuition* (Boston: Harvard Business School Press, 2009).

7. "Going Against the Tide: Avoiding Groupthink," *HRM Asia*, October 22, 2010, http://www.hrmasia.com/resources/leadership/going-against-the-tide-avoiding-groupthink/49852/ (accessed June 16, 2011).

8. Claudia Golden and Cecilia Rouse, "Orchestrating Impartiality: The Impact of 'Blind' Auditions on Female Musicians," *The American Economic Review* 90, no. 4 (September 2000): 715–741.

9. Marilyn Mark, "Blind Auditions Key to Hiring Musicians," *Princeton Weekly Bulletin* 90, no. 16 (February 12, 2001): 7, http://www.princeton.edu/pr/pwb/01/0212/7b.shtml.

10. Rhea E. Steinpries, Katie A. Anders, and Dawn Ritzke, "The Impact of Gender on the Review of the Curricula Vitae of Job Applicants and Tenure Candidates: A National Empirical Study," *Sex Roles* 41, nos. 7/8 (1999).

11. Ibid.

12. Amos Tversky and Daniel Kahneman, "Judgment under Uncertainty: Heuristics and Biases," *Science* 185, no. 4157 (September 1974): 1124–1130.

13. Dan Ariely, George Loewenstein, and Drazen Prelec, "Tom Sawyer and the Construction of Value" (working paper, Federal Reserve Bank Research Center for Behavioral Economics and Decision-Making, Boston, July 2005).

14. Stephanie A. Scharf and Barbara M. Flom, *Report of the 2010 NAWL Survey on the Retention and Promotion of Women in Law Firms*

(The National Association of Women Lawyers and the NAWL Foundation, October 2010), http://nawl.timberlakepublishing.com/files/NAWL%202010%20Final(1).pdf.

15. Todd J. Thorsteinson, "Initiating Salary Discussions with an Extreme Request: Anchoring Effects on Initial Salary Offers," *Journal of Applied Social Psychology* 41, no. 7 (July 2011): 1774–1792.

16. Adam Galinsky, "When to Make the First Offer in Negotiations," *Negotiation* (July 2004).

17. Amos Tversky and Daniel Kahneman, "Availability: A Heuristic for Judging Frequency and Probability," *Cognitive Psychology* 5, no. 2 (September 1973): 207–232.

18. *Lung Cancer: Deadlier to Women Than Breast, Ovarian, and Cervical Combined*, http://www.theajcf.org/lung-cancer-deadlier-to-women-than-breast-ovarian-and-cervical-combined/.

19. Maegan Voss, "5 Worries Parents Should Drop, and 5 They Shouldn't," *Shots, NPR's Health Blog*, August 30, 2010, http://www.npr.org/blogs/health/2010/08/30/129531631/5-worries-parents-should-drop-and-5-they-should?sc=nl&cc=es-20100912 (accessed June 20, 2011).

20. Rosabeth Moss Kanter, *Men and Women of the Corporation* (New York: Basic Books, 1977).

21. See Kanter, *Men and Women of the Corporation*; See also Elizabeth Chambliss and Christopher Uggen, "Men and Women of Elite Law Firms: Reevaluating Kanter's Legacy," *Law & Social Inquiry* 25, no. 1 (Winter 2000): 41, 43.

22. Thomas F. Pettigrew, "The Ultimate Attribution Error: Extending Allport's Cognitive Analysis of Prejudice," *Personality and Social Psychology Bulletin* 5, no. 4 (October 1979): 461–476.

23. Daniel G. Goldstein and Gerd Gigerenzer, "The Recognition Heuristic: How Ignorance Makes Us Smart," in *Simple Heuristics That Make Us Smart*, by Gerd Gigerenzer, Peter M. Todd, and ABC Research Group (New York: Oxford University Press, 1999).

24. Daniel M. Oppenheimer, "Not So Fast! (and Not So Frugal!): Rethinking the Recognition Heuristic," *Cognition* 90, no. 1 (November 2003): 1–9(9).

25. U.S. Census Bureau, http://www.census.gov (accessed June 18, 2011).

26. Lennar, "Our Lennar Name Badges," http://www.lennar.com/careers/culture/badge (accessed June 18, 2011).

27. Ralph Hertwig, Stefan M. Herzog, Lael J. Schooler, and Torsten Reimer, "Fluency Heuristic: A Model of How the Mind Exploits a By-Product of Information Retrieval," *Journal of Experimental Psychology: Learning, Memory, and Cognition* 34, no. 5 (2008): 1191–1206.

28. Herbert Wray, *On Second Thought: Outsmarting Your Mind's Hard-Wired Habits* (New York: Random House Digital, 2010; Kindle edition).

29. Matt Davis, http://www.mrc-cbu.cam.ac.uk/people/matt.davis/cmabridge/ (accessed September 12, 2011). There are many confusing cites to this research; however, this is the best explanation of this full body of research.

30. Ibid.

31. Diemand-Yauman Connor, Daniel M. Oppenheimer, and Erikka B. Vaughan, "Fortune Favors the Bold (and the Italicized): Effects of Disfluency on Educational Outcomes," *Cognition* (September 2010).

32. Ibid.

33. M. S. McGlone and J. Tofighbakhsh, "Birds of a Feather Flock Conjointly(?): Rhyme as Reason in Aphorisms," *Psychological Science* 11, no. 5 (September 2000): 424–428.

34. Ibid.

35. Gerald T. Gabris and Kenneth Mitchell, "The Impact of Merit Raise Scores on Employee Attitudes; the Matthew Effect of Performance Appraisal," *Public Personnel Management* 17, no. 4 (special issue, Winter 1988): 369–386.

36. Margit E. Oswald and Stefan Grosjean, "Confirmation Bias," in *Cognitive Illusions: A Handbook on Fallacies and Biases in Thinking, Judgment, and Memory*, ed. Rüdiger Pohl, 79–96 (Hove, UK: Psychology Press, 2004).

37. Ulrich Hoffrage, "Overconfidence," in *Cognitive Illusions: A Handbook on Fallacies and Biases in Thinking, Judgment, and Memory*, ed. Rüdiger Pohl (Hove, UK: Psychology Press, 2004).

38. Amos Tversky and Daniel Kahneman, "Judgment under Uncertainty: Heuristics and Biases," *Science*, New Series, 185, no. 4157 (September 27, 1974): 1124–1131.

39. W. Edwards, "Conservatism in Human Information Processing," in *Formal Representation of Human Judgment*, ed. B. Kleinmutz, 17–52 (New York: John Wiley).

40. Gary Marks and Norman Miller, "Ten Years of Research on the False-Consensus Effect: An Empirical and Theoretical Review," *Psychological Bulletin* (American Psychological Association) 102, no. 1 (July 1987): 72–90.

41. Jonathan Baron, *Thinking and Deciding*, 2nd ed. (Cambridge, UK: Cambridge University Press, 1994.)

42. Marshall McLuhan, *Brainy Quotes*, http://www.brainyquote.com/quotes/authors/m/marshall_mcluhan_3.html.

43. Kathleen Doheny, "Chemotherapy Can Help Older Breast Cancer Patients, Too," HealingWell.com, February 2, 2005, http://news.healingwell.com/index.php?p=news1&id=529885.

CHAPTER 11

1. Michael Hills, "Overcoming the Stigma of Epilepsy," supplement, *Neurology Asia* 15, S1 (2010): 21–24.

2. John Burton, *Conflict Resolution and Prevention* (New York: St. Martin's Press, 1990).

3. Hills, "Overcoming the Stigma of Epilepsy."

4. Howard H. Stevenson and Mihnea C. Moldoveanu, "The Power of Predictability," *Harvard Business Review* (July–August 1995): 141.

5. Mika Shelley, "The Four Drivers of Innovation, Top Executives and Business Experts Reveal the Keys to Making Your Company More Creative," *Gallup Management Journal* (January 11, 2007).

6. Ibid.

7. Ibid.

8. Christina Cheddar Berk, "Brace Yourself, It's the Next Ugly Shoe Trend," *CNBC*, May 10, 2011, http://www.cnbc.com/id/42683628/Brace_Yourself_It_s_the_Next_Ugly_Shoe_Trend (accessed June 20, 2011).

9. James Joyner, "The Next Ugly Shoe Trend," *Outside the Beltway*, May 14, 2011, http://www.outsidethebeltway.com/the-next-ugly-shoe-trend/ (accessed June 20, 2011).

10. Vibram, "70 Years of Innovations," http://www.vibram.com/index.php/us/VIBRAM/About-Us/The-History (accessed June 20, 2011).

11. Michael Hammer and James Champy, *Reengineering the Corporation: A Manifesto for Business Revolution* (New York: HarperBusiness, 1993), 24.

12. William Samuelson and Richard Zeckhauser, "Status Quo Bias in Decision Making," *Journal of Risk and Uncertainty* 1 (1988): 7–59.

13. See Irina Feygina, John T. Jost, and Rachel E. Goldsmith, "System Justification, the Denial of Global Warming, and the Possibility of 'System-Sanctioned Change,'" *Personality and Social Psychology Bulletin* 36, no. 3 (March 2010): 326–338; P. J. Henry and Andrea Saul, "The Development of System Justification in the Developing World," *Social Justice Research* 19, no. 3 (September 2006): 365–378; J. T. Jost and A. E. Azzi, "Microjustice and Macrojustice in the Allocation of Resources between Experimental Groups," *Journal of Social Psychology* 136 (1996): 349–365; J. T. Jost, M. R. Banaji, and B. A. Nosek, "A Decade of System Justification Theory: Accumulated Evidence of Conscious and Unconscious Bolstering of the Status Quo," *Political Psychology* 25 (2004): 881–919; J. T. Jost, S. Blount, J. Pfeffer, and G. Hunyady, "Fair Market Ideology: Its Cognitive-Motivational Underpinnings," *Research in Organizational Behavior* 25 (2003): 53–91; J. T. Jost and D. Burgess, "Attitudinal Ambivalence and the Conflict between Group and System Justification Motives in Low Status Groups," *Personality and Social Psychology Bulletin* 26 (2000): 293–305.

14. See F. Harinck, E. Van Dijk, I. Van Beest, and P. Mersmann, "When Gains Loom Larger than Losses: Reversed Loss Aversion for Small Amounts of Money," *Psychological Science* 18, no. 12 (December 2007: 1099–1105); Daniel Kahneman and Amos Tversky, "Prospect Theory: An Analysis of Decision under Risk," *Econometrica* 47, no. 2 (March 1979): 263–291; Deborah A. Kermer, Erin Driver-Linn, Timothy D. Wilson, and Daniel T. Gilbert, "Loss Aversion Is an Affective Forecasting Error," *Psychological Science* 17, no. 6 (2006): 649–653.

CHAPTER 12

1. Anita Williams Woolley, Christopher F. Chabris, Alex Pentland, Nada Hashmi, and Thomas W. Malone, "Evidence for a Collective Intelligence Factor in the Performance of Human Groups," *Science* 330, no. 6004 (October 29, 2010): 686–688.

2. Mark Roth, "Groups Produce Collective Intelligence, Study Says," *Pittsburgh Post-Gazette*, January 10, 2011, http://www.post-gazette.com/pg/11010/1116833-115.stm.

3. Ibid.

4. "Cross-Border Inventors," Patently-o, November 21, 2010, http://www.patentlyo.com/patent/2010/11/cross-border-inventors.html (accessed June 21, 2011).

5. Ibid.

6. Ibid.

7. Richard Carlson, ThinkExist.com, http://en.thinkexist.com/quotes/Richard_Carlson/.

8. Agnes Moors and Jan De Houwer, "Automaticity: A Theoretical and Conceptual Analysis," *Psychological Bulletin* 132, no. 2 (2006): 297–326; Agnes Moors and Jan De Houwer, "Problems with Dividing the Realm of Cognitive Processes," *Psychological Inquiry* 17 (2006): 199–204.

9. K. F. Szymanski and C. M. MacLeod, "Manipulation of Attention at Study Affects an Explicit But Not an Implicit Test of Memory," *Consciousness & Cognition* 5, nos. 1/2 (March–June 1996): 165–175; C. M. MacLeod and M. E. J. Masson, "Implicit Remembering: The Fluency of Reprocessing," *The Annual Report of Educational Psychology in Japan* 35 (1996): 166–171.

10. Barry M. Staw, Lance E. Sandelands, and Jane E. Dutton, "Threat-Rigidity Effects on Organizational Behavior," *Administrative Science Quarterly* 26, no. 4 (December 1981): 501–524; Irving L. Janis and Leon Mann, *Decision Making: A Psychological Analysis of Conflict, Choice, and Commitment* (New York: Free Press, 1977).

11. Ibid.

12. Yavin K. Shaham, Jerome E. Singer, and Monica H. Schaeffer, "Stability/Instability of Cognitive Strategies across Tasks Determine Whether Stress Will Affect Judgmental Processes," *Journal of Applied Social Psychology* 22, no. 9 (May 1992): 691–713.

13. Mathias V. Schmidt and Lars Schwabe, "Splintered by Stress," *Scientific American Mind* (September–October 2011): 22–29.

14. Jeff T. Larsen, A. Peter McGraw, and John T. Cacioppo, "Can People Feel Happy and Sad at the Same Time?" *Journal of Personality and Social Psychology* 81, no. 4 (October 2001): 684–696; Tiffany A. Ito, Jeff T. Larsen, N. Kyle Smith, and John T. Cacioppo, "Negative Information Weighs More Heavily on the Brain: The Negativity Bias in Evaluative Categorizations," *Journal of Personality and Social Psychology* 75, no. 4 (1998): 887–900.

15. C. Idzikowski and A. D. Baddeley, "Fear and Performance in Dangerous Environments," in *Stress and Fatigue*, ed. G. R. J. Hockey, 123–144 (Chichester, UK: Wiley, 1983).

16. Jochen Musch and Karl Christoph Klauer, "Locational Uncertainty Moderates Affective Congruency Effects in the Evaluative Decision Task," *Cognition and Emotion* 15, no. 2 (March 2001): 167–188; Timothy A. Judge and Randy J. Larsen, "Dispositional Affect and Job Satisfaction: A Review and Theoretical Extension," *Organizational Behavior and Human Decision Processes* 86, no. 1 (September 2001): 67–98.

17. James E. Driskell, R. Carson, and P. J. Moskal, "Stress and Human Performance," US Naval Training Systems Center Technical Reports (86-022), 1986; James E. Driskell and J. H. Johnston, "Stress Exposure Training," in *Making Decisions under Stress: Implications for Individual and Team Training*, eds. J. A. Cannon-Bowers and E. Salas, 191–217 (Washington, DC: American Psychological Association, 1998); J. E. Driskell and E. Salas, "Group Decision Making under Stress," *Journal of Applied Psychology* 76 (1991): 473–478; James E. Driskell, Eduardo Salas, and Joan Johnston, "Does Stress Lead to a Loss of Team Perspective?" *Group Dynamics* 3, no. 4 (1999): 291–302.

18. Irving L. Janis and Leon Mann, *Decision Making: A Psychological Analysis of Conflict, Choice, and Commitment* (New York: Free Press, 1977); Irving L. Janis, *Victims of Groupthink: A Psychological Study of Foreign-Policy Decisions and Fiascos* (Oxford, UK: Houghton Mifflin, 1972).

19. R. Cropanzano, D. Rapp, and Z. Byrne, "The Relationship of Emotional Exhaustion to Work Attitudes, Job Performance, and Organizational Citizenship Behaviors," *Journal of Applied Psychology* 88, no. 1 (February 2003): 160–169.

20. Robin M. Hogarth, *Judgment and Choice: The Psychology of Decision* (New York: John Wiley, 1987).

21. Arie W. Kruglanski, James Y. Shah, Ayelet Fishbach, Ron Friedman, Woo Young Chun, and David Sleeth-Keppler, "A Theory of Goal Systems," in *Advances in Experimental Social Psychology* 34, ed. M. P. Zanna, 331–378 (San Diego: Academic Press, 2002).

22. Keith E. Stanovich and Richard F. West, "Individual Differences in Reasoning: Implications for the Rationality Debate," *Behavioral & Brain Sciences* 23 (2000): 645–665.

23. Buchanan, J. and Kock, N. (2000), *Information Overload: A Decision Making Perspective*, Proceedings of the 15th International Confer-

ence on Multiple Criteria Decision Making, (Koksalam, M. and Zionts, S., eds.), Springer Verlag, Berlin, Germany, pp. 49–58. [Ankara, Turkey, July 10–14, 2000; included in these proceedings as an invited paper, a version of this paper was also presented at the 34th Annual Conference of the Operational Research Society of New Zealand in Wellington, New Zealand, December 1999.]

24. Itamar Simonson, "Regarding Inherent Preferences," *Journal of Consumer Psychology* 18, no. 3 (July 2008): 191–196. doi:10.1016/j.jcps.2008.04.007; Itamar Simonson, "Will I Like a 'Medium' Pillow? Another Look at Constructed and Inherent Preferences," *Journal of Consumer Psychology* 18, no. 3 (2008): 155–169.

25. Tim Rakow, "Risk, Uncertainty, and Prophet: The Psychological Insights of Frank H. Knight," *Judgment and Decision Making* 5, no. 6 (October 2010): 458–466.

26. Min Gong, Jonathan Baron, and Howard Kunreuther, "Group Cooperation under Uncertainty," *Journal of Risk and Uncertainty* (in press; August 2009), http://opim.wharton.upenn.edu /risk/library/J2009JRU-MG,JB,HK.pdf.

27. Yvonne Harrison and James A. Horne, "Sleep Deprivation Affects Speech," *Journal of Sleep Research and Sleep Medicine* 20, no. 10 (October 1997): 871–877; Yvonne Harrison and James A. Horne, "Sleep Loss Impairs Short and Novel Language Tasks Having a Prefrontal Focus," *Journal of Sleep Research* 7, no. 2 (June 1998): 95–100; Yvonne Harrison and James A. Horne, "One Night of Sleep Loss Impairs Innovative Thinking and Flexible Decision Making," *Organizational Behavior and Human Decision Processes* 78, no. 2 (May 1999): 128–145; J. A. Horne, "Sleep Loss and 'Divergent' Thinking Ability," *Sleep: Journal of Sleep Research & Sleep Medicine* 11, no. 6 (December 1988): 528–536.

28. "One Night of Sleep Loss Impairs Innovative Thinking and Flexible Decision Making"; Renee M. Petrilli, N. Lamond, G. D. Roach, and D. Dawson, "Identifying the Cognitive Skills That Are Most Affected by Fatigue within a Decision-Making Framework," in *Kumpulan Makalah Ergonomi*, ed. I. G. N. Susila, 548–556 (Denpasar, Bali: Udayana University Press, 2002).

29. Kanav Kahol, Mario J. Leyba, Mary Deka, et al., "Effect of Fatigue on Psychomotor and Cognitive Skills" (presented at the Association for Surgical Education Joint Meeting, Capitol Hill, Washington,

DC, April 11–14, 2007), *American Journal of Surgery* 195, no. 2 (February 2008): 195–204.

30. D. R. Davies and G. S. Tune, *Human Vigilance Performance* (London: Staples Press, 1970).

31. Staw, Sandelands, and Dutton, "Threat-Rigidity Effects on Organizational Behavior."

32. American Society of Safety Engineers, "NTSB Urges FAA to Address Air Traffic Controller Fatigue," Resource Library, CBS Interactive Business Network, July 2007, http://findarticles.com/p/articles/mi_hb5618/is_200707/ai_n32256355/ (accessed June 23, 2011).

33. Ibid.

34. Kathy Gurchiek, "Employers Can Control Some Fatigue Factors," *HR News*, January 20, 2011, http://www.shrm.org/Publications/HRNews/Pages/FatigueFactors.aspx.

35. Ibid.

36. Elise M. Clerk, Meghan W. Cody, Jeanine K. Stefanucci, Dennis R. Proffitt, and Bethany A. Teachman, "Imagery and Fear Influence Height Perception," *Journal of Anxiety Disorders* 23, no. 3 (April 2009): 381–386.

37. Andreas Olsson, Jeffrey P. Ebert, R. Banaji Mahzarin, and Elizabeth A. Phelps, "The Role of Social Groups in the Persistence of Learned Fear," *Science* 309, no. 5735 (July 29, 2005): 785–787.

38. Ibid.

39. H. Henry Cao, Bing Han, David Hirshleifer, and Harold H. Zhang, "Fear of the Unknown: Familiarity and Economic Decisions," December 1, 2007, http://papers.ssrn.com/sol3/papers.cfm?abstract_id=985381.

40. Janelle Weaver, "Children Who Form No Racial Stereotypes Found Brain Disorder Eradicates Ethnic but Not Gender Bias," *Nature*, April 12, 2010, http://www.nature.com/news/2010/100412/full/news.2010.176.html.

CHAPTER 13

1. Bill George, *True North: Discover Your Authentic Leadership* (San Francisco: Jossey-Bass, 2007): 68–69.

2. Brad Burnham Blog, "Chris and Malcolm Are Both Wrong," Union Square Ventures, August 9, 2009, http://www.usv.com/2009/08/chris-and-malco.php (accessed June 25, 2011).

3. Ray Reagans and Ezra W. Zuckerman, "Networks, Diversity, and Productivity: The Social Capital of Corporate R&D Teams," *Organization Science* 12, no. 4 (July–August 2001): 502–517.

4. Ibid.

5. Margarita Mayo and Pastor Juan Carlos, "Networks and Effectiveness in Work Teams: The Impact of Diversity" (IE working paper, WPO5-10, September 2, 2005, funded in part by SHRM Foundation).

6. Kenneth Thomas, "Conflict and Conflict Management," in *Handbook of Industrial and Organizational Psychology*, ed. M. D. Dunnette, 889–935 (Chicago: Rand McNally, 1976).

7. "U.S. Greenhouse Gas Emissions and Sinks," Environmental Protection Agency, http://epa.gov/climatechange/emissions/downloads11/GHG-Fast-Facts-2009.pdf (accessed June 26, 2011).

8. "Petroleum & Other Liquids, Analysis & Projections," U.S. Energy Information Administration, http://www.eia.gov/petroleum/reports.cfm?t=66 (accessed June 26, 2011).

9. "EDF and FedEx: Driving toward Cleaner Trucks," *EDF Business*, http://business.edf.org/casestudies/edf-and-fedex-driving-toward-cleaner-trucks (accessed June 26, 2011).

10. "FedEx Hybrid-Electric Fleet Surpasses Two-Million-Mile Mark," FedEx, http://about.fedex.designcdt.com/2MMiles (accessed June 26, 2011).

11. "FedEx Recognized for Environment-Friendly Trucks," *Memphis Business Journal*, December 1, 2005, http://www.bizjournals.com/memphis/stories/2005/11/28/daily30.html (accessed June 26, 2011), and "Environmental Defense and FedEx Express 'Put Commercial Hybrid Trucks on the Map,' Says CALSTART," Environmental Defense Fund, December 1, 2005, http://www.edf.org/pressrelease.cfm?ContentID=4895 (accessed June 26, 2011).

12. "EDF and FedEx: Driving toward Cleaner Trucks."

13. Malcolm Gladwell, *Blink: The Power of Thinking without Thinking* (New York: Little, Brown, 2005).

14. Colin L. Powell and Joseph E. Persico, *My American Journey* (New York: Ballantine, 1996).

15. Peter M. Senge, *The Fifth Discipline: The Art and Practice of the Learning Organization* (New York: Currency Doubleday, 1990).

16. Irving L. Janis, *Victims of Groupthink* (Boston: Houghton Mifflin, 1972); Irving L. Janis, *Groupthink: Psychological Studies of Policy Decisions and Fiascos* (Boston: Houghton Mifflin, 1982).

17. Ibid.

18. Karim R. Lakhani, Lars Bo Jeppesen, Peter A. Lohse, and Jill A. Panetta, "The Value of Openness in Scientific Problem Solving" (Harvard Business School Working Paper No. 07-050, October 2006), https://www.innocentive.com/files/node/casestudy/open-innovation-research-value-openness-scientific-problem-solving.pdf.

19. Dale Ainsworth, "What Is the Collective Wisdom Theory? An Essay by Dale Ainsworth," Placerville, California, January 2010, http://www.collectivewisdominitiative.org/papers/ainsworth%20WhatIs.pdf (accessed June 29, 2011).

INDEX

ABOUT THE AUTHOR

Born in India and raised in India, Libya, and Tanzania before arriving in the United States, Arin learned (and forgot and relearned) several languages before she graduated from high school as an English-speaking-adopted native of Chicago. What stayed with her through the experiences of navigating family scattered across many countries, attending schools taught in various languages and traditions, and forging friendships across different cultures was that different perspectives were not challenges to be overcome but gifts to be treasured. She took these lessons with her as she embarked on her academic and professional endeavors, and she draws on these lessons as she works, writes, and lives a life steeped in curiosity about everything and with a passion for thinking differently.

Arin studied business at DePaul University's College of Commerce, attended law school at University of Southern California, and received her Ph.D. in Sociology from Northwestern University. Arin has designed and led several comprehensive research projects on inclusion in the workplace as part of her education career, an adventure she loved enough to entice her to choose a career that integrated the research aesthetics of her doctoral work with the advisory impact of her practice as an attorney.

Arin is the president of the newly formed consulting firm, Nextions, a new way of seeing and doing leadership and inclusion. Prior to her position at Nextions, Arin served as the president of The Athens

Group, a consulting firm that specialized primarily on the inclusion aspect of talent management. At The Athens Group, Arin developed and implemented strategic plans and programming (including lectures, presentations, trainings, and dialogue facilitations) on recruitment, retention, attrition, promotion, mentoring, marketing, and client development issues in these various arenas, and she has also researched and written on these issues extensively. Prior to The Athens group, Arin served as an adjunct professor at Northwestern University for several years where she taught classes on law and society, and she also practiced law in Illinois.

Arin has been featured on NPR for her work on women of color in the legal profession and is cited often in online and traditional media as an expert in leadership and inclusion in the workplace. She is a Fellow of Leadership Greater Chicago (class of 2003). In 2010, she was recognized as a Rising Star by the Anti-Defamation League, and her column "Diversity in Practice" was recognized by the Herman Kogan Media Awards for excellence in journalism. She also serves on the Boards of Directors of several civic and not-for-profit organizations.

Arin lives in Chicago with a husband who has an amazing sense of humor and two children who have unlimited energy. She is an avid amateur photographer and has been "outed" in the *Wall Street Journal* as a professional addict of all things political.